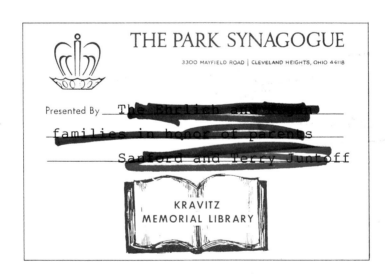

MEMBERS
OF THE
TRIBE

ZE'EV CHAFETS

MEMBERS
OF THE
TRIBE

ON THE ROAD IN JEWISH AMERICA

BANTAM BOOKS
TORONTO • NEW YORK • LONDON • SYDNEY • AUCKLAND

MEMBERS OF THE TRIBE
A Bantam Book / October 1988

*Grateful acknowledgment is made for permission to
reprint lyrics from "We Reserve the Right to Refuse
Services to You" by Kinky Friedman. Copyright ©
1973 by Ensign Music Corporation.*

Library of Congress Cataloging-in-Publication Data

Chafets, Ze'ev.   88-158
  Members of the tribe.
    1. Jews—United States—Social life and customs.
  2. Jews—United States—Politics and government.
  3. Judaism—United States. 4. Jews—United States—
  Identity. 5. United States—Ethnic relations.
  I. Title.
  E184.J5C43   1988   305.8'924'073   88-47647
  ISBN 0-553-05308-6

Published simultaneously in the United States and Canada

PRINTED IN THE UNITED STATES OF AMERICA

WAK   0   9   8   7   6   5   4   3   2   1

For Joseph B. Colten

CONTENTS

ACKNOWLEDGMENTS

In the course of writing this book, I spent nearly six months traveling in America and Canada. During that time I visited more than thirty states and provinces, and in almost every place I found old friends or new ones who extended hospitality, provided logistical and moral support, and shared insights with me. Thanks are due to:

Joe Colten, Gary Baumgarten, Steve and Carla Schwartz, Harvey Wasserman, Macy and Susan Hart, Carol and Ricka Hart, Tom Dine, Minette Wernick, Lori Posin, Christine Rimon, Dale Ackerman, Joe and Linda Chafets, Julie and Allan Grass, Stuart Shoffman, Roberta Fahn Shoffman, Harry Wall, Arthur Samuelson, Warren Feierstein, Abe Foxman, Rabbi Dan Syme, John and Diane Carbonara, Joseph and Betty Miller, Winston Pickett, Valerie Shalom, Yossil and Dora Friedman, Michael Stoff, Rabbi David Maharam, Rabbi Yoel Kahn, Isaac Lakritz, Scott Galen, Rabbi Eric Yoffie, Mike Hall, Roger Simon, Marilyn Miller, Gary Rosenblatt, Jerry Countess, Rafi Rothstein, and John Broder.

Thanks are also due to a number of people who read all or parts of this book in manuscript form and made valuable suggestions. They include Liora Nir, Barry Rubin, Michal Chafets, and again, Joseph Colten, Rabbi Dan Syme, and Harry Wall.

As usual, I am grateful to Esther Newberg of International Creative Management for her professional help and guidance.

Thanks are also due to Margot Levin of Bantam Books for her tireless and efficient efforts throughout the project.

Finally, I would like to thank my editor, Steve Rubin, who believed in this book from the start and played an invaluable role in its completion.

INTRODUCTION

THE SECRETS OF THE JEWS

I was fifteen years old when I first met Vernon and Mary Lou. One Friday night they simply turned up at our temple, sat down in the front row of the sanctuary, and joined in the Sabbath service. In our congregation, which had the social pretensions of a country club and the interlocking family connections of a Berber village, outsiders stood out; outsiders like Vernon and Mary Lou stood out a mile.

People like them usually came to Temple Beth Jacob to fix something, or as gaping guests at the annual Baptist-Jewish Brotherhood Week service. That first Friday night, Vernon wore a black Robert Hall Sunday-go-to-meeting suit, a lurid floral tie that choked his throat and turned his moonpie face purple, brown shoes, and, inevitably, white socks. His wife was dressed in the Bess Truman mode, with accessories by the Beverly Hillbillies. They couldn't have been more conspicuous if they had come dressed in white sheets and carrying a flaming cross.

After services that first time, Vernon and Mary Lou wandered around the social hall, self-consciously speared a few cookies off the hospitality table, and then left. But they came back the following Friday night, and every one thereafter. They always sat in the front row, sang the hymns with fervor, and joined the responsive reading in a modified Tennessee holler. After services they sought out fellow worshipers, he pumping hands ("Hey there, Brother Horowitz, how you doin' this Shabbes?"), she calling the Hadassah ladies "hon." After a month or so the entire congregation knew that Vernon and Mary Lou had decided to become Jews.

The temple was split over the issue. Its president, board of directors, and general membership were adamantly opposed to the conversion of Vernon and Mary Lou, while the pro-conversion camp consisted of me and my friend Ackerman. We delighted in the consternation of the establishment and adopted the couple as heroes. One of our favorite pastimes was putting them in imaginary situations. Vernon on Jewish history: *"Whoo-ee, them Maccabees shore did whomp the shit out of ole Antiochus!"* On religion: "Rabbi, what ain't kosher, the ham or the eggs?" On the family: "Y'all know my boy, Morris Bob? We're havin' his bar mitzvah at the Indy 500." And so on.

Under pressure from the congregation, the rabbi tried to discourage the prospective converts, but they were determined to become Jews. For months they attended temple activities with a fanatical ubiquity. And then one day, mysteriously, they disappeared.

Ackerman and I speculated on their whereabouts. *"Boys, we decided to hook up with them Chasidics. They got that ole-time Yiddishkeit."* We laughed at the picture of Vernon in a *strimel* and blue suede shoes, Mary Lou warning customers at the truck stop not to mix up the milk and meat dishes. We laughed, but in truth we missed them.

Then one day Ackerman spotted Vernon downtown, coming out of the Kresge's on Saginaw Street. "Hey Vernon, you old Yid, where you been hiding?" he shouted. Vernon turned and regarded him sadly.

"Well, tell you the truth, me and the missus decided to quit."

"What do you mean quit?" asked Ackerman. "I thought you liked it at the temple."

A look of grievance passed over Vernon's round face. "We quit because nobody would tell us the secret," he said.

"What secret?" Ackerman demanded, sensing something great.

"Come on, now, you know what I'm talkin' about. The secret. The secret of how you all get so rich."

I laughed when Ackerman told me the story, but a part of me understood what Vernon meant. I knew from my own family that not all Jews were rich by any means; but I also suspected that there *was* some sort of Jewish secret, something that nobody had let me in on. It was a suspicion I had harbored for a very long time.

I was raised to regard myself as an American who happened to be Jewish. Judaism, as taught to me at Sunday school and at home, was simply another American religion, theologically boring and socially respectable. My parents encouraged me to invite Christian friends to our Reform temple, and to attend their church services in return. It was a nothing-up-our-sleeve approach, open and midwestern. We were like Christians who didn't believe in Jesus, and what was the big deal about that?

And yet, I had the feeling there were undercurrents I didn't understand; something a little mysterious about being a Jew.

Somehow this feeling was connected with Passover. Every year we would leave our non-Jewish neighborhood in Pontiac, Michigan, and drive to my father's parents' home in Detroit, half an hour away. And there, at the ritual Passover Seder, I witnessed a peculiar transformation. My uncles, greengrocers and petty merchants, reclined on pillows and chanted strange Hebrew incantations. They proclaimed that they had once stood at Mount Sinai with Moses, flung open the doors of the small apartment to greet Elijah the prophet, flicked drops of sweet red wine on their plates to commemorate the plagues in Egypt, and implored God to pour His wrath on their enemies. In my grandparents' living room I was suddenly no longer an American boy. I was not even in America. By some magic I had been transported to the table of fierce desert strangers.

It was always a shock when the Seder ended and we drove home. Suddenly I was back in the USA, listening to rock 'n' roll on WXYZ as my father and mother lapsed back into their American personae. We whizzed by crowds at the Dairy Queen and the A&W, and I thought: They don't know where I've been tonight, they don't know who I really am. The deception thrilled me, and puzzled me. I wasn't sure who I really was myself.

Once on Chanukah a friend of mine named Jimmy came over to play. As far as I knew his family was originally from Mexico, although his parents spoke American English. Our families didn't socialize but they knew one another, and when Jimmy's father came to pick him up, my parents invited him in for a drink in the small-town midwestern way.

Jimmy and I went on playing, uninterested in the adult conversation going on a few feet away in the living room. Then, suddenly, I heard a sob and turned to see Jimmy's dad with his eyes full of tears. My father put an arm around his shoulder and led him into the den. A few minutes later, he emerged dry-eyed and took Jimmy home.

"Why was Jimmy's father crying?" I asked. "Is something the matter?"

My father explained that Jimmy's father had choked up when he saw the candles burning in our Chanukah menorah. "The man is a Jew," said my father with barely controlled emotion. "He remembered his grandmother lighting candles, but she never told him why."

I couldn't have been more surprised if he had told me that Willie Mays wore a yarmulke under his batting helmet. "He's not Jewish, he's a Catholic," I said with certainty.

My father explained that Jimmy's family had once been Jewish in Spain, but long ago they had been forced to convert to Christianity. "It happened five hundred years ago," my father said in an awestruck tone that reminded me of Passover. "His family has been Christian for *five hundred years*, but he still has a Jewish heart." How do you get a Jewish heart? I wondered; and how do you get rid of one? The incident with Jimmy's father became another part of the Jewish mystery.

My father's family was from Europe, but I could never figure out exactly where. Whenever I asked my grandmother, she would frown and say, "the old country," without specifying which old country she meant. When I got a little older I once brought her a map of Europe and asked her to point out the place where she had grown up. She peered at the map for a moment and gestured vaguely in the direction of Russia. "It doesn't matter," she said. "It isn't there anymore. Hitler wiped it out. Anyway, America is better."

My mother's family, on the other hand, was American. She was born in Milwaukee, and her mother—my grandmother—was born in Sterling, Illinois. But although she had been a suffragette and knew nothing about the "old country," my American grand-mother had her own thing—Jewish cartography.

Pontiac never had enough Jews for a Jewish neighborhood, but from the time I was a small boy I was aware that it had a special Jewish geography, and my grandmother was its da Gama. She would point out an unremarkable brick home on a leafy street and confide, "That's a Jewish house." Downtown she would pause near a certain store and say, "This is a Jewish business." Occa-sionally, when we passed a parking lot, she would point out a Chevrolet or Plymouth and say, "There's a Jewish car." None of these cars, shops, or houses impressed me as being especially Jewish, but I was prepared to take her word for it.

At first I thought that mastering Pontiac's Jewish geography was some sort of Sunday school lesson, like memorizing the Hebrew alphabet or the kings of Judea. But as I grew older, I realized that my grandmother mapped out the town reflexively, more for her benefit than mine. Jewish houses, stores, and offices were safe havens, places she could count on if, for example, she needed to use a bathroom, or was being chased through the streets by a sex-crazed cossack rapist.

There were very few Jewish children in my school, and only one other in my class, a girl named Beverly. Like me, she had only the slightest Jewish education. All we knew in Hebrew were a few scattered prayers, but occasionally we would show off our erudition by turning them into conversation. *"Baruch atah adonai* (Blessed art thou, O Lord)," I would say casually, and she would reply, *"Eloheinu melech ha'olam* (Our God, king of the world)," just as coolly. "What are you talking about?" the other kids would ask, and one day Jesse Stephen, the son of a black preacher, came up with the answer. "They speakin' the secret language of the Jews," he informed the class.

It was Jesse who put me into a special racial category. One day, during a break from a half-court basketball game, he turned to me and, imitating his father's delivery, intoned, "Noah had three sons—Ham, Shem, and Japheth. Now Ham, he was the black boy. Japheth was the Gentile boy. And Shem, now he was the Jewish boy, and he was red. That's what you are, baby— you red."

And there was another mystery—my relationship to other Jews. Once, on a family trip to northern Michigan, we stopped at a country inn for lunch. The restaurant was crowded and we stood in line waiting for a table. While we waited, my father idly ran his fingers over the keyboard of an upright piano that stood near the door. "Da da da da DA da, da da da da DA," he played, picking out the first notes of "Ha-Tikvah," the Israeli national anthem.

We were halfway through lunch in the bustling dining room when another patron stopped in front of the piano. "Da da da DA da, da da da da dum," he completed my father's tune and, without turning to look at us, walked out the door. I felt like I was in the underground.

So there I was. I had a color I couldn't see, a secret language I couldn't speak. I had uncles who hurled ancient curses across the centuries and then settled back to watch the Stanley Cup finals on television, aunts who worshiped America and spit superstitiously every time they passed a Christian cemetery. I had an invisible geography and a family that came to the United States out of thin air. No one wanted to explain anything, and yet everyone seemed proud when I figured something out by myself.

It wasn't until I came to Israel at the age of twenty that things began to fall into place. Gradually my American self became intensely curious about these small mysteries. The Jewish aspect of my life was trivial and the Judaism I knew in Pontiac seemed to be a relatively innocuous kind of modern religion. And yet, I knew that for two thousand years my ancestors had been persecuted and tortured, even murdered, for practicing it. What, I wondered, did Temple Beth Jacob of Pontiac, Michigan have in common with Auschwitz? How was I, an American kid more or less like my non-Jewish classmates, related to the mythological figures of the Bible? What was really Jewish? What was really Jewish about me?

These questions eventually led me to Israel, where I went to spend my junior year of college. And it was there, at the Hebrew University in Jerusalem, that things began to make sense. My first glimpse of the country was like emerging from Plato's cave. Jewishness, an elusive shadow in Pontiac, became a clear, tangible reality. It was in Jerusalem that I found what my ancestors had once had but failed to pass along—the attitudes and skills, spirit and substance of a distinctive, self-contained Jewish civilization.

I stayed in Israel, and gradually I came to understand and adopt its way of looking at Jewishness. Although most Israelis are not Orthodox, people tend to see Jewish life in traditional terms. Holidays are celebrated when and how they always have been; and synagogues look and feel pretty much the way they have for generations. Children are taught what Jewish children need to know—Hebrew, the Bible, and Jewish literature, history, and customs—as a matter of course. The concept of Jewish people-hood is implicit in Israel's attitudes and explicit in its laws and policies. Even the rebellion against religion is carried out in a Jewish language and intellectual tradition. Israel's daily life and underlying assumptions would be understandable, if outrageous and offensive, to any eighteenth-century rabbi.

As I came to understand Jewish reality through the prism of Israeli life, and to acquire the skills necessary to participate in it, a strange thing happened; perversely, I became curious about American Judaism. I left the United States when I was a college student, and although I had been back for sporadic visits, I had never lived there as an adult. I began to wonder what it was really like to be a Jew in America.

I heard differing and, to me, confusing reports about the state of Jewish life in the United States. Some experts argued that Jews were disappearing; others claimed that things had never been better. I read articles proclaiming America a Jewish wasteland; other articles called it a center of Jewish culture. Friends told me that anti-Semitism was dead; other friends spoke fearfully about Louis Farrakhan or the radical right. It was hard to know who or what to believe.

On another level, I was fascinated by the lives of individual Jews in America. I wondered if they were confounded, as I had been, by a sense of their own mysteriousness. I was curious about how they lived, how they were different from other Americans—and other Jews. My interest was partly the product of Zionist concern about the Jewish future; but it was at least as much a personal curiosity about what my own life might have been if I had stayed at home.

In the fall of 1986, I decided to take a trip through Jewish America. I had no itinerary and no special agenda. I wanted to meet as many Jews as possible, talk to them, and see their lives up close. I had no intention of writing an "objective" study, or a comprehensive report. I didn't look for representative samples or worry about giving every aspect of the community its proper weight. I avoided experts, spokespersons, and superstars. I wanted to see and experience things for myself.

For almost six months I traveled randomly, visiting more than thirty states. I was fascinated by the variety and complexity of American Jewish life, and the unpredictable ways it affects individuals.

In many places I had a contact—a friend, a local journalist, or someone active in the Jewish community. In others, I simply picked up the phone or walked in and introduced myself. It didn't matter. Jews understand books, Americans are open and friendly, and the combination made it possible to go places and see things I hadn't expected or imagined.

Some of the customs I encountered during my trip seemed strange, even exotic; there is a do-it-yourself flavor to much of American Judaism that can be disconcerting. And many of the people I met along the way were far from the stereotypical Jews I had expected to find. But no matter where I was—in a Jewish farm town in New England or a black synagogue in Queens, in a gay temple in San Francisco or among the Jews of the Louisiana bayou—I always felt at home. I came to the United States feeling like an Israeli; I left reminded that I am also, as a friend in Detroit put it, an MOT—a Member of the Tribe.

CHAPTER ONE

MACY B. AND THE DIXIE DIASPORA

On a muggy, overcast Thursday afternoon in October, Macy B. Hart set out from New Orleans in a white Chevrolet van to bury the Dixie diaspora. His destination was Donaldsonville, Louisiana, a little town in the heart of Cajun country, the first stop on a long, slow procession through the hamlets of the Deep South. Once, Jewish communities had flourished in places like Donaldsonville, but now they were dying, and Macy B. was determined to give them a decent funeral. Nobody assigned him the burial detail. He volunteered for it, because he knew it had to be done and there was no one else to do it.

Macy came to that realization gradually. A few years before, he heard about an old man in Laurel, Mississippi, who—discovering he was the last Jew left in town and uncertain what to do—took the Torah out of the ark of the small temple and locked it in the trunk of his car. Macy wasn't surprised. For some time, Jewish religious objects had been turning up in boutiques and antique shops around the South, historic temples had been crumbling for lack of attention, and Jewish cemeteries had gone untended. But the Laurel incident made Macy realize that small-town southern Jewry as he had known it as a boy in Winona, Mississippi, was coming to an end, and he resolved to help make the demise as dignified and painless as possible.

First, he tried unsuccessfully to get the Laurel Torah for the Jacobs Camp for Living Judaism in Utica, Mississippi, a summer camp that Macy has run since 1969. Then he began to search the boutiques for sacred articles, which he brought to Utica. Gradually he became determined to create a museum at the camp as a memorial to southern Jewry and to provide aid to those communities that could no longer help themselves. For months he had been planning the museum; now, in the fall of 1986, he was ready to set out on a barnstorming tour aimed at making it a reality. I was invited along for the ride.

The arrangements had been made a few months earlier. I called Macy's office from Jerusalem, smiling when his secretary answered the phone in a murky delta drawl: "Jacobs Camp for Livin' Judaism, shalom y'all." It was a Macy thing to say, funny and defiant, and I was still chuckling when he came on the line. I told him I wanted to write about southern Jews, and he suggested that I join him on the road.

"Come with me and I'll show you some Jews you never seen before," he had promised. "I'm fixin' to hit Donaldsonville, Laurel, Natchez, Port Gibson—all them big cities."

"You mean there are really Jews in all those places?" I asked, and he gave me an easygoing country laugh. "Yeah, boy, there are. And I'll guarantee you one thing. They all eat crawfish."

It was an old joke between old friends. Macy had been calling himself a crawfish eater ever since we first met, in the summer of 1964, at a camp institute of the National Federation of Temple Youth in upstate New York. None of us Yankees had ever encountered a Jew like Macy, or even suspected that one existed. He was razor thin and country slick with a squeaky southern voice like Deputy Barney Fife on *The Andy Griffith Show,* and he quickly became the focus of amused attention. We learned that his was the only Jewish family in Winona, Mississippi, a town where his father owned the local clothing store, his brother was married to the daughter of the Baptist preacher, and Macy himself led an idyllic Tom Sawyer life, playing basketball for his segregated high school, riding with the Confederate Cavalry Club, spinning records as a DJ on the town's underpowered radio station, and chasing girls with innocent abandon.

Macy was perfectly well aware of his impact on us northerners and he played it for all it was worth, deepening his already outrageous Mississippi drawl, calling fifteen-year-old girls "ma'am," and regaling us with tales about his exotic hometown. In the course of these stories it emerged that there was a serious side to Macy B. Hart. Back home, on Sunday mornings, he drove seventy miles over rural roads to Cleveland, Mississippi, to attend religious school and to take part in the youth group; and despite his lack of a hometown constituency, he had somehow managed to get himself elected a regional officer of SOFTY, the Reform youth movement of the Deep South. Macy's knowledge of Judaism was tenuous—he was capable of asking, "What do y'all call Friday night, Shabbes?"—but his sincerity was obvious and touching. He came back to the summer institute year after year, and in 1967 he was elected president of the National Federation.

Macy went to Louisiana State University and later to the University of Texas, where he met his wife, Susan, a former high school majorette from Lexington, Mississippi. After graduation he intended to become a lawyer. But the Reform movement wanted to start a camp in Mississippi for Jewish children, and Macy agreed to set it up and run it for one year. Macy and Susan wanted to live in a large city with a real Jewish community; instead they wound up in Utica, a place where Jews are so rare that Susan, whose southern accent makes Dolly Parton sound like Margaret Thatcher, was once asked by a neighbor if she knew of any other foreigners in town.

That was in 1970. Now, almost twenty years later, Macy was still at the camp, still engaged in a quixotic struggle to preserve and defend Jewish life below the Mason-Dixon line. It was a losing battle and he knew it, but something compelled him to keep fighting. I was interested in seeing the South and its Jews, but I was even more curious to learn what made Macy feel such a sense of obligation. I thought I might find the answer on his somewhat macabre burial tour.

There were four of us in the van as Macy headed onto the highway, up the Mississippi from New Orleans in the direction of the Louisiana bayou. Vicki Fox, a young museum consultant from Los Angeles by way of Hattiesburg, had been brought in to help with the technical details. And Macy had drafted Betty, a New Orleans Jewish matron who grew up in Donaldsonville before World War II, to serve as our guide to Cajun country.

For Betty it was a sentimental journey, and she was in a nostalgic mood. "My daddy had this store in Napoleonville?" she said, ending her declarative sentences with question marks in the southern way. "Well, everybody in town knew we were Jewish, I mean he closed up on the holidays. Rosh Hashanah and Yom Kippur? Of course he closed for Christmas, too. And we had a Christmas tree. I never did have a feeling that there was anything too different about being a Jew back then, you want to know the truth."

"People up north think that the Jews down here were afraid of the Klan," Macy said, and Betty shook her head. "I can't honestly say we ever had any anti-Semitism that I knew of. Well, there was this one time when a little nothin' boy put a note under our door, but nobody got too excited about that."

As we approached Donaldsonville, Betty began to point out local landmarks. She became especially animated when we reached the Sunshine Bridge. The bridge is a monument to the administration of Huey Long, a politician Betty remembers with fondness. "A lot of people had the wrong idea about that man," she said in a challenging tone. "He was portrayed as a dictator and all, but he did a lot of good for this state. And I'll tell you something else, he had a lot of Jewish support down here, and a lot of Jewish officials in his government."

Huey Long seemed an appropriate hero for this part of Louisiana. In the fall of 1986 New Orleans was in a severe economic slump, victim of the world oil glut and the decline of OPEC, but Donaldsonville was unaffected by such contemporary economic exotica—it was still trying to recover from the Great Depression.

The town calls itself "The Gateway to Acadia," but on this dismal Thursday afternoon, with gray clouds brooding low and ominous, it seemed less a gateway than a tenement doorway. Aimless groups of men engaged in indolent, fly-swatting, street-corner conversation, and raggedy children clambered over the Studebakers and Packards that rested on blocks on the front lawns of tar-paper shacks. Betty surveyed the town with dismay, occasionally murmuring "My, my" under her breath. Clearly it had been a long time between visits.

"Miz Betty, do you recollect where the temple was?" Macy asked, and she shook her head in confusion. "I was confirmed in that little ole temple, and now I can't even remember where it is," she said. "I think it was this building here." She pointed to a two-story clapboard structure with the sign ACE HARDWARE above a window. Macy, who knows southern Jewish architecture, looked with a practiced eye. "Yes ma'am, there she is," he said, shaking his head sadly.

Downtown, at the corner of Crescent and Mississippi, Betty brightened. "Now here's a place I do recall," she said, pointing to a large white two-story building with a tattered awning draped over peeling white pillars, iron hitching posts in front, and a sign, THE BERNARD LEMANN BUILDING, over the door. "This used to be the grandest building in town. In those days the Lemanns were still Jewish people, Nowadays, they're all Catholics," she mused, without evident disapproval.

Macy stopped his van in front of Lemann's and called to one of the men slouching against its whitewashed wall. "Do y'all know where Mister Gaston Hirsch lives?" he asked, and the idler readily provided directions in French-inflected swamp brogue.

With the window rolled down I got my first real whiff of Donaldsonville. The local economy is based on fishing and sugar refining, and it smells it; the two aromas mingle in the thick bayou air like some rich creole concoction. I was still sniffing when Macy hung a U-turn on the deserted downtown street and headed out to Cajun suburbia, to the home of Gaston Hirsch, the last Jew in Donaldsonville.

Gaston Hirsch didn't look much like a crawfish eater when he met us at the door of his tract house. Like many of the Jews who once lived in Donaldsonville, he was born in Alsace-Lorraine; for obvious reasons, they gravitated to the French-speaking bayou country. When Hirsch first arrived in town, after World War II, there was still a congregation. But the Jews all died or moved away, and now only he was left. People in Donaldsonville didn't know or care that he was the last Jew in town. To them he was an old man in his late seventies with a charming accent and a shock of white hair, spry and energetic despite his advanced age. But in the long, quirky procession of the Dixie diaspora, Gaston Hirsch was the end of the line.

Hirsch was expecting us, and he greeted Macy warmly. He introduced us to his wife, a non-Jewish woman, and they looked at each other as if they were still on their honeymoon. The interior of their home revealed less than their gaze—a place that was not French, Jewish, or southern, but contemporary sitcom. The bland decor stood in contrast to the mysterious countryside, a denial of the bayou's voodoo legacy as well as the Jewish heritage that Hirsch had brought with him from Europe.

The old man had been careless about his religion—both of his sons were baptized—but in a curious way he was as obsessed as Macy with his Jewish obligations. Foremost among these was the care and maintenance of the Jewish cemetery of Donaldsonville. Nearing the end of his life, he was concerned about the future. "Soon I will be buried there," he told us, "and then someday, my wife will join me. She is not Jewish, but we have been together so long, and when you love a woman for fifty years, religion is not so important, yes? But who will look after us then, after I am no longer here?"

We decided to go to the cemetery for a look around. I rode with Hirsch, and Macy and the others followed in the van. The old man was anxious to tell me, a visitor from Israel, about his life as the last Jewish consul in this desolate outpost.

"I spent five years in a German prisoner-of-war camp during the war," he said. "My wife was sentenced to hard labor, just because she was married to a Jew. We survived, and we came here, to Donaldsonville, Louisiana. Well, you are from Jerusalem, so I want you to know that I am very Jewish in my heart. My sons were baptized, yes, but that is the way it is for us here." He shook his head at the vagaries of the Jewish condition in Acadia. Hirsch mentioned the names of several local families who were once Jewish and no longer are. "These people now call themselves Catholic, Christian. But are they Catholic in their hearts?" He gave me a sly glance. "Believe me, no matter what they call themselves, they are still Jewish in their hearts."

The Jewish cemetery turned out to be a fenced-off section of a larger graveyard, a city of the dead for a few Protestants, a great many Catholics, and the Jews. Gaston Hirsch led us with sure steps past ornate tombstones bearing French inscriptions: *"Thérèse Moyse, éspouse du Salamon Bloch," "Babbette Blumenthal," "Lissette (enfant),"* and hundreds more. "It was easier to find someone to write French inscriptions than Hebrew ones," he explained. Macy seemed bemused by the culture shock. Donald-sonville is in the South, but it is far from the Mississippi Delta, and he was temporarily out of his element.

When we finished our tour of inspection, Gaston Hirsch took Macy aside to confer about the future. He had, he confided, a temporary solution—three men in town had agreed to take care of the cemetery. "They call themselves Christians," he said conspir-atorially, "but they all had a Jewish parent. But these men are in their sixties. The problem is, what happens when they die?" Hirsch looked at Macy with the blatant practicality of the very old.

Macy promised to explore the possibility of arranging perpet-ual care for the cemetery. He planned to raise money for his museum, and if he succeeded some funds would be left over for an endowment to tend Jewish cemeteries and historic buildings. "I promise you one thing, Mr. Hirsch," he said, returning the old man's imploring look. "We're gonna take care of everything. We won't let our cemeteries go untended."

Hirsch nodded, a man who recognizes a Jewish heart when he finds one. As we drove away he stood in the cemetery, among the tombstones of his departed friends, and waved, a white-haired old man among the Jewish ghosts of the bayou.

We headed back to New Orleans in a depressed silence, stop-ping along the way for some RC Colas and barbecued rinds at a Piggly Wiggly. To break the mood, I told Macy and the others about the time, a few years before, when I had come to New Orleans to give a speech. My host that night had been a young woman rabbi who had taken me out to dinner at Pascale's Manale, the best barbecue shrimp restaurant in the city. During the course of the meal, her husband mentioned that he was a professional skin diver, working mostly out of the Gulf. I remarked that skin diving was an unusual profession for a Jew. "My husband isn't Jewish," she snapped, as if it were an impertinence to assume that a rabbi's husband would be.

Macy and the others laughed at the story. "Pretty soon you'll be having Christian rabbis down here," I said, and Betty nodded vigorously. "Considerin' some of the rabbis I've known, I'm not sure that's such a bad idea," she said.

"Heck, they already tried that," said Macy. "Over in Arkansas, a rabbi hired a Christian woman as his assistant to make hospital calls. The congregation made him stop, but a lot of folks thought she was better than the man they had." We laughed together, happy to be leaving the bayou and heading back to the land of the living.

We spent the night in New Orleans at the home of Uncle Carol, one of Macy's ubiquitous southern relatives. There have been Harts in the South for a hundred years, ever since Macy's great-grandfather, Isaac T. Hart, moved to Woodville, Mississippi, from Kingston, Jamaica. A man of strong patriotic enthusiasms, he became an instant rebel, naming his son, Macy's grandfather, H. Van E. Hart, after the Confederate general Henry Van Eaton.

The Jewish H. Van grew up in Woodville and became a "dealer in wood, hides, furs, snakeroots, junk, and country produce"—in short, a peddler. He died young, leaving a wife and four small sons. Unable to take care of them, the young widow sent her oldest boy, Julian, to live with relatives in Arizona, and placed the three younger sons, including Uncle Carol and Macy's father, Ellis, in the Jewish orphanage in New Orleans. It was the only home Carol and his brothers ever had.

"I'm a Jew in my heart, not in my head," Carol told us, as we sat in his spacious living room. He is a successful lawyer who once ran against Jim Garrison for prosecutor but, like Macy, his passion is the Jewish community. A few days earlier, on Yom Kippur, he had accompanied a visiting Israeli poet to a Conservative synagogue, an experience that had left Carol baffled. Despite his Jewish activism, he knows no Hebrew and was unfamiliar with the traditional service; the orphanage was a resolutely secular institution that assigned religious training of its wards to a very assimilated Reform temple.

In those days the temple's rabbi, Julian Feibelman, was strongly anti-Zionist, and Carol left the congregation because of it. "I realized that the rabbi was committed to the preservation of Judaism at the corner of St. Charles and Calhoun," he said. Carol understood that the Jews needed a place of their own, just as he had found refuge at the orphanage. He has been a devoted Zionist ever since.

Carol Hart has an orphan's pride in his heritage, and he showed us a stack of yellowing scrapbooks that chronicle the family saga. He was especially proud of his aunt, Rosa Hart, a local theatrical luminary who attended Sophie Newcombe College and, according to Carol, became—in 1919—the first female cheerleader in America.

The Harts are not just Jews, but southern Jews. Like Macy, Carol is rooted in both traditions, a combination reflected in his home. There is a "shalom" doormat on the back porch, and his living room is decorated in a mixture of Jewish and antebellum southern decor. Chagall lithographs hang next to J. W. Buell's "Louisiana and the Fair," and Irving Howe's "World of Our Fathers" shares a shelf with an ornately framed photograph of a young, saucy Carol at the Texas Centennial, 1936. There is also a wedding picture of Carol's daughter, who recently graduated from the Jewish Theological Seminary in New York, and her husband, a Conservative rabbi. Carol proudly told us the young couple keeps kosher and observes the sabbath. His daughter is a throwback to Isaac T., certainly the most observant Jew the Hart clan has produced in the last hundred years.

The Harts have deep roots in the South, but they are comparative newcomers. Jews, most of them Sephardim from the Caribbean and Europe, began settling in southern seaport towns in the seventeenth century and gradually moved inland. Some were merchants, others became planters and farmers, and they took an active part in the political and cultural life of their region. In the eighteenth century, Judah Touro of New Orleans gained national fame as one of America's first philanthropists, establishing charitable institutions, including the Jewish orphanage where Carol was raised. Fifty years later, Judah P. Benjamin was elected secretary of state of the Confederacy. "We've been a part of things down here ever since the very beginning," Carol said proudly.

Even before the Civil War, a wave of German Jewish peddlers came south, and many of them stayed, establishing small stores in the towns and hamlets of the region. Later they were joined by a larger group from Eastern Europe. Together they formed Jewish

communities centered around Reform temples, tight-knit little en-
claves where people knew each other and forged family alliances
through marriage.

That was the Jewish South of Carol's boyhood, but it no longer
exists. Highways and chain stores and a flagging farm economy
have forced the small merchants of the South to give way, and the
"Jew Stores" of the region are no longer viable. The sons and
daughters of the merchants went away to school in the 1960s and
1970s and had no incentive to return. Instead they gravitated to
New Orleans, Memphis, Atlanta, and Jackson. The Jewish communities in these cities are holding their own; but elsewhere,
congregations that numbered several hundred families only a generation ago are now down to their last few members.

"Where y'all goin' tomorrow?" asked Carol, and Macy told
him that we would be heading up to Natchez. "I used to go up
there for dances when I was a young man," Carol said with a
faraway look. "They had an elegant temple. I don't guess they
have too many dances these days, though. I hear that things are
pretty bad up there now."

The next morning we set out early to see for ourselves, following the Mississippi River up the Interstate to the Natchez junction
and then on into the town. We passed a Dr. Bug Exterminator
shop, the headquarters of an "Indian Spiritual Advisor," and half
a dozen Skoal Chewing Tobacco billboards before turning into a
charming antebellum neighborhood of tree-lined streets and tourist
attraction mansions.

Temple B'nai Israel isn't quite in that class, but it is, as Carol
had remembered it, an elegant building, a relic of the days when
Natchez was an important cotton port with more than three hundred Jewish families. The temple's sanctuary has a powerful tracker
organ, stained glass windows, and a marble ark that holds five
Torah scrolls. Polished oak pews seat three hundred downstairs,
and there is a special section upstairs which was once reserved for
noisy children and their black mammies.

There are no more mammies in Natchez, however, and only
four Jewish children. When we arrived we found one of them, a
pretty ten-year-old blond named Keely Krouse, solemnly decorat-
ing a small succah with holly bush leaves. Her father, Jerry, was
waiting for us along with his wife, Betty Jo, and two genteel ladies

in their sixties. These were the leaders of what's left of the congregation—thirty-four people in all, twenty-four of them over the age of fifty.

In his early forties, Jerry Krouse is a dark, attractive man who looks a little like Henry Winkler. He was born and raised in Natchez, where his family has a scrap business. In those days there were about twenty Jewish kids in town, but most of them went away to college and never came back. Jerry and two contemporaries are the only ones who stayed behind.

Jerry and Macy were old friends, and they chatted easily as Jerry led us into the basement social hall, where Betty Jo and the two older women sat under a SAVE ETHIOPIAN JEWRY poster sipping their mid-morning coffee. The women greeted Macy softly, inquiring about his mother and aunts. After a few minutes of small talk, he cleared his throat and the group came to attention. "I want to thank y'all for taking the time to hear me this morning," he said, talking Southern, a language as natural to him and the others as Yiddish was to their grandparents.

Macy began by explaining how other communities around the South were going under. They listened raptly as he ran off the list of temples that were closing down, congregations that were reduced to three or four members. Once or twice they interrupted to ask about some specific family, but mostly they sat in shocked silence.

Macy spoke gently, aware that he was telling these people something they knew but had never been able to admit. They had all grown up in this temple, and they had bittersweet memories of the intimate, vibrant congregation that was now gone. For years they had seen the signs, watched the numbers decline, but somehow they had continued to hope. Now Macy was here to tell them that there was no hope, that they were the last generation, the end of the line, and that they had an obligation to make an orderly exit.

They listened to Macy and they believed him. He was no sociologist here to predict the demise of their way of life, no rabbi armed with dire warnings about the future. The future was already here, and Macy, Ellis Hart's boy from Winona, had come to tell them that it was too late for remorse or remission.

"We want to keep our religious articles out of Christian homes where they'll get used as objects d'art—is that how you pronounce that word, Jerry?'' he said, and the ladies smiled. ''We want to keep the Jewish South *in* the South. What we intend to do is to provide for these things in Vicksburg, Meridian, Greenwood, and all the other places that are coming to an end. Now, we don't want y'all to give us anything right now—I'm talking about the future. I want these things to stay right here in Natchez, as long as there is a single Jew to use them.'' He lowered his voice and looked slowly at each one. ''But when the time comes, we want to gather them at the camp where your grandchildren can come and worship in a temple where the '*ner tamid*' (the ritual eternal light) comes from Natchez and the ark comes from the temple in Greenwood and maybe the Torah is from Meridian.''

When he finished talking, there was a long silence. ''Macy's absolutely right,'' Jerry said finally, and the others nodded in agreement. ''Now, some of the people here in town are going to be opposed to this, but we need to explain it to them the way Macy's explained it to us. As far as I'm concerned, we ought to give up these things as soon as y'all open up your museum.'' One of the older women murmured her assent. ''We've got to be practical about this,'' she said in a genteel tone. ''We simply cannot allow ourselves to be ostriches.''

The meeting broke up and Jerry took us on a tour of the temple. We entered a classroom where Hebrew letters were written in chalk on a blackboard. The letters had been there for years. Natchez no longer has a religious school and Jerry drives his children to Alexandria, Louisiana—160 miles round trip—for Sunday school each week. They've been attending school there for six years, and in that time enrollment has dropped from fifty-five to thirty-eight. ''It won't be long before Alexandria goes the way of Natchez,'' Jerry sighed.

In a storeroom off the social hall I spotted some Purim games stacked on a shelf—Queen Esther Roulette, Pin the Tail on Hamen, Loop the Groger—that are used every year when the temple puts on a Purim carnival for Keely Krause and the other three children. ''Purim used to be a fun holiday,'' recalled Jerry. ''Now, to tell you the truth, it's downright discouraging.''

Jerry Krouse is far from religious, but he tries to go to temple every Friday night. ''My Jewish identity is just about the most important thing in my life right now,'' he said. ''That's partly why

I go. But the main thing is, I'm afraid that if I *don't* go, no one will be there, and I don't want our temple to be empty on Friday night. I just couldn't handle that at all.''

We entered the sanctuary, where Keely and her mother were still working on the model succah. ''How does it feel to be one of the last Jewish women in Natchez?'' I asked Betty Jo, and she looked at her husband before answering. ''Oh, I'm not Jewish,'' she said finally, laying holly branches over the roof of the small structure. ''I belong to the First Assembly of Christ. Charismatic Christians?''

''You ever hear of a Christian woman who keeps kosher?'' Jerry demanded. ''Well, you're looking at one right here.'' His tone indicated that he was not pleased by her piety.

''Why are you kosher? For Jerry?'' I asked, and she shook her head emphatically. ''Him? Please, he'll eat anything.'' She said it in a determined tone of voice; obviously this was territory they had been over before. ''I just feel like the Lord had a good reason to forbid those foods. I can't help it, that's mah belief.''

We said good-bye to Betty Jo and Keely and drove across the river for a barbecue lunch that Jerry's wife would not have appreciated. ''Betty Jo is a very religious woman, and religious people have a tendency to get carried away,'' Jerry said, chewing thoughtfully on a hickory-smoked rib. ''Now, I'm not saying I'm perfect, either. In fact, I'm about the most prejudiced person my wife knows. I believe most Christians hate Jews. They think we killed Christ if you want to know the truth. I'm anti-Christian myself, and I guess that's pretty strange considering that both my wife and my mother are Christian women.''

Macy almost choked on his Dr Pepper. ''You mean to tell me Miz Krouse wasn't Jewish?'' he said incredulously, and turned to me. ''Miz Krouse was one of the most active Jewish women in this state. She helped us with the camp, and I believe she was president of the sisterhood right here in Natchez.''

Jerry nodded his assent. ''My mother practically ran the temple. Hell, she organized everything, but she never *was* Jewish—at least not that she'd admit. But she raised me Jewish because that's what she promised my father, and that's just exactly what I intend to do with my children.''

"Why?" I asked him. "I mean, what kind of Jews can they be down here, anyway? There's no community left. What's the point?"

"Do you play chess?" Jerry asked, and I nodded. "Well, I'm a chess player, three-time champion of the state of Mississippi. Down here I'm considered good, but let me tell you, I'm nothing compared to the really great players. Look at them and what do y'all notice? Every last one of those boys is a Jew." He ticked the names off on his fingers. "Fischer, Spassky, Kasparov—his real name is Weinstein—Mikhail Tal, all Jews. Now what does that tell you about the Jewish mentality?"

"Good at board games?" I asked, but Jerry was serious. "Hell no, what it tells you is that Jews are naturally smart. That's our heritage, and I intend to pass it along to my children."

After lunch we dropped Jerry off at his scrap yard and headed down the highway for Port Gibson, a small town that U. S. Grant reputedly spared because it was too beautiful to burn. Near the entrance to the town we stopped in front of the temple, a small, domed building that is, according to Macy, the only example of Moorish architecture in the state.

The temple, which was built in the 1890s, looked foreign among the surrounding southern mansions. Back when there were Jews in Port Gibson, the building must have excited local curiosity; it speaks of strange rituals and exotic customs. But over the years, the Jewish community dwindled down to two people and recently the temple had been turned over to a local man with an interest in historical renovation who promised to maintain it as a Port Gibson monument.

We found the restoration man at the temple. He was a Faulkneresque old gent named Bill, dressed in work clothes and sporting a porkpie hat. Macy greeted him warmly, turning up his good ole boy personality half a notch. Carpenters were already tearing up the floor, and the two men sat down to go over the plans.

"Looks like y'all doin' a great job," Macy said, and Bill nodded happily. "Yessir, won't be long before this ole church is as good as new." Macy made no comment, but a few minutes later, when Bill again referred to the building as a church, Macy couldn't keep silent.

"Now Bill, I don't mean to be disrespectful at all, but the correct name for this building is a synagogue."

"Synagogue? Not a temple?"

"Temple is all right, too. But not church," Macy said with polite firmness.

"Well, I'll go with temple, ah guess," said Bill. "It's easier to say."

Macy shot him a grin of southern complicity. "Yep, easier to spell, too."

While Macy busied himself with the blueprints, Vicki and I went for a walk. Port Gibson is lucky that U. S. Grant never got downtown, which is depressingly ugly even by the exacting standards of rural Mississippi. Many of the stores along Main Street were boarded up, and most of the others had display windows so dirty you had to go inside to see what they were displaying. Here and there dispirited blacks meandered down the dusty street and an occasional dump truck rumbled by, but nothing broke the oppressive silence of the town. Even Vicki, who was raised in Mississippi, seemed taken aback by the utter hopelessness of the scene.

Vicki told me that years ago, when Port Gibson was a thriving place, many of the stores downtown had been owned by Jews. As we walked down Main Street, we searched for vestiges of the Jewish mercantile past that might belong in Macy's museum, and in the middle of the block she spied one—a sign that said FRISHMAN'S DRY GOODS.

Frishman's turned out to be an old-fashioned department store, totally empty of customers. A black salesman dozed in front of a full-length mirror in the shoe department, a peroxide blond woman of indeterminate age arranged merchandise in a bin, and at the front of the store a man in his late fifties leaned over the counter in an almost stupefied state of boredom. He had thinning brown hair combed in a George Wallace pompadour, and his face showed squint lines from innumerable eyefuls of Chesterfield smoke. He wore a cheap sport jacket, and I would have been willing to bet that he had a service tattoo on his forearm.

When we entered the store the man regarded us with faint interest, perhaps taking us for travelers with a sudden rip or stain, in the market for an emergency replacement. But when Vicki told him that she was a museum curator interested in the sign outside and asked permission to take a photograph, he lapsed back into apathy. "Y'all welcome to take your pitcher," he said in a soupy drawl.

"Do you have any idea what happened to the Frishman family that used to own this store?" Vicki asked. The man looked at her closely through the cigarette smoke. "Why do you ask?" he said, showing curiosity for the first time.

Vicki explained that she was collecting material about southern Jews and their history. "I'm a Frishman," he said after a moment's hesitation, and Vicki blinked in surprise. Macy had briefed us on the Jews of Port Gibson, and there weren't supposed to be any Frishmans left. Finding one behind the counter of this old-fashioned store was exciting, and Vicki reintroduced us, mentioning that I was from Jerusalem. The man accepted the news calmly, as if Israelis were frequent shoppers at his dry goods emporium, but Vicki was undeterred by his indifference. For the next fifteen minutes, she bombarded him with questions about himself and the town.

As we talked, the blond woman ambled over to the cash register to listen in and the shoe salesman stirred briefly before lapsing back into a deep sleep, but Frishman refused to let sudden celebrity go to his head. He answered Vicki's questions in a laconic way, and after a quarter of an hour all we really knew about him was that he was a native of Port Gibson, had served in the Marines, was unmarried, and was related to a gaggle of other Frishmans, Shiffmans, and Marxes around the South. He vaguely knew that the temple, only a few blocks away, was undergoing some restoration and that there had been a dispute about its sale, but he seemed reluctant to discuss it. "I didn't really want to get mixed up in all that ruckus," he said. "I go for my religious needs to the temple in Hattiesburg." It was a southern sentiment; in the Bible Belt, respectable people belong to a house of God and have "religious needs," but Mr. Frishman seemed notably unenthusiastic about his.

On the way back to meet Macy it occurred to me that Frishman had accomplished the considerable feat of remaining unaffiliated in a town of only three Jews. Perhaps because we had stumbled on him by accident, he seemed to me a kind of Marrano, an underground figure poised in the netherworld between Jew and gentile,

a Dixie version of the missing link. Macy was amused by the
conceit. "I told you that you were gonna meet some crawfish-
eating Jews down here," he said, laughing, as we crossed Little
Bayou Pierre on the way out of town.

It was almost nightfall when we reached Jackson, where Macy
and Susan Hart live when they are not at camp. The capital of
Mississippi, it is a charmless city of half a million, but after Port
Gibson, Natchez, and Donaldsonville, it seemed like Paris. Macy
had recently been elected vice president of the temple, a Reform
congregation of 250 members, and he intended to go to services
that night. I suddenly realized that it was Simchat Torah, and
I decided to go along to see how the holiday is celebrated in
Mississippi.

"You're gonna have to wait till next year for that one," Macy
said. "We celebrated Simchat Torah last week."

"What are you talking about? Last week was Succot," I told
him, certain that he was confusing the two holidays, which are
always a week apart, but Macy was sure of his ground.

"See, we kind of combined them this year. It made for a bigger
crowd."

My Israeli sensibilities, strained all week by Christian Hadassah
women and Mississippi Marranos, came undone. "You can't change
the date of holidays! It doesn't work like that!" I insisted, but
Macy raised a placating hand. "Now, Ze'ev, if you want to
understand what's goin' on down here, you have to realize one
thing—this isn't New York City or Israel. We're doin' the very
best we can."

After services that night, Macy and Susan took their small
children to an ice cream parlor for sodas. It is a weekly ritual, an
integral part of the southern Jewish experience.

"Actually, it's a bribe," Macy confided. "The kids don't like
coming to temple and I don't blame them. It's even hard for us
sometimes—there aren't many people of our generation there either."

"Then why go?"

"Well, it's an obligation to the community. Now, the children
have to realize that they're Jews, and that that entails an obligation. So, we force 'em to go and then we bribe 'em afterwards."

Most of Macy's and Susan's close friends are Jews, although
Macy isn't sure why. Certainly, to an outside observer, the Jews

of Mississippi seem just about like everyone else. They have no language of their own, no special ethnic customs. But at some indefinable level they feel connected to each other, see themselves as separate, and they communicate on Jewish wavelengths beyond the range of the northern ear.

After ice cream that night, Eric Hearon and Rona Bloom came over for a visit. Rona is a stylish blond in her early forties who looks and sounds like Lee Remick playing the part of a southern senator's wife—coquettish, demure, and charming. Actually, under the taffeta is a tough political intelligence. Rona is a veteran of Democratic politics and that fall she was managing the reelection campaign of Congressman Wayne Dowdy.

Rona Bloom has the conventional southern Jewish biography. She grew up in a small Mississippi town where her father ran a dry goods store, went away to school, married a Jewish boy from another little town, and settled in Jackson. Recently divorced, she met Eric at temple and they have been going together for some time.

Eric's story is a little more unusual. A Jimmy Carter look-alike, he is a CPA who flies for the Air Force reserve on weekends. Although he is one of the most active members of the temple, he was born and raised a Baptist. He grew up in Jackson, but his family was originally from a Mississippi town so small that, as he told me with a grin, "one day it plain went out of business."

As a boy Eric never saw a Jew, and he assumed that they had gone out of business as well, a group of people who existed only in Sunday school stories. But in college he met some live ones, and they kindled his interest, especially after he heard Abba Eban's speech at the United Nations during the Six-Day War.

Three years later he married a Jackson girl whose parents had once been—but no longer considered themselves to be—Jews. By this time Eric was thoroughly intrigued by Judaism and wanted to convert, but his wife resisted. "She said that Jewish children were subject to harassment in Mississippi, and at one point she even threatened to divorce me if I converted," he said. Eric was persistent, though. He began to attend services in Jackson and studied with the rabbi. In 1977, he became a Jew.

"Before my conversion, people at the temple used to tell me,

'You're really going to be surprised by what you find out about us once you get inside.' But actually, I wasn't surprised by very much at all. Now, there was a time when I believed that Jews were way above average in their interpersonal relations, and I was a little taken aback by all the gossiping and backbiting, but that's just human nature, I guess. Yeah, and I was surprised when I found out about all the intolerance of the Orthodox Jews for Reform and Conservative,'' he said.

"How about intolerance of Jews for non-Jews? Did you find any of that?'' I asked. He shrugged and grinned. "Not really. And sometimes the goyim deserve a little intolerance, you know what I mean?''

Eric was divorced in 1983 and he is raising his children to be Jews, but it isn't easy. "Macy and Susan, they can relate to their children from a Jewish family background. But in all honesty, I never had a Jewish childhood and the conversion program doesn't prepare you for everything. For instance, I still have a hard time keeping up on the holidays, and I feel a little left out on some of the household ceremonies, not knowing just the right rituals and all.

"I wouldn't want my children to marry out of the faith, but I've got to be realistic about it,'' he said. "Their own mother married a non-Jew who converted. I can't tell my kids, 'What your ancestors were, that's what you should be.' I can't tell them that their great-grandfather was a rabbi in Poland. Hell, when we get to the kaddish prayer in temple I've got nobody to say it for—I doubt my Baptist grandparents would appreciate it. But other than that, I feel pretty comfortable at services. Actually, they're a whole lot like the Protestant services I grew up with, and I'm kinda sorry about that. Except for the Hebrew, you can't really tell the difference between theirs and ours.''

When Eric Hearon says "ours'' there is no doubt what he means. Like Macy, he sees being Jewish largely in terms of commitment to the Jewish people. Israel is his passion. He is a national board member of the American Israel Public Affairs Committee (AIPAC), helped establish a local political action committee on behalf of Israel, and has visited the country four times in the last few years.

"I've taken congressmen from Mississippi over to see it,'' he told me, "but my most exciting visit was when I had the honor of commanding the first plane in our Air National Guard unit to fly into Israel. I got out of the cockpit and kissed the ground. That turned a few heads."

As we talked, I noticed that Eric was wearing an I.D. bracelet inscribed with the name of Russian refusenik Boris Kelman. "I got it from the Council on Soviet Jewry," he said with a shrug, and Rona started to laugh. "Honestly," she said, "people down here are just so backward sometimes. We met these people at a dinner one night? And the woman just kept *staring* at Eric's wrist? And the next time I met her she said, 'Now you say hello to Boris for me, hear?' " Macy, Susan, and I burst out laughing—you have to see Eric Hearon to know what an unlikely Boris Kelman he makes.

Eric flushed, and then laughed along with everybody else. "Now how do you know what Boris Kelman looks like?" he asked, and someone said, "That's easy. He looks like Irv Feldman," and they all laughed again.

The next morning I went to pay a visit to Irv Feldman and his wife Judy, who are the proprietors of Jackson's only Jewish restaurant, the Olde Tyme Delicatessen. Feldman has a hook nose and sad eyes—not the kind of deli man who wisecracks with the customers. He was raised in St. Louis and came south when he married Judy. She is a Clarksdale girl, the daughter of a Jewish dirt farmer who went bust in the Depression, moved into Jackson, and opened the Olde Tyme. Irv and Judy run it now, and under their guidance it has become one of the principal Jewish institutions in Mississippi.

"Watch out, though," Susan Hart cautioned me before I went to see them. "They serve Christian samwiches."

"What's a Christian samwich?" I asked her.

"A thin one," she said with a giggle.

Irv Feldman disagrees. He considers himself a deli man with a sense of proportion. "I was up in New York at the Carnegie Delicatessen," he told me. "And I'm going to tell you something—they give you too much. You can hardly eat it, it falls apart in your hands, you can't even finish it. Who needs it?" He contemplated the waste with a pained expression.

"Now, I'm not saying the New York delis aren't great, not at all. I was up there a few years ago and I went to the Stage every day for a week, just to watch how they make their Reuben sandwich. And today, the Reuben is my third leading sandwich,'' he said, his sad eyes sparkling at the memory of his successful venture into industrial espionage.

Feldman told me that ninety-five percent of his customers are Christians with an imperfect grasp of deli idiom. ''A lot of people order 'kosher ham,' '' he said. ''They think 'kosher' means 'better' in Yiddish.'' The Olde Tyme's menu is a concession to local tastes, with grits and gumbo alongside matzoh ball soup and kosher beef rib. Jewish patrons go for corned beef (Feldman sells four hundred pounds a week) and bagels and lox. When they first opened up twenty-five years ago, the Feldmans catered mostly weddings. Today, with the trend at the temple toward a more traditional style of Judaism, they do five or six bar mitzvahs a year.

Irv Feldman was obviously proud of his role in the Jackson Jewish community, and indeed throughout Mississippi. He imports kosher meat for the three families in the state who keep the dietary laws, and on Passover he stocks his deli with a full line of Manischewitz and Rokeach products. ''I try to make sure we get everything people need,'' he said in a serious voice. ''It's not like New York down here—if I don't carry it, you can't get it. I believe that we've got the only Yahrzeit candles between here and Memphis.''

Feldman's clientele has included a number of visiting celebrities, such as Jan Peerce, Rosalyn Carter, and the Allman Brothers, but his fondest memories are of the time back in the sixties when the restaurant was a hangout for Jewish civil rights lawyers and activists. The Jews of Mississippi supported civil rights, and in those violent days such support could be dangerous.

Macy and Vicki Fox talked about growing up during the civil rights era as we drove to Meridian on Sunday morning. Black church music on the radio provided a sound track as they discussed the fear and confusion of those days. For Macy, much of it was secondhand—Winona made a relatively peaceful adjustment, and the Harts, as the only Jewish family in town, were never identified with the northern agitators. But Vicki, who grew up in Hattiesburg, had vivid recollections of firebombings and frightened conversations among her parents' friends.

As southerners invariably do, they assured me that things have changed radically since then. But the memories and scars are still fresh, and Meridian is a particular symbol of the time when it was dangerous to be a Jew in Mississippi.

Back in the 1960s, Meridian had a flourishing Jewish community, self-confident enough to have built an impressive temple, complete with a modern Sunday school wing. But not long after it was finished the temple was firebombed, and one of the town's leading Jewish citizens received death threats. The Jews of Meridian banded together, raised money, and funded an FBI investigation that led to the capture of the would-be assassins, who included a local grade school teacher moonlighting as a Ku Klux Klan hitperson.

Those were days of high drama for the Jews of Meridian—days that contrast sharply with the present drab reality of the community. The religious school, built with such optimism only a generation ago, stands empty and padlocked—there isn't a single Jewish child left in town. The Meridian Jewish community is coming to its end, not with a white-sheeted bang, but a whimper.

As we pulled into town, Macy informed me that we would have not one, but two meetings. Meridian, despite its depleted condition, has both a Reform temple and an Orthodox shul. The split is a relic of the flush days when Meridian had enough Jews to indulge in theological contentiousness.

We went first to the Herzogs', transplanted New Yorkers whose Honda Accord SE bears the vanity plate CHAI 18. About twenty members of the temple, most of them in their fifties or sixties, were gathered in the spacious family room, munching bagels and lox imported from the Olde Tyme. Macy greeted each person by name and asked about their children—his contemporaries—now scattered across the South. Most of the people had known Macy since his teenage youth group days, and they treated him with respect, even deference.

Al Herzog called the meeting to order in a hoarse Yankee voice and gave Macy the floor. As Macy described the decline of communities in Port Gibson, Laurel, Natchez, and elsewhere, his audience listened with dismay. But no one contradicted him. He spoke quietly, almost dryly, leading them step by step to the need to face the future and prepare for the end.

It was an exercise in grass roots leadership that reminded me of the Rabbinical injunction: "Where there is no man, be a man," and the people in the room responded with gratitude. When Al Herzog proposed that the community draw up a "last will and testament," several flinched, but again no one disagreed.

As the meeting was breaking up, a man in a golf outfit took me aside and introduced himself as Arnold Frishman. He asked if I had run across his son, Arnold, Jr., in Jerusalem. "He's a student at the Or Samach Yeshiva," he said in a deep drawl, naming an ultra-Orthodox rabbinical academy that caters to born-again Jews. Mr. Frishman didn't seem very happy with his son's choice of life-style. A hundred years ago his people had left a European ghetto for a new life in America. Now Arnold, Jr., was swimming against the tide, recrossing the ocean to the Eastern European pietism of long-departed ancestors. Arnold, Sr., clearly didn't understand how or why this genetic time bomb had gone off in his son.

I promised to say hello to Arnold Jr., and suddenly I remembered Port Gibson. "I met a man over there who runs a store called Frishman's," I told him.

"Yeah, he's a cousin of mine," he said.

"He goes to Hattiesburg for his religious needs," I said, and Arnold, Sr., whose boy has gone to Jerusalem for his, looked at me blankly.

Macy approached with Sammy Davidson, a wizened old man with a bulldog face. Davidson was born and raised in Meridian and he was related to many of the guests at the Herzogs', but as the president of the rival Orthodox synagogue he had discreetly waited outside until the temple people had finished their business.

"Ah'm gonna carry y'all over to the shul now," he said, "so's Macy B. can talk to the minyan."

As we followed Sammy's car through the Sunday morning quiet, Macy described him admiringly as "the stubbornest old Jew in Mississippi." The shul's membership was down to eleven and finding the requisite ten men for prayers is an ornery problem, but Sammy refused to give up. Occasionally one of the men from the temple dropped by, but most days were a scramble. That year Davidson had taken out ads in several national Jewish newspapers, offering to pay transportation and expenses for Jews willing to come down to Meridian for Rosh Hashanah and Yom Kippur. But there had been no takers, and the regulars were forced to spend all day in synagogue, a team with no bench.

Sammy stopped alongside a tiny white shingled building with no identifying sign, located on the corner of two run-down residential streets. As we walked around front, I saw half a dozen old men leaning against a red pickup truck, like characters in a Jack Daniels advertisement. These were the good ole boychiks of Meridian. One wore a fishing cap over his yarmulke, another sported a baseball hat compliments of "Red Pylate's Machine and Welding." They greeted us with a chorus of howdys, pushed themselves off the truck with effort, and ambled into their clapboard shul.

The synagogue consisted of one room. Six wood benches faced a small platform decorated with dusty Israeli and American flags. On the far wall was a small ark and a memorial plaque. The wood floor was unvarnished, and the other walls, made of pea-green plasterboard, were bare. A small storage closet contained some prayer books and a King Edward cigar box full of filmy shot glasses for the morning schnapps. Off the sanctuary was a small restroom with a brass spittoon on the floor next to the sink.

Only two of the men were under seventy, and only one, Jeff Winters, was not a native. Winters, a Brooklyn-born flight instructor at the nearby naval base, was discovered and recruited by Sammy in the course of his relentless pursuit of a minyan. He told me he wasn't particularly religious and was married to a non-Jewish woman, but he felt a sense of solidarity with the boychiks and came to services when he wasn't on duty. His presence lent a touch of vitality to the congregation, and the old men were obviously fond of him; but military life is unpredictable, and they knew he might well be gone before they were.

Sammy introduced Macy to the men, and for the first time on the tour there were several people who didn't know him. Still, they were able to place him with a couple of questions—"Are you Ellis Hart's boy from over in Winona? Is Miss Riva your momma?" —and he went to go into his appeal. Looking around the chapel there seemed little of historical value, although the spittoon would make an interesting addition to Macy's aggregate temple in Utica. But the men were noncommittal, unwilling to consign any part of their little synagogue to a museum. Instead, they preferred to reminisce.

"When I was a boy, we used to walk to this shul every Saturday morning," said one old-timer, with a distant look in his eyes. " 'Course we didn't have no automobile back then anyways, just this ole Cushman motor scooter my daddy had is all."

"Yeah, his daddy was somethin' else," said another man. "I remember back during the Six-Day War, he packed his forty-five and flew over to Israel to fight. Hell, he must have been in his seventies at least."

The others nodded, recalling the way it had been back when there were still enough Jews to make a minyan, and young fellows didn't come by to inform them that they were a dying breed. Macy, sensitive to their mood, didn't push them. "Y'all talk this over amongst yourselves and let me know," he said. "We're not talkin' about anything urgent, just trying to plan for the future is all." We shook hands all around and then walked out into the overcast Meridian morning, climbed into the van, and headed down the highway for Jackson.

It had been an exhausting few days out on the road in the Dixie diaspora, and Vicki napped in the backseat while Macy and I discussed the next stage of his plans. For the foreseeable future he would be busy with the new project, crisscrossing Mississippi, Arkansas, Louisiana, and western Tennessee, touring museums, spending interminable hours writing grant proposals, and meeting with lawyers, contractors, and benefactors. No one would pay him for his time or trouble, and he didn't expect them to. He was merely fulfilling an obligation. As we talked, I looked at him closely, as old friends entering middle age sometimes do, and I saw that he had lost his country-boy looks. I was startled by something I saw in him. Balding, with a gray beard and prominent nose, Macy B. looked like a Jew.

Strangely, he wasn't sure that he felt like one. "Sometimes I don't even know if I believe in all this," he said in a soft voice, careful not to wake Vicki. "I mean, I'm not religious. I don't know Hebrew or anything. You come right down to it, I'm a Jewish illiterate. And I guarantee you, I never planned my life this way. I got out of college and I thought about a dozen different things, but I sure as hell didn't think I'd wind up doing this. I've been involved in Jewish things now for goin' on twenty-five years, goin' back to my youth group days, and I'm amazed that I have. My only reason, I guess, is that I'm doing it for my kids.''

"Hey, Mace, you were doing this for more than fifteen years before you had any kids,'' I reminded him, and he thought about that for a long moment.

"Damn, boy, you right,'' he said in his squeaky southern twang, and he turned to face me with a grin. "I guess I just got me one of them Jewish hearts everybody keeps talkin' about.''

CHAPTER TWO

THE GREAT
IOWA JEW HUNT

I left Macy and flew up the Mississippi to Moline, Illinois. My destination was the Stardust Motel, where I was supposed to meet Lori Posin of the American Israel Public Affairs Committee (AIPAC). At the time Lori was based in Washington, but she spent most of her time on the road, searching out and organizing Jews in the boondocks of America. At AIPAC they call it Jew hunting. I came to Moline to join her annual Midwestern Jew Hunt.

The idea was proposed to me by AIPAC's director, Tom Dine, over drinks at the King David Hotel in Jerusalem. Dine is a Brooks Brothers Jew in his forties, a bright, fastidious fellow with a highly developed aesthetic sense, who judges synagogues by their architecture and rabbis by their political connections. In another Jewish organization, Dine's unemotional approach might be a drawback. But AIPAC is about politics, and Dine is a consummate Washington insider. Since taking over in 1980, he has turned the group into a sophisticated, powerful voice for Israel.

AIPAC's success has excited dark conjecture about a Jewish

conspiracy on the part of anti-Semites, causing some Jews to fear the lobby's high profile. But Dine, who was born and raised in Cincinnati, is far too confident to be intimidated by such fears.

"American Jews are American citizens, and American citizens have the right to organize, express opinions, and take part in the political process of their country. There's nothing wrong with that," he told me. "The secret of our success is organization and hard work. You ought to go out in the field and see for yourself."

This kind of self-assurance is relatively new for American Jews. A generation ago they were still political outsiders and the American-Israeli relationship was far from intimate. During the Suez Crisis, for example, President Eisenhower not only threatened Israel, but he refused to discuss the issue with American Jewish leaders (his biographer, Stephen Ambrose, attributed this to Ike's dislike of Jews). Even John F. Kennedy, whose party had a strong Jewish component, declined to allow Israeli Prime Minister David Ben-Gurion to pay a state visit to Washington, preferring to meet with him in New York.

The Six-Day War was a turning point for Jewish involvement in American politics. The threat to Israel's survival galvanized Jews around a national issue. Just as important, the Jewish community had outgrown its immigrant jitters; by 1967, most Jews felt sufficiently self-confident to speak out, something they had failed to do a generation earlier when Franklin Roosevelt charmed and bullied Jewish leaders into silence about the Holocaust.

The year nineteen hundred and sixty-seven also marked the beginning of AIPAC's transformation from a small, marginal political group into a powerful Washington lobby. Lyndon Johnson was a sympathetic president (his administration was the first to sell Israel sophisticated weapons) and Israel was widely admired in America for its military victory. AIPAC's growth accelerated once again in 1973, as a result of the Yom Kippur War and the Arab oil boycott. By the 1980s the Reagan administration's pro-Israel policies, Israel's high standing in American public opinion, and Dine's astute leadership combined to make AIPAC one of the nation's most effective political machines.

The emergence of Jewish political power in America has more than one cause. The United States is a more tolerant and pluralistic country than it was under FDR or Eisenhower. The Holocaust taught American Jews the price of political impotence. And last but by no means least, Israel has proved an ideal issue—the country is pro-American, widely admired by non-Jews, and emotionally compelling for the Jewish mainstream. There may be occasional distress over Israeli policy, such as in the West Bank and Gaza; but basically, there is no downside to support for Israel in America.

In many ways, politics in a democracy are a mirror of society, and talking to Tom Dine on the patio of the King David, it occurred to me that AIPAC could provide an interesting view of the American Jewish state of mind. I was curious to know how Jews talked to each other about issues, how they perceived their interests, and how they pursued them. Of course I knew the basics—most Jews support Israel and tend to be liberal Democrats on domestic issues. What I wanted was to get a feel for Jewish politics at the grass roots level. An AIPAC Jew hunt seemed like a good place to start—which is how I wound up in Moline, at the Stardust Motel, in the middle of October.

The Stardust is a kind of Big Ten Versailles, with marble pillars in the lobby and bogus Greek statuary in the parking lot—not Tom Dine's kind of place at all. When I arrived, I found Lori Posin in a private room, conducting a working dinner with fifteen or so middle-aged people. The seventh game of the World Series was on television that night and another Jewish organization might have been tempted to cancel or postpone. But AIPAC plays a kind of hardball of its own, and it attracts people who would rather talk politics than watch Boston get clobbered by the Mets.

Lori gave me a brief smile of recognition when I came in but continued explaining the intricacies of the upcoming foreign aid bill to her audience of ophthalmologists, downtown retailers, and lawyers. She looked like a young Jane Fonda playing the part of a political organizer—wholesomely attractive, crisply professional, and self-confident in a way that didn't threaten or antagonize anyone.

As I listened to her, I felt a poke in the ribs. A pecked-at-looking man sitting next to me tapped my copy of the *Quad-City Times* ("The Midwest's Most Exciting Newspaper") and whispered, "this is a Jewish newspaper." The paper looked unremarkable to me—just another *USA Today* clone—but the man was referring to its ownership, not its content.

Unsophisticated people, Jews and non-Jews alike, sometimes imagine there is a connection between the Jewish community in America and the Jews who own or run many of the country's most prestigious magazines and newspapers. In fact, most of these journalistic Jews are about as involved in Jewish life as Jackie Kennedy is in the Knights of Columbus Ladies' Auxiliary. But AIPAC is made up of pros, people who deal in Washington reality; they would never consider the *Quad-City Times* (or *The New York Times*) to be, in any useful sense, a Jewish paper.

Determined to make an impression, the man poked me again. "See this motel?" he asked. "It's a Jewish motel." Here, it seemed to me, he was on more solid ground. Jewish politics in the United States are financed largely by businessmen—the American equivalent of the merchants of Eastern Europe who underwrote struggling Talmudic scholars or built new roofs on village synagogues. In the world of AIPAC, a Jewish journalist means trouble; a Jewish hotel owner means a discount.

Jews originally came to the Midwest for the same reason they went south—to find economic opportunity. My own great-grandfather settled in Sterling, Illinois, a small town not too far from Moline, more than one hundred years ago. He was the only Jew in town. Nominally a tailor, he became a popular figure in the local saloons. It is a little-recorded fact of Jewish history that he organized the first Simchat Torah parade in southern Illinois, holding aloft a Torah he had brought from Europe and leading a procession of staggering Elks down the main street of the dusty little hamlet singing "The Battle Hymn of the Republic."

My great-grandfather spent too much time with the Elks to ever really get ahead, but most of his fellow Jews had a more sober turn of mind and they prospered. In recent years, however, prosperity has turned into decline. As in the South, automobiles, chain stores, shopping malls, and falling farm prices have undermined the small merchants of the heartland. Their children have mostly moved to big cities—Chicago, Minneapolis, or the West Coast. Those who stay tend to marry non-Jews. As a result,

Jewish communities in the farm belt are shrinking, their average age is progressively older, and some are already approaching a total collapse like that in Mississippi.

And yet, during the Jew hunt I didn't feel the same sense of melancholy that had infused Macy's tour of the Dixie diaspora. Midwestern Jewry has always been a poor cousin of Chicago, and by extension New York; it lacks the southern sense of its own specialness and tradition. And, more important, I was with Lori Posin of AIPAC, a traveling saleswoman with the sexiest item in the American Jewish catalog. In a region of shrinking synagogue rosters and disappearing ethnicity, AIPAC is a dynamic, growing organization. It deals in the substance and glamour of Washington, national politics, and international diplomacy. Lori Posin was able to introduce the provincials to that world, like a drummer showing Paris fashions to farmers' wives.

Despite its depleted state, midwestern Jewry is an important element in AIPAC's planning. The organization thrives because it is able to muster a national constituency. The areas of highest Jewish density—New York, New Jersey, Philadelphia, Southern California—are easy. But there are Jews in the boondocks, too—people who vote and contribute money and identify, or can be taught to identify, with Israel. The job of the Jew hunter is to track them down and throw the AIPAC net over their heads.

That night at the Stardust, Lori and I went over her itinerary for the coming few days. Most national Jewish groups divide the country into congregations or federations, but AIPAC sees the world in terms of electoral units. During her midwestern swing, Lori was scheduled to visit every one of Iowa's eight congressional districts, with side trips into Illinois, Nebraska, and South Dakota. It is arduous work, but it has its rewards, not least of which is the gratitude and respect she receives from people eager to be caught.

The next morning, Lori wheeled her rented Chevrolet onto Interstate 80 in the direction of Iowa City in the Third Congressional District. In her three years at AIPAC Lori had visited forty-two states and driven hundreds of thousands of miles. Usually she is alone. Most nights she winds up in a motel, curled up with road maps and congregational rosters, eating greasy meals off room service trays, and watching Johnny Carson.

Lori Posin has visited Israel, too, and she likes the country, but she would never consider living there. Although she believes strongly in AIPAC's message, she is first and foremost an American political organizer; it would be easy to imagine her working for the AMA, the Republican National Committee, or the Teamsters. Like her boss, Tom Dine, there was no schmaltz in her presentation or her personality, no appeal to ethnic ties or religious imperatives. "AIPAC is perfect for people who are looking for a Jewish activity without becoming involved in the Jewish community," she told me on the way to Iowa City.

Lori's farm belt tour, like all her visits to the hinterland, began with a single contact, a Des Moines woman who wrote to AIPAC and applied for membership. Lori developed a telephone friendship with the woman, who put her in touch with a local Reform rabbi. That led to contacts with other rabbis around the state, and with interested laypeople.

Eventually Lori was able to set up a series of parlor meetings in various cities, where she could meet prospective members and explain the AIPAC program. During her trip, she would also continue to seek out Jews who were not yet in the AIPAC network, which is why our first stop was the Hillel House on the campus of the University of Iowa.

University people are notoriously uninvolved in Jewish community affairs. Like journalists, they tend to be critical of the establishment, and their primary identification is most likely to be with their profession and its values. Besides, most of them are not willing or able to give large sums of money to the United Jewish Appeal or other fundraising groups. But university people are just what Lori is looking for.

"Money is no problem for us," she said, as we pulled into the parking lot of the Hillel. "I'm not out here looking for rich Jews. I'm looking for activists. Political science professors can be very good, rabbis, anyone involved in local politics. A few people in a district like this can make all the difference in the world."

People who can make a difference become what are known as "key contacts." Ideally they have a personal relationship with a member of Congress or a senator, or have political chits they can cash on behalf of Israel. Given the extraordinarily high degree of Jewish involvement in politics, it isn't too hard to find key contacts—Lori estimated that AIPAC has them for about ninety percent of the members of the House of Representatives and ninety-eight percent of the Senate.

Our meeting in Iowa City was with Jeff Portman, a Reform rabbi who serves as the local Hillel director. "A couple of years ago we had problems with some of the more liberal rabbis and laypeople who disagreed with Begin's policies," Lori told me, "but today things are much easier. Maybe one percent of rabbis give you a hard time and just about all the Jews out here are very supportive."

Portman, a studious-looking man in his mid-thirties, is a supporter. Unlike some other Jewish organizations, AIPAC does not compete with him for members or money; on the contrary, it enhances his power and prestige by enabling him to introduce congregants to the American political game.

Lori and the rabbi sat in his study poring over a computer printout of Iowa City's affiliated Jews. Lori wrote down the names of a couple involved in Democratic politics and a woman who once served on the city council. "The faculty here are liberal, but the students are just incredibly conservative," Portman said with regret, but Lori couldn't have cared less. AIPAC is an aggressively nonpartisan group, and there is room for everyone. Besides, she got her start as a Reaganite. "Give me the names of some active students and I'll see them on my next trip out here," she said.

The meeting took less than an hour, and when it was over she had a list of half a dozen key contact prospects—people whom she could call when she got back to Washington. Not all of them would want to get involved, but Lori knew from experience that at least several would be interested and flattered—and in a place like the Third District, that would be enough. No place is too small or remote for her. After all, every town and hamlet in America has a representative in Congress, and all of them vote on Israel-related issues.

Lori wound up the Hillel meeting with brisk efficiency. We had to make Waterloo by nightfall, and she wanted to stop for lunch at the Amana Colonies. Her years on the road have made her an experienced traveler, and the colonies, founded in the 1850s by a Protestant religious sect from Germany, were the closest thing to a tourist attraction in this part of the state.

After a heavy Teutonic lunch we took a walk through the village, browsing through stores with German names. We stopped for coffee at a tavern with stuffed moose and wild boar heads above the fireplace and a plastic reindeer propped against one wall. I kept reminding myself that the colonies were founded in 1854 by God-fearing Christians who had nothing to do with the Third Reich, but I couldn't help feeling uncomfortable, and I noticed that Lori did, too. The gloomy, Wagnerian tavern seemed somehow sinister, and I was relieved when we got back to the car and the flat-voiced disc jockey who played country tunes and hawked farm implements on the radio.

It will be a very long time before American Jews feel comfortable around Germans. The trauma of the Holocaust is still sinking in. Its visible manifestations are television documentaries, monuments, museums—and organizations like AIPAC, whose subtext is that only Jewish political power and the existence of the state of Israel can prevent a future catastrophe. In her presentation, Lori never mentioned anti-Semitism or the Nazis; she didn't have to. Hitler and Arafat were always present, at every AIPAC gathering, uninvited guests who provided a sense of cohesion and purpose.

We arrived in Waterloo around sunset and rendezvoused with Lori's contact, Martha Nash. They had never met before—Lori got Nash's name from a local rabbi and called her cold—but within a few minutes the two women were chatting like old friends. Martha, a diminutive grandmother with seemingly boundless energy, took us to the best restaurant in Waterloo, Lodge 290 of the Elks Club. There we were joined by a round, jolly professor of Spanish from the local college, his equally round, jolly wife, and a dignified, Pillsbury-prim widow in her sixties. The professor and his wife were transplanted New Yorkers and they had a Broadway flamboyance. Martha and the widow, by contrast, seemed as austere as Grant Wood figures.

The talk at dinner was mostly about the Jewish community of Waterloo, which is in a state of decline. Once there were ninety pupils in the synagogue religious school; now there are twenty-three. Most Waterloo Jews marry Christians, and the widow lady, who genteelly lowered her voice whenever she said the word "Jew," confided that her bachelor son would almost certainly marry out of the faith. Neither she nor her dinner companions seemed to feel that this was in any way unusual or undesirable; in a place like Waterloo, Jews have long since made their accommodation with the realities of American life.

Farm belt anti-Semitism was a hot topic that fall—there had been several articles in national publications, and *60 Minutes* had recently done a segment on disgruntled Iowa farmers who allegedly blamed Jewish bankers for their financial hardships—but none of our hosts had any personal experience of it. Martha Nash explained that the Elks Club, the pinnacle of Waterloo society, has been open to Jews for years, and even the Elkettes, once restricted, now welcome Jewish members.

A sense of confidence in American tolerance is a necessary condition for Jewish political activity, and it makes up a large part of AIPAC's appeal. The formula requires just enough atavistic fear to keep Jews on their toes, but not enough real anti-Semitism to frighten them or make them lose faith in the system.

This equilibrium is at the heart of the AIPAC effort. Jews in America remember the Holocaust and the price of powerlessness in the face of an indifferent U.S. government. The determination to develop political power is in large part a reaction to that experience. But it is the sort of power that only works under the existing ground rules. As long as America remains decent, tolerant, and pluralistic, political clout of the AIPAC variety has value. But it is an umbrella designed for a sunny day. AIPAC's power is conditional, not independent, and even its most assertive members must always keep that in mind.

After dinner we drove to the temple, where about thirty people, most of them middle-aged, were gathered. Martha Nash introduced Lori, who spoke in a low-key, direct way about the AIPAC program. She briefed the audience on foreign aid ("At three billion dollars a year, Israel is a *real* bargain for American security"), the fight against arms sales to Israel's enemies ("We support the proposal to require congressional approval for arms sales to the Arabs"), and the effort to grant Israel a status equal to that of the NATO countries. These were Washington issues, well known to capital insiders but somewhat abstract out in Iowa, and she did her best to simplify them. The crowd followed her presentation carefully, and with obvious affection. There was something of the good Jewish daughter about her, and as she spoke many of the older people nodded their heads encouragingly, wanting her to do well.

There was only a month or so until the 1986 elections, and Lori gave a rundown on AIPAC's view of various contests. She was careful not to endorse specific candidates, but she made the organization's preferences clear. She was especially concerned about Senator Alan Cranston of California, who was fighting for reelection. "How many of you have received direct mail appeals for Cranston?" she asked, and most of the hands in the room went up. "He's been very, *very* good on issues that concern the pro-Israel community," she reminded them.

AIPAC rarely talks about "the Jews." The phrase "pro-Israel community" sounds more professional, and in any event about half the people Lori deals with have non-Jewish partners. Intermarriage is not an issue for AIPAC (Dine himself is married to a non-Jewish woman); the organization seeks to build the widest possible coalition, and it takes its supporters where it finds them. One of the great ironies of the "Jewish lobby" is that an increasing number of its activists aren't Jewish.

After her pitch for Cranston, Lori reminded the audience that Senator Jim Abdnor of neighboring South Dakota was lukewarm on foreign aid to Israel. A few years ago, Israel had some real enemies in the Senate—William Fulbright of Arkansas, James Abourezk of South Dakota, Charles Percy of Illinois—but, one by one, they bit the dust. From AIPAC's viewpoint, the 1986 elections were for the most part a choice between good and better. Abdnor was the closest thing it had to a villain.

Lori concluded on a Mr.-Smith-goes-to-Washington note. "You have representatives in the House and Senate, and they want to hear from you," she said. "Your job is to let them know what you want. Remember, that's your right as American citizens. Your opinion can really make a difference."

The next morning we hit the road for Sioux Falls, South Dakota. Lori took the wheel, driving across southern Minnesota with a calm competence. By mid-morning we were both hungry and decided to stop for lunch in Blue Earth, a small town whose entrance is guarded by a huge statue of the Jolly Green Giant. A sign informed us that Blue Earth's population was three thousand and change.

"Do you think you could find a Jew out here?" I asked, and she grinned at the challenge.

"Give me a stack of dimes and a phone book and a couple hours and I could," she said confidently. She had noticed a Cantonese restaurant on the main street, a sure tip-off for a Jew hunter. "You find a Chinese restaurant, there's got to be some Jews around," she said.

When we arrived in Sioux Falls, Lori changed from her driving outfit of jeans and a sweater into her work clothes, a navy blue suit and high heels. An AIPAC volunteer met us downtown and took us to the home of a local lawyer named Duke Horowitz, where twenty or so people—roughly ten percent of Sioux Falls's diminishing Jewish community—were sipping coffee and eating sponge cake.

President Reagan was campaigning that day in Rapid City on the other side of the state. According to radio reports, monster crowds had turned out for his rallies, while Lori addressed a group of twenty. But a handful of dedicated people in a state like South Dakota are all you need; it is quite possible that there weren't twenty people in Rapid City that day—including the president— who would have been willing to give up an afternoon to discuss Middle Eastern policy.

Here, as elsewhere, Lori was greeted with affection by people hungry for a Jewish winner. Most of them seemed to be second- and third-generation midwesterners, but despite their prairie isolation they identified with Israel in a deeply personal way. When Lori mentioned the peace treaty with Egypt, for example, a woman with blue hair and a corn belt twang interrupted with a loud "If you can call what we have peace." During this trip and all across the country, Jews constantly referred to Israel as "us" and "we," usages I found alternately touching and gratuitous.

In Sioux Falls, Lori gave her standard presentation and answered the usual questions. The audience was willing, even eager to sign up. She was offering them a Jewish activity they could understand and appreciate, something that didn't threaten them or put them off.

The accessibility of AIPAC's work is a key factor in its popularity. A couple of months later, in Los Angeles, I discussed this phenomenon with Norman Mirsky, a sociologist who is an expert on the subject of Jewish affiliation. Mirsky once spent four months at Factor's Delicatessen on Pico Boulevard in L.A. studying the restaurant's patrons. He discovered that most of them are highly assimilated Jews, often with non-Jewish partners. "They want to identify as Jews, but they don't know how," he said. "They don't feel comfortable in a temple or synagogue, don't know how to behave or what to do. But they know enough not to order pastrami on white bread, and they can impress their non-Jewish spouses with their familiarity with Jewish foods. That's why they come."

For Jews in places like Sioux Falls, AIPAC is a kind of political Factor's Deli. They belong to temples because affiliation is the sine qua non of Jewishness; but they are not religious people, and any ethnic differences between themselves and their neighbors are more imagined than real. These people are Jews without Jewish skills, and they feel comfortable with AIPAC because the organization doesn't require any.

We left South Dakota and returned to Sioux City, Iowa for Lori's last meeting of the day. Sioux City's main claim to Jewish fame is as the hometown of "the twins"—Ann Landers and Dear Abby. Back when they were growing up there were three thousand Jews in town; but in recent years the number has shrunk to seven hundred.

"It's a dying community," said our host at dinner. The man, a local merchant who had lived for a few years in Israel, grew progressively more morose as he described the decline of Jewish life in his city.

"Believe me," he said, "it's a total disaster. The young people all move away, it's very demoralizing. Even the ones who stay don't have the same spirit, the same 'ta'am.' There's such a thing as waking up in the middle of the night when Israel is in trouble and not being able to get back to sleep again. I don't think the younger generation really feels that way anymore."

In light of his pessimism, I was surprised by the turnout that night. More than fifty people showed up at the home of a wealthy businessman, and a good many of them were in their late twenties or thirties. When Lori passed her list around at the end of her presentation, two dozen people signed up.

That night, back at the hotel, Lori and I said good-bye. I was going on to Milwaukee, and she had to leave at dawn for Nebraska, on the last leg of the Great Plains Jew hunt. She would drive for hours through the bleak countryside to meet with one person, a key contact she had cultivated over the phone, and then drive hours more to Des Moines to catch a plane for Washington.

"Has it been a successful trip?" I asked her.

"Very successful," she said. "I've already got more names than I expected. And tomorrow I might get one or two more. It's slow work, but it's necessary. If you want to build a coalition, you've got to build it with people. It's the only way."

AIPAC deals in political retail but there is another, mass market approach to Jewish political activity. Its improbable center is Fox Point, Wisconsin, a Milwaukee suburb. There, in a blue hangarlike building, two jovial Jewish yuppies named Bruce Arbit and Jerry Benjamin have put together a company called A.B. Data that may eventually make the Jew hunter as obsolete as the blacksmith.

A.B. Data's headquarters has the anti-architecture common to computer firms, from Cambridge to Silicon Valley. But it is a high-tech company with a difference. The coffee table in its waiting room is stacked with copies of the *Baltimore Jewish Times* and the *Jerusalem Post Overseas Edition,* and its walls are decorated with Israeli art posters. A.B. Data is a specialty operation, America's leading Jewish direct marketing firm.

Like many successful ventures, A.B. Data came about almost by accident. It was founded by Bruce Arbit, a potbellied man in his early thirties who chain-smokes Kools and punctuates his conversation with frequent belly laughs. Arbit is a native of Milwaukee who was raised in a Labor Zionist home and moved to Israel after high school. He attended Haifa University and intended to stay. Instead, he fell in love with an American girl who "dragged me home kicking and screaming."

Back in Milwaukee, Arbit started a small Jewish publishing business. He wanted to sell books by direct mail, but he soon realized that there were no Jewish lists available. Slowly he began to assemble his own, using synagogue rosters and telephone books. By 1978, he had accumulated so many names that he began to sell his lists to organizations and politicians.

At about the same time he met Jerry Benjamin, a Harvard-trained educator and Jewish activist. Jerry was raised in a small town in Ohio, where he developed strong ideological passions— liberal in politics, conservative in religion. When the two met, Jerry was working as an administrator at the Maimonides Academy, a prestigious New England Orthodox school. Bruce convinced him to leave and join him in Milwaukee.

"In those days, A.B. Data was just a hole in the wall," said Jerry. He is a plump, sandy haired fellow with a boyish, open manner and an obvious delight in his success. He and Bruce are business partners, but they are also close friends who trade genial insults, finish each other's sentences, and laugh loudly at each other's jokes. They could have been a borscht belt comedy duo; instead, they are the proprietors of a multi-million-dollar business that employs 225 people.

The reason for this growth can be summed up in one word— information. Jerry Benjamin and Bruce Arbit know more than anyone else about where American Jews are and how they can be reached. "Let's say you want to get in touch with red-haired Jewish doctors who play golf," Bruce said, bubbling with the enthusiasm of a magician about to perform a well-rehearsed trick. "Okay, first we pull our file on Jewish doctors, which is compiled from medical registries, phone books, and synagogue rosters. Then, for the red hair, we go to the motor vehicle registries— most states list hair color for driver's licenses and you can get that stuff easily. And then, for the golf, you turn to the subscription list of *Golf* magazine. Lay one on top of the next until you come up with a list. Jewish doctors with red hair who play golf. Simple."

Bruce and Jerry estimate that there are roughly 5.6 million Jews in America, or, as they prefer to count, between 2.3 and 2.6

million households. Their computers list the names and addresses of 1.7 million households—approximately two-thirds of the total. "There are no absolutely foolproof figures on this," said Bruce. "The only thing we know for sure is that the number of Jews in this country is declining, mostly as a result of intermarriage. It's interesting to note that fewer and fewer of the non-Jewish partners convert. That's a trend."

"How do you find Jews?" I asked, thinking of Lori Posin's painstaking approach. Bruce and Jerry looked at each other and smiled. "Simple. It's all a matter of names and probabilities," said Bruce.

"Exactly," said Jerry, breaking in to finish the thought. "Take the name Cohen, for example. What percentage of the Cohens in this country would you say are Jewish?"

A few weeks earlier I had been looking for Jews in a midwestern inner city and had come across the name "Glorious Cohen" in the phone book. When I called I was informed by an irate Mr. Cohen that he wasn't a Jew and never had been.

"Not all of them," I said, recalling that conversation. Jerry seemed disappointed that I had managed to evade his trap.

"Right. Eighty-six percent of Cohens in America are Jewish. But Cohen is easy. There are 80,000 common Jewish names, each with its own degree of frequency. We match them up with neighborhoods and professions, first names, and other indicators, and we get pretty close to the exact percentages."

"Take the name Gordon," said Bruce. "It's a borderline name. Sheldon Gordon from Long Island is likely to be a Jew. Bubba Gordon from Tennessee, probably not. It's a matter of probability and common sense."

"Right. First names are very important," said Jerry. "Only about half of all Jews have Jewish family names, so we look for Yiddish or Hebrew first names. It's interesting that Jewish yuppies like Hebrew names for their children."

Arbit and Benjamin not only find Jews, they try to find out about them, and they take a gleeful pride in the information they have accumulated. "What percentage of Jews have Christmas trees?" demanded Benjamin. "Come on, take a guess. Eleven percent."

"And what percentage keep kosher?" asked Arbit, smiling broadly at his partner. "Bet you can't guess that one, either. All right, twenty-two percent."

"I'm a little skeptical about that one," said Jerry. "The other day I saw a neighbor of mine who claims to be Orthodox at the drive-in window at McDonald's. I think we should start a new category—people who eat McD.L.T.s only in the privacy of their own car."

Both Arbit and Benjamin delight in this kind of speculation, but they haven't built up their data bank to amuse visitors. They sell information about Jews, and to judge by their company's rapid expansion it is a sellers' market. They have two kinds of clients— Jewish groups and politicians—and their company is strategically located at the point where the two intersect.

Neither Arbit nor Benjamin is simply a technocrat. A.B. Data sells mailing lists to all the Jewish organizations, but its owners have their own agenda, and this poses a potential threat to the establishment. "Direct mail is the great equalizer," Jerry said in a matter-of-fact tone. "We can enable Jews in Montana and Idaho and places like that to take part in Jewish life without an intermediary organization located on the eastern seaboard. We make it possible to bypass the gatekeepers of the Jewish community."

The A.B. Data agenda is based on three principles: Zionism, traditional Jewish values, and American political liberalism. In the fall of 1986, the company was still promoting these indirectly, as a resource for politicians and mainstream Jewish organizations. But knowledge is power, and Benjamin and Arbit are potentially very powerful men. When I mentioned the possibility that they might someday create an independent Jewish power center in Fox Point, Wisconsin, they both smiled modestly, but neither one denied the possibility.

We interrupted our conversation to take a tour of A.B. Data's facilities. At the heart of the operation are giant computers that contain the vital statistics of millions of Jews. I found the concentration of so much information disconcerting. "I bet the Klan or the PLO would love to get their hands on this stuff," I said to Arbit, who was guiding me through the building. But he dismissed my concern as Israeli paranoia. "America doesn't work that way," he assured me. "Besides, there's nothing here you can't get out of the phone book."

Benjamin and Arbit, like the people at AIPAC, view America's current philo-Semitism and political stability as natural and permanent. It is not dangerous to compile Jewish lists because there is no real threat to Jews; not presumptuous to organize Jews politically, because as Americans it is their right. Although Benjamin and Arbit consider themselves Zionists, they do not accept the Zionist notion that Jews are merely guests in America.

Much of A.B. Data's work is done for politicians who want to appeal to Jews for support and financial contributions, and Benjamin and Arbit have been exceptionally effective in helping them do it. I mentioned to them that during the Iowa Jew hunt, Lori Posin had asked her audiences if they had been contacted by Alan Cranston. The question always elicited good-natured groans from people who had been inundated with appeals. "My children should write me as much," one woman had said in Waterloo. "They should send that much money, too," laughed Benjamin. "We raised four million dollars for Cranston in twenty-dollar checks."

A.B. Data is picky about its clientele. "We have two conditions for working with politicians," said Jerry. "They have to be pro-Israel and they have to be liberal on American issues."

Bruce readily agreed with the first principle. "There is no single Jewish community in this country," he said. "There are different groups with varying ideologies. The only thing that unites them is support for Israel." But he disagreed with the second. Like Jerry, he is a political liberal and Jewish conservative; but he is the less doctrinaire of the two, and it wouldn't be surprising if he occasionally slipped into the McD.L.T. line. "Jerry's a knee-jerk liberal," he said fondly. "I consider myself a moderate and I have no trouble working with candidates who are moderate if they are pro-Israel."

In fact, most of A.B. Data's political clients *are* liberals: Cranston; Lowell Weicker of Connecticut; Barney Frank from Boston; Jim Hunt, who ran against Jesse Helms for the Senate in North Carolina; Carl Levin of Michigan; and Paul Simon of Illinois.

"Most Jews are genetically Democrats," said Bruce. "Jesse Jackson's performance at the 1984 convention was perceived by

Jews as the Democratic Party shitting all over the Jews, and they were freaked out by it. Believe me, it's had an impact ever since. The worst response we ever got to a direct mailing was one we did to raise money to fight apartheid. Jews in America don't support apartheid, but as long as Jesse Jackson is a major black spokesman they won't give money on the issue. Still, in spite of everything, they voted for Mondale three to one. Why? Because Jews in this country, despite what they say, are still basically insecure, and their main fear is of right-wing Christian anti-Semitism.''

I mentioned to them that my next stop would be Washington, D.C., where I was scheduled to meet with Ben Waldman. Jerry Benjamin searched his encyclopedic memory of American political operatives and brightened when he recalled the name. ''Ben Waldman did Jewish political organizing for Reagan in '84,'' he said. ''What's he up to these days?''

''He's in charge of Pat Robertson's Jewish campaign,'' I said, happy to be one up on the A.B. Data whizkids. They looked at each other in amused wonder. ''Pat Robertson's Jewish campaign,'' said Benjamin. ''Now I've heard everything.''

In political circles, Ben Waldman is known as Pat Robertson's Jew. It is a common usage—I heard other people mentioned as ''George Bush's Jew'' or ''Jack Kemp's Jew,'' as if Jews, like chartered airplanes, are standard issue for presidential candidates.

Actually, Jews are intensely involved in virtually every aspect of American politics. In 1986, there were eight Jews in the U.S. Senate—many from states with very small Jewish populations (one, Edward Zorinsky, has since passed away)—and twenty-eight in the House of Representatives. And in twenty-seven of the thirty-six Senatorial races, at least one of the candidates (and often both) had a Jewish campaign manager or finance chairman.

Many of the Jews in politics are professionals who happen to be Jewish and have no particular connection with the Jewish community and its concerns. On the other hand, there are political people who specialize in being Jewish. Some, like the AIPAC activists, lobby for Israel. Others work directly with candidates, as fundraisers or Jewish issues experts; Ben Waldman is that kind of political Jew. In the fall of 1986, there were dozens like him in Washington, but none of them was working for Pat Robertson; I went to see him because I wanted to find out what that was like.

We met in a restaurant not far from Capitol Hill. Waldman looks like the kind of Jew Pat Robertson could relate to, a handsome, fair-haired man in his mid-thirties, with startling blue eyes and the reasonable, patient manner of someone who expects not to be believed. As a boy, growing up in Claremont, California, he wanted to become a Conservative rabbi. Instead, he went into conservative politics.

Waldman's political baptism came during the 1980 presidential race, when he ran Ronald Reagan's "Jewish campaign" in California. "You can't believe how much hostility there was," he told me. "We went door to door in the borscht belt on Fairfax Avenue in L.A., and people spit at us. Literally. They said Reagan would be bad for Israel."

In 1984 Waldman headed Reagan's national Jewish campaign, stressing the president's pro-Israel record. It proved to be an insufficient argument. Jewish voters appreciated Reagan's support for Israel, but the Democrats neutralized it by playing up the influence of the radical right on the GOP. "Church-and-state killed us in '84," he said in an analytical tone. "It was a negative contest between Jerry Falwell and Jesse Jackson, and we lost."

For his efforts in 1984, Ben Waldman was rewarded with a middle-level administrative job on the White House staff. But he was dissatisfied. In August 1986 he was contacted by Robertson, who invited him out to his headquarters for a chat. Waldman was impressed, and he signed on.

"Actually, working with Pat makes a lot of sense for me," he said, sincerity shining from his blue eyes. "I was raised a Conservative Jew, but I'm more to the right on Jewish issues these days. I believe in the Bible literally, in creationism. I believe in the Orthodox interpretation of the Bible."

My gaze fell to the cheeseburger he held in his hand. "My wife is a convert and she doesn't understand kashrut," he said apologetically, "but in my beliefs, I'm very close to Pat."

If it was hard to convince Jews to support Ronald Reagan, getting them to vote for Pat Robertson seemed a truly imposing challenge. Waldman told me that his main problem was one of education. "Jews are incredibly bigoted in their attitudes toward born-again Christians," he said. "For one thing, they think they're all the same—they don't know that they vary greatly among themselves. Christians like Pat don't understand Jews, either. They have a deep-seated religious love for Jews, and they are hurt when it isn't reciprocated."

Waldman was well aware that many Jews considered Pat Robertson's vision of a Christian America to be a threat to them. "My favorite uncle stopped talking to me when I went to work for him," he said sadly. "He called it anti-Jewish. It's true that many Jews don't feel comfortable with Christian verbal affirmations of God's glory. We don't do that—we're a more subtle religion. Most Jews don't know what their prayers mean, anyway. But they misunderstand Pat and his program."

Ben Waldman's job is to make them understand, and he had marshaled some novel arguments for the task. "There's a panic in the Jewish community today about intermarriage," he said. "In my own extended family, almost all of my cousins, twenty or so, married non-Jewish spouses, and that is very typical today. Some converted and some didn't. But even the ones who did, a lot of them don't really consider themselves Jews. Our greatest threat is that we are losing the traditional Jewish family."

According to Waldman, Christian prayer in school is the solution. "Prayer in school or teaching Christian religion is positive for Jews because it reinforces our sense of being different from the gentiles. And that's what the Bible commands us to be—different," he said in a tone of utmost piety.

Another Waldman innovation was his Brooklyn strategy—a plan to attract Chasidic votes for Robertson. "I'm not saying we have widespread support there or anything, but there is potential," he said. "They tend to be very conservative, anti-communist, like Pat. And they share a lot of his beliefs—they are pro-life, pro-federal aid for parochial schools, anti-ERA, and of course very pro-Israel. Pat is probably closer to them on most issues than any other candidate. After all, they're both fundamentalists."

It was a strange scene to contemplate—fresh-faced, born-again Robertson-for-President volunteers in red, white, and blue blazers and straw hats canvassing among the Sotmar and Lubavitch Chasidim of Brooklyn; strange, but not impossible. In many ways,

America has become a post-satiric society. Nothing is too sacred to be trivialized or too improbable to be true. I thought of Macy's Baptist rabbi; Elie Wiesel, tossing out the first ball at a World Series game; McDonald's Fievel Mousekewitz Christmas Stocking promotion and I wondered: Why not Yiddish bumper stickers that say VOTE FOR A CHRISTIAN AMERICA in Williamsburg?

The boys from A.B. Data, politicians like Ben Waldman, and the Jew hunters of AIPAC have very different interests and approaches, but they all have one thing in common—they are involved in national politics. They deal in large issues and aim for big results. But I was also curious about grass roots Jewish politics. For a closer look I took a train up to Lawrence, Long Island, deep in the heart of the Ninth District, to Carol Berman-for-State-Senate headquarters.

The Ninth District was my last stop during the 1986 campaign. Berman, a Jewish Democrat and former state senator, was locked in a tight race with incumbent Dean Skelos, a Greek Orthodox Republican, who had defeated her in 1984. The Ninth District is in Nassau County, home of the formidable Republican machine that produced Senator Alphonse D'Amato. Democrats start out there at a disadvantage, and to compensate the party sent in Cliff Williams, a political gunslinger from Queens, to run the campaign. Williams, in an inversion of Ben Waldman's role, was Carol Berman's goy.

I found him at campaign headquarters, located on the second floor of a shopping center. When I arrived, the small, improvised office was in chaos, with teenage volunteers frantically stuffing envelopes and hollering into telephones. As soon as I walked in I was buttonholed by two middle-aged couples on their way to Israel. Refusing to believe I wasn't with the Bermanites, they demanded that I tell them how to file an absentee ballot.

I was rescued by Williams, who turned the couples over to a staffer and ushered me into a cramped panel-board office, which looked like the cell of a slovenly monk. A fat man with an unbarbered mustache and the unflappable calm of the true political pro, he made small talk for about thirty seconds before getting down to his favorite topic. Like all New York politicians, he began his assessment of the campaign with a tour d'horizon of the district's ethnic composition.

"We've got approximately two hundred fifty thousand people in the Ninth—one hundred sixty thousand registered voters," he said, and began ticking off the percentages on his stubby fingers. "We're almost forty percent Jewish, eighteen percent Italian, twenty percent Irish, and the other twenty percent or so are white Protestants. That's what I am," he added, an ethnic disability that may account for the fact that he had recently lost his seat in the state assembly.

Berman's official campaign theme was that she would be a full-time state senator, while Skelos, a practicing attorney, would not. Her subtext, direct and unmistakable, was an appeal to Jewish solidarity. This, Williams explained, was based not on parochialism but on cold political calculation.

"To be blunt, we got an Irish problem in this campaign," he told me. "Okay, we got the endorsement of the Irish-American Congress, but that sounds more important than it is. A lot of Irish people still have a problem with Jews."

Williams said that his working assumption was that half the Irish people in the district were anti-Semites who would vote against Berman out of bigotry. That sounded high to me and I said so, but he shook his head. "There's one difference between you and me," he said. "I'm not Jewish, and these people talk openly around me. Believe me, Carol's going to lose a lot of Irish votes because of the Jewish angle. Coupled with the fact that most Italians will vote Republican, Berman will have to do well among the Jews—better than she did in 1984."

The defeat of 1984 was viewed by Bermanites as an aberration of historic dimensions: "Reagan swept the entire country," said Williams. "I mean, it was a Republican year. And if that wasn't bad enough, he actually came to the Ninth District. The president. He had dinner with a local rabbi and visited his synagogue. A local *Republican* rabbi," he added darkly.

"Was Reagan's endorsement really that important?" I asked. Williams, who had been told that I had worked in politics in Israel, blinked at the question. "Yeah, you could say it was important," he said. "It was the first time in history that an

American president appeared in a synagogue. You could call that important."

The Reagan visit made me wonder what other endorsements might matter in a Jewish district. Cliff Williams stared into space, considering. "Let's see . . . Shimon Peres. Abba Eban. Sharansky. In parts of the district, Menachem Begin. That's about it," he said.

"Those are all Israelis," I reminded him. "What about American Jewish leaders?"

"American Jewish leaders?" he asked, unfamiliar with the notion. "Ah, I guess George Schultz is pretty popular. I can't really think of anybody else."

In addition to the Reagan factor, Berman had also been hurt in 1984 by a Skelos campaign circular to Jewish voters. "They sent out this letter saying that Carol was practically an enemy of the Jews because she hadn't denounced Louis Farrakhan," Williams said indignantly. The charge was unfair; worse—much worse—it had been effective. This time, the Berman campaign was determined not to be out-Jewed by the Greek.

There was a grudge-match edge to the campaign that I had detected a few weeks earlier when I first contacted the headquarters of the two candidates. The Berman people had suggested that I accompany her to Candidates' Night at a local B'nai B'rith chapter.

"Will Skelos be there, too?" I asked.

"No way," a Berman aide told me, her voice ringing with contempt. "He's been ducking Carol all over the district. He's afraid to debate, especially at a B'nai B'rith gathering. I doubt if you'll see him at all. He does most of his campaigning by mail."

The Skelos forces had been equally scathing. "Dean is at his best at these gatherings," a spokesman told me on the phone. "He's extremely popular in the Jewish community. But don't look for Carol Berman—she's afraid to appear on the same platform with Dean Skelos. She's been avoiding him for weeks."

"That's what they told me about your guy," I said, eager to stir up a little trouble. The spokesman snorted in righteous indignation. "We don't avoid anyone. We'll be there, you can bet on that. But don't be surprised if Carol Berman has a headache that night."

Naturally, I timed my visit to the Ninth District to coincide with the Great Debate. I mentioned this to Cliff Williams and told him that I would be going over to Skelos headquarters before the event. He didn't try to dissuade me from fraternizing with the enemy, but he did give me some reading material to fortify me. One pamphlet began with a quote from Carol Berman: "For years we relied on our 'friends' to protect us and our way of life. We learned that in the end we had to rely on ourselves. Our friends forgot us. I will never forget. I can't forget."

"Don't you think it's just a little blatant?" I asked. "It's almost as if she's blaming Skelos for the Holocaust."

Williams shook his head in vigorous disagreement. "It's perfectly legitimate for Carol to remind the voters that she's Jewish. Especially since she's running against an opponent who spends all his time pandering to Jewish voters. You go over there, you'll see what I mean."

On my way out, I was introduced to a spry old man named Harold Forma, the Democratic leader of Woodmere, a Long Island town. Forma told me that he has been in politics for sixty-one years, ever since he broke in with Tammany Hall on the Lower East Side.

Woodmere is a predominantly Jewish area, and Forma predicted that Berman would carry it ten to one. This seemed like an extravagant goal until he explained that, in the past, the town had sometimes voted for Democrats twenty to one.

"We've got good voters out here, but this boy Skelos has made some inroads," he said. "The guy practically sleeps in a yarmulke."

"Will it do him that much good?" I asked.

"Well, crime is the biggest talking issue out here, but abortion and especially foreign policy are the big voting issues, particularly for Jews. By foreign policy, I mean Israel. And Skelos has put in a lot of work on foreign policy, know what I mean?"

I thanked Forma for his analysis and asked him if he would be at the B'nai B'rith showdown.

"Naw, I'm getting an award someplace else. Outstanding community leadership, et cetera, et cetera. And you know what, boychik. I paid for it, believe you me." He laughed, a man who knows his value in the political marketplace.

After talking with Williams and Forma, I wouldn't have been surprised to find Senator Skelos dressed like a Chasid and eating a gefilte fish. But his office in Rockville Centre proved to be a model of Republican decorum. Conservatively dressed young people sat behind desks arranged in two rows, speaking softly to one another and typing away at silent word processors. The room was carpeted, and the overall effect was that of a suburban savings and loan association. Only the walls, decorated with a calendar from Yeshiva Toras Chaim, plaques from the Nassau County Podiatry Society and the Marco Polo Lodge, and signed photographs of Skelos with Ronald Reagan, Bob Hope, and Jack Kemp revealed the political nature of the office.

Skelos welcomed me cordially and told his secretary to hold his calls. He is a boyishly handsome man in his late thirties with a face that looks like it was designed in a laboratory for post-Kennedy political aspirants.

Carol Berman is originally from Brooklyn, but Skelos is a native son, born and raised in Rockville Centre, who settled in his old hometown after law school. As a young attorney he joined the county Republican machine and progressed rapidly. In 1982 he ran against Carol Berman and lost; in 1984 he won. Now, only a few weeks away from the rubber match, he seemed poised and confident.

Part of that confidence was based on his Jewish support. There aren't many Greek Orthodox in the Ninth, and over the years Skelos had sought to expand his ethnic base by becoming a keen student of Jewish voters. Not surprisingly, he had nothing but good things to say about them.

"Jewish citizens are literate and smart," he said over the hum of the air conditioner. "They read campaign material and they care about the issues. Most of all, they want a positive campaign. I think Carol Berman's negative campaign against me is a boomerang. She wraps herself in Jewishness, and I think a lot of voters object to that. Jews are Americans, and they vote and think as individuals, which is why I, a Republican, got thirty-five percent of the Jewish vote in the last election, and almost fifty percent here in Rockville Centre where they know me best.

"If you want to know what Jewish voters really want, I can sum it up in one word—respect. Respect for their traditions, their institutions, their sensitivities."

Skelos is nothing if not respectful. For example, he refrained from campaigning on the high holidays, and closed his office on Succot and Simchat Torah for good measure. During his term in the state senate he opposed testing at state universities on Jewish holidays, worked to stop price-gouging of kosher turkeys on Thanksgiving, and fought to withhold tenure to a professor at Stony Brook who denied the existence of the Holocaust.

His only major disagreement with his Jewish constituents has been over the abortion issue. "I'm against abortion, even though most Jewish voters are pro-choice," he told me. "I'm honest with them about my position, which is a way of showing them respect, and I think they respect me in turn," he said.

Skelos agrees with Harold Forma about the importance of foreign policy in the Ninth District. In 1984 he traveled to the Soviet Union, accompanied by a local rabbi, as the guest of the Long Island Committee on Soviet Jewry. Two years later he went on a junket to Israel that was organized by the local Jewish Federation. The trips were lavishly documented, and Skelos proudly showed me photos of his grinning self with Shimon Peres, Yitzhak Shamir, Natan Sharansky, and an array of lesser notables.

The Skelos foreign policy was not only pro-Israel and anti-Soviet, it was also anti-Greek. Throughout the campaign Carol Berman had been attacking the policies of the Athens government for which she held Skelos personally responsible. The incumbent responded by declaring a personal boycott of his ancestral homeland.

"I won't even visit Greece as long as the present government is in power," he said. "I disagree with their policies toward Israel and especially their closeness to the PLO. But I resent Carol Berman's insinuations that individual Greek-Americans are anti-Semitic."

I decided to accompany Skelos to a campaign meeting at the Green Acres Senior Citizens Center in Hempstead, where he was scheduled to give a talk with the admirably Republican title "What's in the Legislation for You?" The audience was composed mostly of Italians and Jews, but Skelos didn't even mention foreign policy; senior citizens vote age interests, not ethnic ones. On the way into the meeting hall he stopped in a card room where half a dozen men were playing poker. "I have some things to say that I think will interest you," he promised, but they were unconvinced. "We know what you're gonna say, Senator, and we're wit ya," said one, chewing on a King Edward corona and dealing a new hand.

After Green Acres, Skelos swung through a residential neighborhood, where he rang doorbells and shook hands with housewives. He then went to a branch campaign office, where I was introduced to Al Ball, a retired importer who was serving as a Republican committeeman and Skelos cheerleader. Ball, a Jew, took me next door, to Roma's. There, over pizza, he told me about his candidate.

"You want to know about Dean Skelos? Fine, this is Dean Skelos. When he went to Russia he took all sorts of things with him, prayerbooks, tefillin, you name it." He looked around the restaurant and lowered his voice to a conspiratorial whisper. "Listen, I'm not even allowed to repeat all the things he did when he was over there. But believe me, he wasn't just a tourist, okay?" I nodded, and he resumed his normal voice. "Let me tell you something else. Jews know that you've got to have Christian support. Not just vote for fellow Jews. That's the basis of Carol Berman's campaign, and to me it's abrasive."

Al Ball was once a liberal, but for the past ten years he has been a conservative Republican. "Look around at the crime, at the situation in the schools, at the secularism in society today," he said, as if these evils were lurking just in back of the pizza oven. "I don't think that liberal policies are the answer. And I'll tell you the truth, I also don't like Carol Berman from the Jewish angle. She's too abrasive. That's *it*."

By the time I got back to Berman headquarters for my first meeting with the Democratic candidate, I was expecting a cross between Don Rickles and Ariel Sharon. But Carol Berman proved to be a petite, somewhat brittle grandmother, a Jewish Nancy Reagan with frosted curly hair, prodigious energy, and a Brooklyn accent that made "war" into "woe-ah" and "sure" into "shoo-ah."

Berman introduced me to John Carbonara, a burly retired New York police lieutenant who was serving as her driver-bodyguard, and the three of us piled in her car for a round of campaigning.

Like Skelos, Berman had a Cadillac ("I've already worn out a Lincoln town car in this campaign," she said), but when I mentioned this to her she scowled, offended by any comparison to the Rockville Centre usurper.

"Look," she told me as Carbonara guided us to our first meeting of the evening, "Skelos is attempting to woo the voters with all sorts of cheap tricks. But I'm not just Jewish at election time—I've been Jewish for five thousand years. And I have the right to remind voters that I was a Jewish senator, not just a senator who happened to be Jewish."

Our first stop was a women's club bazaar at a local restaurant. Berman charged in, kissing cheeks, fingering merchandise, and calling everyone by their first names. This was her fifth senate campaign, and she worked the room with a deft touch, wasting no effort, talking to everyone but pausing with no one. After watching her for a few minutes I felt thirsty and retired to the adjoining bar, where I found John Carbonara sipping a 7-Up. A powerful man running to fat, he wore horn-rimmed glasses that gave him an incongruously studious look.

I asked Carbonara how he, an Italian cop, liked working for a Jewish woman Democrat. "Hey, no problem," he said seriously. "First, I pride myself on being a liberal thinker. Second, when it comes to Jews, I got a real soft spot. I see TV programs about the Holocaust and I can't help myself from crying. And third, as far as her being a woman, well, Carol is competent. Maybe some women aren't, ya know, but let me tell you something, pal, this lady works her ass off."

Just about then, Berman came steaming out of the bazaar, cast a disapproving look at my shot glass, and began towing the huge Carbonara in the direction of the Caddy. We were behind schedule for a neighborhood kaffeeklatsch and she urged Carbonara to step on it. He said nothing, and kept the car at a steady thirty-five.

There were about twenty people—all of them Jewish—at the gathering, which was held in the basement rec room of a supporter. Berman greeted most of the people there by name, was briefly introduced by her hostess, and then took the floor for ten minutes of canned campaign rhetoric. Most of it consisted of anti-Skelos barbs. The Republican was, according to her, soft on crime and real estate interests, a part-time senator, and a coward:

"He's afraid to debate me," she insisted, shaking her head with condescending pity.

Halfway through her presentation she introduced me to the group, making my presence sound like an endorsement by the Israeli government. From there she led into her Jewish theme.

"My Jewish identity is very strong and well known," she said. "When I was in the senate I single-handedly stopped the Arabs from buying the Bank of Commerce in New York. I almost single-handedly got questions about the Holocaust on the Regents Exam. As a Jewish housewife, I held hearings about price-gouging of kosher food at holiday time. I was responsible for Raoul Wallenberg Day." Berman ticked off these achievements on her fingers, and the audience murmured its approval.

After the speech, several people came over to say hello to me. One or two claimed to have read my books, although their tentative tone told me it was a claim born of courtesy. Two or three asked if I knew their relatives in Israel (I didn't) and one man wanted to know if Menachem Begin had Alzheimer's disease (I didn't know). In the meantime, Berman shook hands all around, nibbled on a symbolic cookie, and then went charging into the night. It was time for the great B'nai B'rith confrontation at the Rockville Centre Central Synagogue.

Like many long anticipated and loudly ballyhooed political confrontations, this one proved an anticlimax. When we arrived at Candidates' Night, it emerged that the event was not a debate at all, but serial appearances by various office seekers. Dean Skelos had come and gone. Now it was Carol Berman's turn, and she would appear alone.

Berman opened with the same attack on Skelos's platform and performance that she had used at the kaffeeklatsch. Once again she introduced me to the audience, and when she hit the "I've been Jewish for five thousand years" line, she gave me a significant look, as if I could authenticate her antiquity. I maintained what I hoped was a neutral attitude as she went on to describe her bona fides.

"I don't run on my Jewish credentials," she told the assembly, "but all of you know that I was a Jewish senator, not just a senator who happened to be Jewish." There was a smattering of applause, and she continued. "I never forget my responsibilities to my roots and my heritage. I don't need to travel to the Soviet Union and Israel on taxpayers' money to learn about Judaism.'' Once again there was applause, mixed with a few boos. ''Senator Skelos is practically professing to be Jewish. Well, I can tell you that I'm not professing to be Greek. I wouldn't even go to Greece, with its anti-Semitic government.''

This time there were loud cheers and also loud boos—Rockville Centre was Skelos territory, after all. A furious middle-aged man in a dark business suit leaped from his seat. ''I take exception to your remark about Dean Skelos,'' he said in a tone of lawyerly aggressiveness. ''He doesn't profess to be a Jew, that's nonsense. So he visited Israel and Russia, is that a crime? He went there to learn about our community and our concerns, and that's what a legislator is supposed to do.'' This time the boos and cheers were reversed. Carol Berman regarded the man with narrowed eyes and snapped, ''He did the smart thing,'' before taking the next question.

Afterwards, during the coffee hour while Berman mingled with the voters, I was again approached by several people who wanted to ask about Israeli relatives or tell me about their trip to Jerusalem. One of them was the Skelos man, Elliot Winograd. He introduced himself as an Anti-Defamation League activist and former president of the congregation. Having established his credentials, he explained his outburst at the meeting. ''Everything being equal, I'll vote for the Jew,'' he said. ''But this woman is impossible—she's totally incompetent. Besides, I'm a Republican. I admit it.''

Once again Berman burst loose from the pack, shot Winograd a Sonny Liston hate stare, and led me and Carbonara in a half-run to the parking lot. By now it was past ten, and she still had to address a meeting at the Therese the Little Flower Chapter of the Knights of Columbus.

When we arrived, a man at the microphone was making some announcements. ''I wanna remind you to attend our annual horse show,'' he said, and there were groans from the sixty or so people who sat on folding chairs in the wood-paneled room. ''Hey, it's an enjoyable evening, and it's free.'' This time there was applause, and he used it to bring on Carol Berman, ''an old friend and former senator from our district, now running in a rematch . . .''

Berman grabbed the hand mike and launched into a brief speech. There was no "I was a Jewish senator" stuff this time; she concentrated on crime, reminding them that she favored mandatory life sentences for drug pushers and tough punishments for violent rape. "Don't forget, when I was your senator, I voted for the death penalty five times. . . ."

As she went on in this law-and-order vein, I felt a powerful hand grip my elbow. I spun around and saw John Carbonara's face about five inches from my own. He fixed me with a heavy-lidded stare and said nothing. For a moment I thought he might be angry with me. Finally, blinking away a slight stammer, he said, "I was wondering, ah, where are you staying tonight?"

We had barely spoken since our drink at the ladies' bazaar. I assumed that he wanted to know because he would have to drop me off. I told him I had a room at the Motorway Motel in Lawrence, not far from Carol Berman's house.

He digested this for a minute, and then began to shake his head slowly. "Uh, well, I'm gonna ask ya to stay with us tonight. Ya understand what I mean? What I'm saying is, you look like you could use a good home-cooked meal instead of eating alone in some motel. Am I right?" I was too surprised to answer. "Hey, I'm gonna go call my wife, tell her I'm bringin' ya home, okay?"

"That's really nice, but I couldn't let you do that," I protested. It was past eleven by now, and I figured that it would be close to midnight before we got back to his place. I was going to say "I hardly even know you," but it sounded like a line from a bad movie. Besides, John was already shaking his head again, like a bull brushing away flies.

"Uh, maybe you noticed that I didn't say 'I'll *ask* my wife'—I said 'I'll *tell* my wife.' Wait'll you meet her. I call her Soupy, which is short for super-wife. I already know she wants you to come stay with us and I didn't even need to call. So it's all set, right?"

I had been on the road for weeks, and the truth was that I dreaded another night in a motel. There was no way John Carbonara could have known that, of course; but the idea of spending the evening with real people instead of some late-night movie was suddenly very attractive. I looked at this big blunt stranger and felt very moved. "Sure," I told him, "I'd love to stay with you."

By this time Berman had finished working the room. We dropped her off, exhausted, at her house and then drove half an hour to Carbonara's. Soupy, a.k.a. Diane, met us at the door with a kiss for Carbonara and a welcoming hug for me. She was a dark, very pretty woman who looked about thirty-five, and I was surprised to learn that her oldest son was away at college and that the baby, Joe, had just graduated from high school.

Diane returned to the kitchen, where she was preparing an impromptu Italian feast, and Carbonara went into his bedroom, put away his pistol ("I was on the job almost thirty years and I never once had to use this," he said proudly), and stripped off his shirt. He spent the rest of the evening in his T-shirt, his massive belly peeking out and his powerful arms flexing from time to time.

We joined Diane in the kitchen, and Carbonara hauled out an old scrapbook. He especially wanted to show me a yellowing article from the fifties—the account of a baseball game between shipyard teams from Brooklyn and Philadelphia that had been won by a John Carbonara homer. He wasn't at all self-conscious about the small boast; his attitude was that I, as a friend of the family, would naturally be interested in and proud of the accomplishment.

Diane produced steaming plates of food, which we wolfed down without ceremony. The Carbonaras gossiped happily about family matters—including me, as if I were a cousin from Brooklyn instead of a stranger from Israel. Although he doesn't drink, Carbonara produced a bottle of sweet yellow wine and poured me a glass, determined to make me feel at home.

It was past one when their younger son, Joe, joined us in the kitchen. He has his mother's dark good looks and his father's intense stare and slight hesitation of speech. He also has a Brooklyn accent that makes his father sound like a graduate of Sandhurst. In conformity with the Carbonara dress code, he was shirtless.

Earlier in the meal, John had spoken angrily about Joe's decision not to attend college. "He's a smart kid but all he wants to do is bum around with his friends, go out every night and chase girls," said Carbonara. Seeing him now, I thought that he had made the right choice. He reminded me of the kids who used to dance on *American Bandstand*; there was something sulky about him that, coupled with his thick Brooklyn dialect, made him seem unlikely college material.

Diane introduced me as an Israeli writer, and Joe regarded me with a surprising interest. I expected a wisecrack, but instead he blinked in concentration, his father's mannerism, and then burst into a rapid-fire monologue, stammering occasionally over the words. It sounded something like—

"Ugh, uh, okay. Now, you're from Israel, right? Okay, I want ya to straighten me out on somethin'. Now, Hizbollah, up in Lebanon, Hizbollah is supported by the Iranians, am I right? And the Iranians and the Syrians, they're allies, right? Okay, now, wait a minute, Hizbollah works out of, like, Syrian turf—I mean, it's in the Bekaa Valley but Syria controls it. Okay—now wait—the Syrians are also supporting the Amal, right? I mean, Nabih Bari, those guys. But then, what I don't get is—why do the Syrians let Hizbollah attack the Amal guys who are supposed to be their allies? I mean, is this, like, a trick to soften up the Iranians, or does it have something to do with the, uh, rivalry between the two Bathist parties, you know, Hafez Assad and Saddam Hussein. Can you answer me that?"

I sat there, mesmerized by the performance. It was the kind of question American undergraduates pay thousands of dollars to learn how to ask; but Joe hadn't been showing off. He was just curious.

"How do you know so much about the Middle East?" I asked, and he shrugged, embarrassed. "Hey, I'm innerested in foreign policy, okay?"

Carbonara listened to the exchange with frustrated pride. "Imagine, a kid like this not in college, not using his brains. Is it a waste or not a waste?"

Joe, in an effort to derail his father, broke in. "Here's one more thing I don't get, okay? I mean, Israel's got the strongest army in the region. So why don't you guys just go back into Lebanon and clean it up, ya know, just kick ass and clean the entire place up?"

This was too much for John. "Hey," he bellowed, "I thought

you were smart. What kinda question is that. We can't get you to stop smoking in your room, you want the Israelis to clean up Lebanon.'' He may not know much about Hizbollah, but thirty years on the street have made a realist out of John Carbonara.

We sat up talking until almost four in the morning, and the next day around noon I awoke to the smell of breakfast. In the kitchen I found my place set at the table, and a copy of *The New York Times* next to the plate. Carbonara reads the *Daily News*—he had gone out especially to find me a *Times*. But when I thanked him, he brushed me off with a dismissive gesture. ''It's got a lousy sports section,'' he said, digging into his scrambled eggs.

While we were eating, Diane brought in another scrapbook. ''John's a writer, too,'' she said, and Carbonara nodded assent, without a trace of false modesty. ''I like to write poems. Nothing published or anything like that, just for special occasions, ya know?'' He opened the book and began to recite in his rough Brooklyn voice. The poems were mostly about family events, or couplets written to commemorate something that happened on the job. ''Here's one I wrote in honor of my friend Bernie's son's bar mitzvah,'' he said, clearing his throat. ''Yes, my friend Bernie, it was quite an affair; filled with love and affection, steaks so tender and rare . . .''

I had to get into the city, and I thanked Diane for her hospitality. John offered to drive me to the train. On the way we chatted about the Ninth District election. Although he was a Berman man, he admitted that he liked Skelos, too. And in a discreet way he let me know that he thought Carol was making a mistake with her ''I've been a Jew for five thousand years'' routine.

''There's all kind of Jews, I've noticed,'' he said, driving carefully through the sparse traffic. ''Some of them are what I call real Jews, but a lot of them, they're Americans.'' There was sarcasm in his voice when he said the word. ''They might not like that Jewish stuff so much, you know?'' (He turned out to be right; Skelos won the election, carrying a larger percentage of the Jewish vote than he had in 1984).

We arrived at the station and shook hands, but Carbonara had one parting thought. ''You know, to my mind there's nobody better than a good Jew, a real Jew. But last night? I dunno. I mean, there you were and Carol's introducing you to everybody, like, here's Ze'ev the writer from Israel. And everybody came up to you and says, 'Hey, Ze'ev, how ya doin', Ze'ev, ya know my cousin in Tel Aviv?' Like that. But I noticed one thing—none of those Jews asked ya if you had a place to stay, nobody said, 'Come on back to the house for a meal.' Who asked ya that? Carbonara, the Italian. Sometimes I just don't know who the real Jews are anymore, know what I mean?''

CHAPTER THREE

SUCCAH IN THE SKY

From the street, the Grace Building looks like any other New York City skyscraper. Located on the corner of Sixth Avenue and 42nd Street, its lobby promises nothing more than the standard Manhattan offices listed on the building's directory. But unknown to most of its tenants, for one week every year, during the Feast of Tabernacles, the Grace Building is transformed into the pedestal of a penthouse shrine—the fabled Succah in the Sky.

The heart of the Succah is located twenty-four floors below, in the offices of Swig, Weiler, and Arnow, real estate. The company owns the Succah. It also owns the building on which it sits, and many other buildings in New York and around the country. And its principals, the Weiler and Arnow families, own a considerable chunk of Jewish community leadership in the United States as well.

In the pluralistic, mobile society of America, Jews can live anywhere and be anybody; but belonging to the Jewish community requires involvement in the decentralized but intensely organized web of synagogues, institutions, and organizations that circle the country and are headquartered in Manhattan. Woody Allen, Sandy Koufax, Bob Dylan, and Henry Kissinger have all profoundly influenced the Jews of America, but none of them belongs to the community. David Arnow, the thirty-eight-year-old grandson of real estate mogul Jack Weiler, is the head of the New Israel Fund. He is not only a member of the community, but a leader.

Leadership in the American Jewish community is about money—raising it, distributing it, and then raising more. Every year, Jewish federations throughout the United States conduct fundraising campaigns that collect hundreds of millions of dollars. About half goes to Israel via the United Jewish Appeal; the rest is used to finance local community projects. In addition to the federation campaign, independent organizations like the New Israel Fund raise money for their own agendas. The money comes from federated Jews, people whose credo is, "I give, therefore I am."

Those who give the most can, if they choose, become Jewish leaders. Dozens of megarich businessmen form an informal national network, dominating organizations, setting priorities, and overseeing the activities of the multifaceted community. Some of their names are well known, at least in establishment circles—Edgar Bronfman, head of the World Jewish Congress; Jerald Hoffberger, chairman of the board of governors of the Jewish Agency; Larry Weinberg of AIPAC; and Detroit's Max Fisher. A few, like Ivan Boesky, former head of the New York federation, are notorious. And some, like David Arnow, are just beginning to come into prominence.

Arnow is a new-breed leader, a child of the sixties with a Ph.D. in psychology from Boston University, a left-leaning ideology, and an inherited fortune well into eight figures. His grandfather, Jack Weiler, came to America as an immigrant from Eastern Europe, made millions in real estate, and helped establish the United Jewish Appeal in America. The family tradition of philanthropy was carried on by Jack Weiler's son Robert. Now the torch is being passed to a third generation, to David Arnow, a prince of the American Jewish establishment.

When I arrived at the office of Swig, Weiler, and Arnow I was greeted in the waiting room by Jonathan Jacoby, Arnow's advisor on Jewish affairs. The room was quietly tasteful, decorated in subdued pastels and grays and dominated by a picture window with a dramatic view of the skyline. A marble coffee table was stacked with Sotheby catalogues and copies of *The New Yorker* and *Moment,* a liberal Jewish journal published in Boston.

Like the decor, Jacoby was understated and mellow, a soft-spoken Californian in his early thirties with an open, friendly manner. Rich people dominate America's Jewish organizations, but day-to-day operations are run by professionals with strong Jewish backgrounds. Jacoby, who was raised in a Conservative home in Los Angeles and spent three years in Israel, is no exception. Like David Arnow, he is a political liberal, dedicated to supporting left-wing causes in Israel. Unlike Arnow, however, he has to work for a living, and his job includes taking visitors like me on tours of the premises.

Our first stop was a small model of what was once Einstein Hospital in New York. "They took off Einstein's name and now they call it the Jack D. Weiler Hospital," Jacoby said without a hint of irony. Sic transit gloria—if Einstein had wanted a hospital, he should have gone into real estate.

Next to the model hospital hung a warmly inscribed photograph of Chaim Weizmann, the first president of Israel. The picture is a family heirloom, a symbol of the Weiler-Arnow association with Israel since before the founding of the country.

There is an obvious lack of symmetry in the relationship. Israel's prime ministers and presidents don't hang pictures of American Jewish millionaires on their walls. In fact, they don't regard them as leaders. The businessmen are considered go-betweens, tax collectors, field officers in the campaign for Israel's survival and prosperity. This junior partner status is implicit in the American Jewish community's relationship with Israel; clearly, people who have paid their dues take precedence over those who only foot the bills.

This disparity rankles Arnow and Jacoby, and they would like to change it. They grew up with Israel and take it for granted. Unlike their elders, they are not in awe of the country or its officials. They feel they have wisdom as well as money to contribute. Their goal is not to make life easier for the Shamirs, Pereses, and Rabins, but to prod them into making Israel their kind of place, the sort of country that would meet the approval of the ACLU, *The Nation* magazine, and the Sierra Club.

Jacoby led me down a carpeted hall to a large empty conference room, which he entered with the reverence of a high priest
coming into the Holy of Holies. "If you're looking for American
Judaism, this is a good place to start," he said, gesturing broadly.
"This *is* American Judaism. In this room, Abba Eban and Yitzhak
Rabin and just about every other important Israeli has come to
meet with the establishment. And now, thanks to us, they can hear
others, too—people like Rafik Halabi, for example." Halabi, a
Druze television newsman and author, is the kind of Israeli the
New Israel Fund is anxious to support: bright, hip, and at odds
with his country's traditional policies and attitudes. As I contemplated the possibility that his autographed picture might someday
hang next to Weizmann's, we were joined by David Arnow.

Arnow is a small, neat baby-boomer with the suspicious,
pseudodeferential manner of a rich kid who wants to be liked for
himself. He let Jacoby talk about the New Israel agenda while he
sized me up. After a few minutes, he suggested an elevator ride to
the Succah in the Sky. "I think you'll like the view," he said
shyly.

Fifty-eight floors is only halfway up in Manhattan, and when
we reached the roof of the Grace Building we were still surrounded by buildings twenty or thirty stories higher. But none of
them have a succah—Arnow's is the tallest tabernacle in the
world. During the holidays, VIPs take their meals there. When we
arrived, just after lunch, white-jacketed waiters were clearing away
the kosher dishes and gathering up the empty Israeli wine bottles.
Jacoby and Arnow and I stood looking out at Manhattan from
under a canopy of plastic apples, pears, and grapes. The artificial
fruit is a ceremonial reminder of the sweet harvests of the ancestral
fields of the Holy Land. But the Succah in the Sky is a modern
symbol as well—a monument to the confluence of Big Money and
Big Judaism that constitutes community leadership in America.

After a tour of the Succah, Arnow led us back down to his
office on the thirty-fourth floor. He poured coffee into styrofoam
cups, leaned back in his chair, and explained his version of Jewish
leadership.

"My family has been involved with Jewish things for years, and
I share their commitment," he said. "I'm totally dedicated to
helping Israel. But the question is, what kind of Israel? And what

kind of help is appropriate? Things aren't as simple as they seemed twenty or forty years ago.''

In those days the Weiler family gave huge sums of money and helped to raise even more. Israel is dotted with monuments to their philanthropy. I mentioned that there is a Ben Swig Memorial Park—donated by Jack Weiler in honor of his late partner—on the corner of my street in Jerusalem. ''There's a whole neighborhood, Kiriat Jack Weiler, named after my grandfather in Jerusalem,'' Arnow said, putting the park into perspective.

David Arnow could have a park of his own, or even a neighborhood; it's all a matter of money. But he wants influence, not honors. He has a vision of Israel, and he wants to use his organization to further it.

''I'm focused on Israel because the ultimate value of the Jewish people will be decided there,'' he said. ''We can't create an oppressor state. I have a vision of us as a light unto the nations, a vision of pluralism where the lion lies down with the lamb sort of thing. We can live together—I believe that, I really do.

''Look, I have a Ph.D. in psychology. And it's well known that usually people who go from the bottom to the top tend to do the same things to the people at the bottom that were done to them. It's a problem of going from a position of relative weakness to relative strength.

''We want people to face reality—in Israel and here, too,'' Arnow continued. ''American Jews don't know, and they don't care to know, that Arabs live in Israel. The country could become like South Africa, and we just can't let that happen.''

Arnow reached over to his desk and took out a sheet of paper that listed the goals of his organization. '' 'We are primarily concerned with strengthening the democratic fabric of Israel and supporting efforts to create a society based on justice and tolerance,' '' he read. ''That's the kind of country we should have.''

I winced at the ''we,'' and Jacoby quickly intervened. ''I want to stress that the New Israel Fund is an international organization, not just an American one,'' he said. ''Israelis are involved in every aspect of our activity. They have input into the grant process and we have an Israeli vice president.'' He sounded very much like the earnest white liberals who once dominated civil rights organizations in America and were devastated when blacks, intent on running their own lives, kicked them out.

For more than an hour we sat discussing David Arnow's agenda for Israel. From time to time I tried to nudge the conversation in the direction of American problems—intermarriage, shrinking numbers, the state of American Jewish education—but they didn't elicit much interest. Arnow's concept of what Israel should be may differ from his grandfather's, but Israel is no less central in his view of the Jewish people.

"Don't you think it would be more appropriate for you to move to Israel and work from the inside?" I asked as our conversation drew to a close. Arnow paused to consider, and Jacoby took over.

"I've just about given up on mass immigration to Israel from America," he said. "It's unrealistic. American Jews won't go, they'll give money—love money and guilt money. But they don't want to know the truth about Israel, they don't want to be confused by reality. Now personally, I'm torn. I have one foot in Israel and the other here. I'll probably move there for good someday."

David Arnow felt no such conflict. "We're all one people, but we can't all live in one place," he said. "I don't advocate moving to Israel, making *aliyah*. After all, how can I send people to a place that I'm not prepared to live in? That doesn't seem fair."

David Arnow and Jonathan Jacoby have a vision of Israel— they want the Jewish State to be a light unto the nations. But like other American Jewish leaders, they prefer to see that light from a distance, from the vantage point of the great American Succah in the Sky.

"You want to know how I got my organization? Simple—I stole it!" said Israel Singer when I stopped by to see him at the headquarters of the World Jewish Congress on Madison Avenue in New York. The Congress is located in a suite of offices considerably less grand than Arnow's, but that is more a matter of style than of necessity. The organization belongs to Singer and his senior partner, Edgar Bronfman; and when you're in business with Bronfman, what do you have to prove?

Singer's monthly trips to Israel are guided by this same tasteful understatement. Although he flies first class, he prefers to stay in modest five-star hotels. "Bronfman can afford the King David," he said with a mischievous grin. "That's where all the big American *makhers* stay. But I don't stay there on principle. I don't need to."

I found Singer's cheerful cynicism a refreshing change from the patrician earnestness of the New Israel Fund. Unlike David Arnow, Singer is a self-made man, the son of Chasidic Jews from Brooklyn. He attended a yeshiva as a boy—his family was so Old World that he spoke nothing but Yiddish until he was twelve. But once he began to talk English, thirty-five years ago, it has been hard to shut him up. Singer is an amusing monologuist with a conversational style that is part Talmudic erudition, part Brooklyn street jive. He sees himself as a kind of organizational Robin Hood, a man who steals from the rich to give to the Bronfmans.

Until Israel Singer came along, the World Jewish Congress (WJC) was a moribund outfit that labored for years under the brilliant but eccentric leadership of Nahum Goldmann. Then Singer teamed up with Edgar Bronfman, who was looking to get into the Jewish leadership game. Israel Singer, who knew a great deal about Jewish life, convinced Edgar Bronfman, who knew almost nothing, that the WJC would make a perfect vehicle. "I studied the techniques of Garibaldi," he told me enthusiastically. "I studied the techniques of Juan Perón. And here we are." He waved his hand grandly at his cramped office, a man with an empire.

Under Singer's guidance, Edgar Bronfman has emerged as a major American Jewish figure, and the Congress has become an important, if somewhat maverick player in the Jewish community. Its greatest coup was its role in uncovering Kurt Waldheim's Nazi past, an achievement that Singer dismissed with uncharacteristic modesty. "Waldheim was important," he told me, "but believe me, I've got bigger things on my agenda."

Singer's master plan involves another theft. "I want to steal one hundred twenty million dollars from the Jewish Agency," he said with an expansive grin. "I want to take it out of their budget for education and aliyah and use it to set up Jewish schools."

Singer is an Orthodox Jew of some flexibility, who believes that Orthodoxy is the wave of the American Jewish future. "There are 120,000 kids in Jewish day schools in this country today, and ninety percent of them are Orthodox," he said. By the year 2000, according to his projections, the American Jewish community will have shrunk from its present 5.5 million to about 1.5 million unless there is a drastic change in the education of American Jews. "That's my priority—not catching Nazi war criminals," he said.

What does Bronfman think of all this? I wondered. Edgar Bronfman, whose family made a huge amount of money in the liquor business, is not exactly renowned for his piety. Singer gave me a cheerful smile and fingered the fringes of his prayer shawl. "Bronfman and I are partners. My *tzitzes* make up for his *shikseh* wife."

Despite Singer's blithe attitude, this is a sore point. Bronfman is far from the only Jewish leader in America with a Christian wife; and a very large number of these leaders have children who are not Jewish or are married to non-Jews. This may account for the thunderous silence of many Jewish organizations on the subject of intermarriage.

Singer was interrupted by a transatlantic telephone call. "It's Hungary on the line," he said grandly, covering the mouthpiece with his hand in a conspiratorial gesture, obviously delighted to be at the fulcrum of international diplomacy. "We're going there next month for a meeting."

Jewish leadership in America offers rewards not normally available to the owners of distilleries, or even run-of-the-mill billionaires. There are consultations at the White House, international conferences, meetings with heads of state, a chance to play on the world stage. Israel Singer hijacked an organization for himself and Edgar Bronfman and, like the legendary chariot of Sir Moses Montefiore, they use it to ride to the rescue of Jews in distress—accompanied, as Sir Moses was not, by minicams and wire service reporters.

The Bronfman-Singer collaboration, and particularly their independent leadership style, have not endeared them to their fellow Jewish leaders. Singer is well aware of his reputation as a prima donna, but he dismisses his critics with a contemptuous wave of his hand. "I'm prepared to include others in our initiatives, like the meeting in Hungary," he said, "providing they're willing to pay the price."

"What price?"

"Loyalty," said Singer in a level tone.

"Loyalty to what?" I asked, and he paused for a dramatic beat.

"Loyalty to my program; that's the price," said the Jewish Perónista from Brooklyn with a smile.

The center of American Jewish communal life is, and always has been, New York City. A few dozen blocks in midtown contain the headquarters of big league Judaism—the Jewish Agency, the United Jewish Appeal, and the offices of various national organizations. In recent years, as American Jews have become more political, Washington, D.C., has become a second power center. AIPAC is located in the capital, and the important national Jewish organizations have branch offices there. Still, New York remains the hub.

In the past few years, however, the primacy of New York and the eastern seaboard has been challenged by Rabbi Marvin Hier—founder and director of the Menachem Begin Yeshiva High School, the West Coast branch of Yeshiva University, and most importantly the Simon Wiesenthal Holocaust Center. Over the past decade, Hier has employed aggressive marketing, astute media management, and emotional appeals to West Coast patriotism in order to create one of the country's most successful Jewish organizations.

The Wiesenthal Center and its sister institutions are located in a single squat brick complex on Pico Boulevard in Los Angeles. The building, with its dark, lugubrious interior, seems strangely out of place in California, a reminder that Judaism has traditionally been an indoor activity.

The building also reflects the personality of its founder. Marvin Hier, an Orthodox rabbi who looks like a middle-aged Duddy Kravitz, is a small, intense man with piercing black eyes, a prominent hook nose, and a little potbelly that strains at the buttons of his monogrammed shirts. He was born and raised on New

York's Lower East Side, and he remains a traditionalist. On Saturday afternoons, for example, in the bean sprout capital of America, Marvin Hier eats cholent—the heavy meat-and-potato stew that his mother used to make back in New York. But the rabbi is also an iconoclast and a visionary—traits that have enabled him to become one of Jewish America's most successful entrepreneurs.

Marvin Heir began his career as a congregational rabbi, and eventually he wound up in an Orthodox synagogue in Vancouver, Canada. In those days he used to visit Los Angeles frequently, and during his trips to Babylon he made two interesting discoveries. First, that L.A. was a Jewish boomtown, with hundreds of thousands of people and more pouring in every day; and second, that there was no important national Jewish organization headquartered on the West Coast.

The young rabbi was immediately impressed by the potential this situation offered. Thirty years earlier a fellow New Yorker, Walter O'Malley, had exploited a similar vacuum by moving his baseball team, the Brooklyn Dodgers, across the continent to Chavez Ravine. Hier has emulated him by establishing the first big league Jewish franchise on the West Coast.

"I saw that California, especially Los Angeles, was very underdeveloped from a Jewish point of view," he said. "The American Jewish investment out here was spread very thin. Until we came along, the entire American Jewish world was tilted toward about thirty square miles on the East Coast. Take them away and there goes your *Yiddishkeit*."

Unlike O'Malley, Hier had no organization of his own. But he did have a backer, Sam Belzberg, a multimillionaire congregant in Vancouver. Belzberg, already one of the most prominent Jewish philanthropists in North America, agreed to bankroll the L.A. franchise, provided that it was run on a businesslike basis. Hier accepted the condition, and by the late 1970s the two men were busy setting up shop in Los Angeles.

The move was far from popular. "The local Jews out here didn't want us and neither did the national organizations," said Hier. "But the truth is, Jewish growth is in California, not back East. There are already close to one million Jews on the West Coast, and that number is going to grow."

Hier began by creating a West Coast affiliate of New York's

Orthodox Yeshiva University. Unlike the main school, the West Coast branch, which has an enrollment of about forty, offers only Judaica. The Menachem Begin Yeshiva High School is more ambitious. Established in 1980, it has around three hundred students and a basketball team, the Yeshiva Panthers, that is the class of its division.

"We've won the championship three out of the last four years," Rabbi Abraham Cooper, the school's headmaster, told me proudly. "And out here, it's not like in Brooklyn. I mean, it's not like we're competing against Flatbush Yeshiva." In addition to basketball, the school offers secular and Jewish studies—Talmud, Bible, Jewish history—"the whole shmeer," in Cooper's words.

The high school and college are important elements in Marvin Hier's operation, but its centerpiece is the Simon Wiesenthal Holocaust Center, named in honor of the renowned Nazi hunter. Hier wanted an organization that would appeal not only to Orthodox Jews but to the mainstream; and only Israel and the Holocaust have that kind of broad appeal.

"In Jerusalem, Jews gather around the *kotel* (the Wailing Wall)," he told me. "Here in America, they gather around the Holocaust." In setting up the Wiesenthal Center, Hier set himself up with the West Coast Holocaust franchise.

Both Marvin Hier and his disciple, Rabbi Cooper, believe in the need to act aggressively in order to counter anti-Semitism in America. In the capital of cool they employ a hot, angry style just short of Meir Kahane's, and they are constantly on the lookout for issues that appeal to the Jewish sense of vulnerability. Hier took on CBS over its decision to cast the virulently anti-Israel actress Vanessa Redgrave as a Jewish concentration camp inmate; led the attack on Jesse Jackson's anti-Semitic remarks in the 1984 primary campaign; and has been active in fighting Arab propaganda on the West Coast.

"We address issues that people respond to," Rabbi Cooper told me. "We monitor anti-Semitic statements, the activities of the neo-Nazis, Arab activities, whatever. The Anti-Defamation League does the same thing? Good, great. There should be four more groups doing it. I mean, there should never be a time when the president of the United States can pick up a telephone and make one call to one Jewish leader and have spoken to everyone. We tried that in the 1930s and it didn't work out too well.

"Look, after the Holocaust, we have two strikes against us. And Rabbi Hier says that a ballplayer with two strikes has to choke up on the bat, be a little more aggressive, not take any close pitches. That's our philosophy here, and it makes us a little more militant than some of the other organizations around the country."

When I mentioned the two-strike analogy to Hier he seemed somewhat vague—his hero is O'Malley, not Pee Wee Reese. But the attitude behind the analogy was plainly his. Hier believes that the threat to Jewry is worldwide, and his advocacy of Jewish rights extends far beyond the borders of California.

"Our focus is on the defense of Jews in America and abroad," he said. "The threat is everywhere and we will fight for the rights of Jews anywhere. We have contacts in the Middle East, for example, that other Jewish organizations just don't have. That's how we got ahold of that anti-Semitic book by Tlas, the Syrian defense minister, even before the Israelis did. We have contacts in Europe, we deal with the Vatican, the British, and French governments. Our efforts are international."

This kind of ambition requires big money, and the Wiesenthal Center has been especially successful in raising it. Like A.B. Data in Milwaukee, the center operates mostly through direct mailings, a technique that brought in 350,000 individual contributions in 1986, according to Rabbi Cooper. But not all of the center's money comes from ten-dollar gifts. "Who runs the biggest fundraising dinner on the West Coast Jewish scene with all the big *makhers* in attendance?" Hier demanded rhetorically. "We do, that's who. Why do they come? Because we are effective."

Marvin Hier's carpetbagging has excited the anger and jealousy of fellow Jewish leaders. "Some people complain that the Wiesenthal Center duplicates the activities of the Anti-Defamation League, the American Jewish Committee, and other organizations. And, in total honesty, we do to some extent," he admitted. "But our critics don't advocate giving all cancer research money to one medical center—they know it's important to diversify. Hatred and anti-Semitism are not the exclusive concern of any one group. Besides, all Jewish institutions need money to survive,

And a NATPAC solicitation from Joan Rivers; a letter from Jack Klugman asking for money for the Institute for Jewish Hospice; and a note from Arthur Waskow on behalf of the Shalom Center, for "Jewish perspectives on preventing a nuclear holocaust." *And* an invitation to a Polish-Jewish-Ukrainian dialogue sponsored by the American Jewish Committee; a solicitation from the Anti-Defamation League; an imitation leatherette address book from the Yeshiva Gedolah of Greater Detroit (with an attached form for donations); an invitation to a United Hebrew Schools luncheon featuring "Original and Traditional Folk Music Performed Vibrantly by Laslo and Sandor Slomovitz"; and appeals from the Crown Heights Jewish Community Council of Brooklyn, the American Friends of Magen David Adom Society, and the Israel Mobile Mitzvah Centers of the Chabad Chasidim of New York.

"What are you going to do with all this stuff?" I asked when he was finished going through the correspondence. "I've never even heard of most of these organizations."

Joe smiled. He had heard of them all, and then some. "You don't have to know about Jewish organizations," he said mildly. "You live in Israel. But for us it's different. If you can't do more, at least you can write a check or go to a meeting."

"Don't tell me you send money to these outfits. I mean, the Crown Heights Jewish Community Council of Brooklyn? Mobile Mitzvah Centers? You've got to be kidding."

Joe gave an embarrassed laugh. "I won't send them very much—just a few dollars. Nothing significant. It's just part of being a member of the community. It's something you do. Most of my time and whatever donation I make go to the federation anyway; that's what really counts."

In Detroit, the federation is a kind of municipal Jewish government in exile. When I was growing up in the 1960s, there were eighty thousand Jews in Detroit, most of them clustered in homogeneous neighborhoods in the city's northwest corner. But in the summer of 1967, just as I was leaving for Israel, the adjacent black ghettos erupted in one of the worst urban riots in American history. Forty-three people were killed, and large parts of the city were transformed into smoldering ruins.

For people like Joe Colten, who were born and raised in the city, it was a heartbreaking and threatening development. The

Jewish community fled Detroit en masse, moving so far and so fast that a lot of people spent the winter in unfinished houses in deserted pastureland ten or fifteen miles north of the old neighborhood.

In the suburbs, the Jews rebuilt their communal life around shopping malls, car pools, and designer synagogues. Meanwhile, in the city, Detroit elected its first black mayor, the flamboyant Coleman Young. Young gave Detroit an aggressively black administration that many whites (including many Jews) considered hostile. The tone was set in Young's inaugural address, when he advised the criminals of Detroit "to hit Eight Mile Road and keep going." Eight Mile Road separates the city from its northern suburbs, and many of the uprooted Jews took a dim view of the mayor's suggestion.

The years since 1967 have been hard on Detroit. The aftermath of the riots blended into the prolonged recession of the 1970s and early 1980s, and the city lost both confidence and economic momentum. It also developed a deserved reputation as one of the most violent places in America. I arrived in town shortly after No Crime Day—a Coleman Young–sponsored cease-fire that turned into a fiasco when three people, including a Detroit policeman, were murdered and eight others were shot.

"They've even got a murder meter on the Lodge Freeway," Joe Colten told me unhappily. "It's like the old automobile production meter except it measures homicides."

"How are the numbers this year?" I asked. Detroiters follow the statistics of mayhem with the pained expertise of stockbrokers in a bear market.

"We're still number one in the country, I'm afraid," he said. "I just don't think things are getting any better."

The prosperity and security of the Jewish community contrast markedly with the violence and decay of the city it left behind. Although it is shrinking—there are about fifty-five thousand Jews in the Detroit area, twenty-five thousand less than a generation ago—the community radiates middle-class respectability and good citizenship. Most Jews belong to a synagogue or temple, and perhaps ninety percent donate money to some Jewish cause. The bulk of these donations come during the annual federation fundraising drive, which is the most important activity of the Jewish year.

Detroit has always been a good fundraising town, and in 1987 the federation was going for a new record—twenty-five million dollars. That sounded like an astonishingly large amount of money, but Colten, who was a member of the planning committee, was confident it could be raised. "We're having our first committee meeting this week," he told me. "Why don't you come along and see how it's done."

The meeting was held on a Monday morning at eight. As we drove to the suburban Hebrew school where it was to take place, Joe filled me in on how the $25 million would be spent.

"Half of what we raise stays here in Detroit to fund local projects and services. We run two Jewish centers, a year-around camp, three day schools, old-age homes, and vocational and family counseling services. Twelve million dollars may sound like a lot, but you'd be surprised how much it costs to maintain the community. And the other half goes to Israel."

"Don't people mind sending so much to Israel?" I asked.

Joe shook his head. "Israel raises money for local projects, not the other way around. If we didn't have Israel, people wouldn't give as much."

"Why *do* people give so much?" I asked. "I mean, there's no Jewish I.R.S. Nobody can force them."

Joe smiled again—a gentle, worldly smile. "People in Detroit have discretionary money, and we expect them to give. It's a kind of self-tax. People in the community respect that. And if they don't, well, there's no reason to be lenient with tax evaders."

When we arrived at the Hebrew school I found about forty people eating bagels and sipping coffee around long tables. Most of them were men in their forties, fifties, and early sixties. They wore conservative business suits and serious expressions. There was only one woman, Jane Sherman, the daughter of multimillionaire philanthropist Max Fisher; and only one of the men wore a yarmulke. In Detroit and other cities around the country, federation leadership is mostly in the hands of Reform and Conservative Jewish men with a lot of money.

"How rich do you have to be to join this club?" I asked Joe, and he winced at my crassness.

"Put it this way," he said. "There are three *W*'s—work, wisdom, and wealth. To be involved in the campaign, you need two of them." A man sitting nearby overheard the answer and laughed. "Right, two *W*'s are enough—provided one of them is wealth."

The cochairman of the campaign, a supermarket mogul, called the meeting to order. The first item on his agenda was a report on a recent UJA junket to Israel. He called on the group's leader. "We had thirty-nine people on the mission," the leader said, "and it was a fantastic experience. The total pledges came to, ah, approximately two hundred thousand dollars."

The room erupted in applause. "Tremendous," said the co-chairman, "that's just wonderful." The leader sat down beaming, but the cynic sitting nearby snorted. "Two hundred thousand from forty people? Chicken feed."

There was a little more old business, and then the chairman gaveled the room to attention and began to discuss the upcoming precampaign. The federation's computers list approximately ninety percent of the city's Jews, and there is a special file for eight hundred or so who have given $5,000 or more in the past.

The eight hundred are the primary targets of the precampaign. The chairman called their names out from index cards and people raised their hands, claiming them like bidders at an auction. The idea is to match solicitors with friends or business associates. This makes for a more personal approach; it also makes it harder for solicitees to bluff their way out of contributing. In addition, campaign volunteers pool information about the financial condition of potential donors. In a close-knit community like Detroit, it's not too hard to come up with this sort of intelligence.

The next order of business was a report on the series of open-house meetings scheduled for the late fall. The first—and by far the most prestigious—is held by tradition at the home of Max Fisher, the godfather of the Detroit Jewish community. To have a successful campaign you need a trickle-down effect, with the richest people providing a yardstick for the rest of the community. In Detroit, the big givers give big; a ticket to the Fisher reception would be a minimum pledge of $100,000, and about thirty people would pay the price of admission.

Joe Colten's notions of good citizenship aside, there are a number of reasons people give large sums of money to the campaign—egotism, social climbing, and self-interested public relations are mixed with altruism and a sense of community responsibility. But the motives are of no concern to the federation. People are expected to do the right thing. Those who do are given the benefit of the doubt; those who don't are punished.

Sanctions take varying forms. Some are social—you cannot, for example, join a Jewish country club in Detroit without making a respectable contribution to the campaign. And for those who don't care about golf, sterner measures are available.

That morning a man mentioned the name of a large firm whose principal partners—Jews—had refused to give to the campaign. There were angry murmurs. "Does anyone here do business with them?" someone demanded, and one of the others nodded. "I'd like to discuss this with you after the meeting," he said grimly. It was not difficult to imagine what that conversation would be like. There are, after all, plenty of other firms in Detroit, not all of them Jewish by any means, that know how to do the right thing for the campaign and the community.

As the meeting progressed, I noticed a small group of young lawyers and businessmen who were sitting together. In their late thirties or early forties, they were easily identifiable as Young Leaders, an elite that has sprung up in every American city with an active federation.

The Young Leaders are a conscious creation of the United Jewish Appeal. The question "Who will carry on?" is a constant refrain in Jewish history; but about a decade ago, the UJA realized that for this generation the question has a special acuity. The baby boomers have no personal memories of Eastern Europe, the Holocaust, or the founding of Israel. They are not assimilating into American life—they are already assimilated. Unlike their grandparents, membership in the Jewish community is neither necessary nor automatic; they have other options. Raised on the words "cool" and "relevance," many of them find the bourgeois world of federated Jewry stodgy, parochial, and somewhat embarrassing.

The old-line community leadership, composed mostly of businessmen, looked at the problem in entrepreneurial terms—how to sell Jewish involvement to a new generation of picky consumers. As David Hermelin, a leader of the federation in Detroit, told me, they realized that they would have to make the community "the in place to be." It is hard to sell B'nai B'rith softball leagues and sisterhood kaffeeklatsches to kids who grew up in the sixties; but Israel is something real and concrete and it has become the primary marketing tool for selling Jewish community involvement to the yuppies.

In the 1970s, the UJA began to run tours and "missions" to Israel designed especially for the young Americans. They attracted—and were meant to attract—mostly nonreligious professionals and businesspeople with some money and the prospect of earning or inheriting a great deal more.

The UJA Young Leader missions are aimed more at consciousness raising than fundraising. There is a whole generation of Americans who feel Jewish (or can be made to feel Jewish) but don't know why. A UJA mission—which often begins with a visit to Polish concentration camps and culminates in Israel, at Masada and Jerusalem—is a crash course, Judaism 101. By offering it, the UJA—nominally a fundraising organization—has become one of the dominant groups in American Jewish life, primarily through its ability to play on the strings of Jewish emotion. A typical mission begins with a visit to Poland and the concentration camps and then proceeds to Israel and the symbols of survival and sovereignty—Masada, an Israeli army camp, a kibbutz, Soviet immigrants, and the like. Usually the trip culminates in a ceremony at the Western Wall or some other symbolic site.

Over the years, UJA groups have become an easy target for Israeli satirists. No one is more aware than Israelis—who live with the crushing burdens of Jewish state building—of the inherent fraud of the UJA slogan—"We are one." It is easy to resent the wealthy, secure young Americans who want to share in the drama and romance of the contemporary Jewish struggle without paying a price higher than a tax-exempt donation.

And yet, it is hard to deny these missions are an effective way—perhaps the only effective way—of attracting yuppies to the Jewish community. Israel, a place where Jewishness *is* relevant and cool, a country that can provide a powerful emotional experience, has become the recruiting ground for the next generation of community leaders.

Not incidentally, this form of training and selection ensures that the leaders of federated Jewry will continue to be Israel-oriented. Many of them try to re-ethnicize themselves along Israeli lines—using little Hebrew phrases, hanging Israeli paintings in their living rooms, and serving humos and felafel at their cocktail parties. They take a keen interest in Israeli politics, send their children to Hebrew day schools, and generally visit Israel once a year or more.

These Young Leaders are the fruit of fifteen years of patient labor. They are made Jews: sincere, committed, but not quite authentic, even to themselves. Their presence at the campaign meeting that morning in Detroit was a message to the other Jewish yuppies of the city: It's hip to be Jewish. You *can* have it all: Jamaica and Jerusalem, Harvard and Hebrew school, Porsches and Passover. Israel as the Jewish state, and suburbia as the Jewish state of the art.

Federated Judaism is strongest in the American hinterland. New York and Los Angeles—the two biggest Jewish concentrations—have notoriously weak organized communities. Middle-sized cities like Detroit, Pittsburgh, and Cleveland are far more cohesive. But the highest levels of affiliation and Jewish activity are often found in places where Jews feel most isolated—places like Waco, Texas.

"Small towns make good Jews," said a friend who drove me down to Waco from Austin on a rainy Saturday morning in January. My friend was originally from Massachusetts, and he has a keen eye for the various peculiarities of Texas Judaism.

"Jews down here tend to assume the characteristics of the general population," he said. "Take Dallas, for example. The worst thing that can happen to a father in North Dallas is to have an ugly daughter. It's the world's plastic surgery capital. And a certain amount of that rubs off on the Jews who live there, too. Or Laredo, for example, down near the Mexican border. I went there once to address a Hadassah meeting, and probably a quarter of the women were Mexican converts. When I went in the temple I didn't know whether to put on a yarmulke or a sombrero."

Waco, according to my companion, is one of the best communities in the state—well organized, generous, and active. "Young Judea was founded there, of all places, and it still produces a lot of national Jewish leader types," he said. One of them, Dr. Stanley

Hersh, was scheduled to meet us out in Downsville (population 130) at the farm of Justin "J.R." Rosenfeld.

Rosenfeld and Hersh are a sort of Texas-Jewish odd couple. When we arrived at his spacious brick farmhouse, J.R., a powerfully built man in his late sixties, had just come in from chores. He was dressed in a flannel shirt and suspenders, faded jeans, and worn, hand-tooled Justin cowboy boots.

Hersh, a transplanted Cleveland ophthalmologist in his late forties, was a city slicker by comparison. Dressed in a cashmere sweater, worsted slacks, and polished pennyloafers, he looked like the kind of man somebody like Rosenfeld might run off his property with a twelve-gauge shotgun.

Justin Rosenfeld was born and raised in Germany, where he was a teenage soccer star before Hitler forced him to flee in the late 1930s. Like many other German refugees, his first stop was Washington Heights. But Rosenfeld wanted to be a farmer, and there were no cows in New York City. He worked his way west instead, and wound up in Waco, where he was welcomed by the Jewish community. At the time, there were almost two thousand Jews in town; today, the number is closer to six hundred.

It took me a minute to realize that Rosenfeld does not have a speech impediment; he has two accents. One is a thick Texas drawl, the other a Germanic hiss, and they are laid one on top of the other, like simultaneous renditions of the same song by Waylon Jennings and Henry Kissinger.

"Ah vas vatchin' TV the othah day," he told me, "an' ah saw dem ole boys mit the fur hats ovah in Jerusalem, raisin' a ruckus an' all jus' becauss some folks vas a-drivin' on Shabbes." The accent is a fair representation of Rosenfeld's life, divided into two unequal parts by his flight from the Nazis.

J.R. follows the news from Israel, but he has a limited familiarity with Jewish politics. He admitted being baffled by a recent midnight phone call from New York, in which someone solicited his vote for the Labor Party slate in the upcoming Zionist Congress elections. "Ah don't know nothin' about no Zionist elections," he told the caller, and then he hung up.

Dr. Hersh laughed fondly at the story. He is an insider, one of the leaders of the Waco Federation and a national UJA activist. He began to explain the complicated web that links Downsville, Texas, to the World Zionist Congress, but Rosenfeld waved his hands in mock protest.

"Now, ahm very Jewish in mah vay," he said, "but ah just don't care nothin' about no organizations. I've been to Israel and I giff a little to hep out; but the truth is, I'd rather travel around the U.S. with another dairy farmer who's a gentile. I can talk to Jews for about a day or two about Israel and whatnot, and then I'm plumb out of conversation. But if I'm with another farmer, I don't never run out of things to talk about."

Rosenfeld knows a great deal more about the Dairy Farmers Association than about the Jewish Agency, the Council of Jewish Federations, or any of the other national organizations that his friend Stanley Hersh belongs to. "But ahm right proud to be a Jew," he said, "and if something comes up at a dairyman's meeting, vell, I let them know vere I stand right quick."

"Let me tell you something about Justin Rosenfeld," said Hersh. "He's the kind of man who's there when you need him. He may live way out here and spend his days with cows, but he's a member of the community. You want to know my definition of a Jew in a small town? Somebody who affiliates, who gives money to support Jewish causes and fellow Jews."

Hersh is a very smart, articulate man who takes a hard line on Jewish slackers. "A few years ago I was president of the Conservative synagogue here in town, and one day I got a call from someone I had never heard of, asking if he could bury his father in our cemetery. It turned out that he and his family had been in town for years, but they had never bothered to make contact with the community or to join any kind of Jewish institution. I said, 'Sure we'll bury him, it'll cost four thousand dollars.' The son almost blew up. 'Four thousand dollars for a funeral is outrageous,' he said. I told him, 'It's one thousand for the funeral and three thousand for the back dues you owe us for keeping up the cemetery all these years.' You know what? He paid the money."

Hersh, a Jewish political sophisticate, is well aware of the controversy surrounding Reform and Conservative religious legitimacy in Israel. But in Waco, criteria for affiliation are somewhat less rigid. When I asked him if the Jewish community ever checked into anyone's Jewish credentials, he seemed surprised by the question.

"Actually, I don't think anyone *has* ever been checked. If somebody says he's Jewish, that's good enough," he said.

And what, I wondered, would get somebody kicked out of the community? Again, Hersh seemed puzzled. "Kicked out? Frankly, I can't think of anything," he said.

"What if someone got up in shul and said he believed that Jesus Christ was the Messiah?" I asked.

"Well, in that case, I'd send him over to the Reform temple," he said, laughing.

As a community leader, Stanley Hersh is primarily concerned with consensus and unity. When he saw me jotting down his joke about the temple, he quickly pointed out that he had been kidding.

"As Jews, we should avoid the issues that divide us, and concentrate on the ones that unite us, especially in a small town like Waco," he said. "And Israel is the great unifier, the cause that every Jew can rally around. I happen to be a Republican, but I support liberal Democrats who are bad for my interests as a physician if they are good for Israel."

For Hersh, who grew up in Cleveland in the 1950s, Israel is more than a tool for achieving Jewish solidarity. "It made us acceptable in this country as Jews," he said. "The Six-Day War was the turning point, wouldn't you say, Justin?"

Rosenfeld nodded emphatically. "Yup, Israel's wars haff changed mah image here in Waco, no doubt about that."

The federated Jews of Waco, like federated Jews everywhere, express support for Israel primarily through fundraising. In 1985, the community collected $650,000, not including a special appeal for Ethiopian Jewry. "On that one, we got everybody together at the synagogue and said, 'You can save a human life for $6,000. We raised $70,000 in one night," Hersh said proudly.

"Yeah, this Hersh is tough," said Rosenfeld with an affectionate grin. "Every year he comes by for the UJA and if you giff him five dollahs, he asks you for fifteen. Then, ah come around for a contribution for the fire brigade dance, and the Jews in Waco make a beeline in the other direction." It was an old joke between friends. The Jews of Waco are civic-spirited, and contribute to any number of local causes, including the Downsville volunteer fire brigade dance. And J.R. Rosenfeld, despite his lack of interest in New York Jewish organizations and the intricacies of national

Jewish politics, gives a great deal more than fifteen dollars to the community each year.

We sat around the massive wood table in Rosenfeld's kitchen, sipping coffee and eating huge slabs of pumpkin pie. Although both Hersh and Rosenfeld are transplanted Texans, they have a native love of anecdote, and they swapped tall tales about life in Waco.

"Justin, you remember that convert we had, the one who had ten kids?" asked Hersh, and Rosenfeld grinned, anticipating a well-known story. Hersh turned to me. "See, there was this guy, a real hillbilly, he converted to Judaism. He was sort of strange and he never had a job, but he had ten kids and he was a Jew. So we helped him out, gave him food packages and money to tide him over. And then, one day he got himself a job as a truck driver. And do you know the first thing he did after he got his paycheck? He quit the synagogue and joined the Reform temple." Both men laughed and I joined in, remembering Vernon and Mary Lou, the converts of my boyhood.

"Yeah, ah remember that feller," said Rosenfeld. "Wonder whatever happened to him?"

Hersh shrugged. The man eventually resigned from the temple and is no longer a member of the Jewish community. And for Dr. Stanley Hersh—a federation man in a small town—a Jew without a paid-up membership is no more real than a tree falling in an empty forest.

The day after my visit to Downsville I flew out of Dallas to Las Vegas in the company of two hundred more-than-usually-optimistic Texans. The sky, rainy all weekend, was suddenly blue, Bloody Marys flowed; and the hopeful, many of whom seemed to know each other, hooted and hollered across the aisles in a camaraderie of shared expectation and greed. Some would return in an even better mood; most would lose a little and enjoy the trip; and an unlucky few would tap out and come home to Texas by Greyhound.

On the other end of the line, Las Vegas was waiting. Like Mecca, the Vatican, or any other place organized around and dedicated to a single infallible principle, it is a patient city. A certain percentage of humanity will always want to get rich quick; greed is a constant. Once the gambling houses along the strip were owned by hoodlums named Siegel and Lansky and Dalitz. Today they have been taken over by faceless corporations. But the principle is the same, the logic of the odds just as inexorable.

Actually, there are two Las Vegases. One is the outgrowth of the original town, a frontier outpost now firmly in the political grip of the dour elders of the Mormon Church. It is a conservative place, full of playgrounds and churches, schools and libraries, built mostly from money generated by what is euphemistically called "the gaming industry."

The other Las Vegas is the Strip—casinos and showgirls and come-on $3.99 steak dinners. This Vegas is an outgrowth of the vision of Benjamin "Bugsy" Siegel, who founded the first major casino, the Flamingo, in the late 1940s. Siegel's dream of creating a gambling empire in the desert came true, but he wasn't there to see it. The Flamingo lost money, a violation of the inexorable principle, and his partners relieved him of control by having him shot through the head.

Today there are approximately twenty thousand Jews in Las Vegas. Roughly eighteen thousand are residents of the Strip—gamblers, casino employees, and transients in a town where people change addresses on an average of every three months. The other two thousand live in Las Vegas proper and make up the city's federated community.

Las Vegas is not an easy city to organize; a man like Stanley Hersh would go out of his mind chasing down the unaffiliated Jews. For years Jerry Countess had that job, and he is glad to be out of it. A wiry little man with a George Burns delivery, he came to Vegas from New York in the early seventies to run the federation. Now retired, he still keeps in close touch with the Jewish community, and he has fond memories of its glory days.

"It used to be very easy to run a federation campaign in this town," he said. "We'd get a dozen biggies from the casinos together and someone would say, 'Okay, this year you give twenty-five grand, you give fifty grand,' like that. In a couple of hours we had our whole campaign. But the biggies are all gone now. How can you solicit some corporation in Cleveland? We can't even get them to comp us for rooms anymore."

In the sixties, when Jews still ran the casinos, fundraising in Las Vegas was not only easy, it was fun. Some of the top stars in show business were drafted and one year Frank Sinatra himself hosted the main fundraiser.

"That caused somewhat of a problem because Carl Cohen was the chairman of the campaign that year," said Countess. I looked at him quizzically. "You don't know who Carl Cohen was," he said. "Well, Carl was a wonderful man out of Cleveland. And one night at the Sands Hotel, he got into a fight with Sinatra and knocked his front teeth out. That's who Carl Cohen was.

"Anyway, Carl was the chairman of the campaign, and Frank agreed to host the meeting, so there was a problem. Somebody called up Carl and explained the situation, and he decided not to attend in order not to hurt the campaign. He was a real mensch."

"How did the fundraiser go?" I asked.

"You mean with Sinatra? It was great. He walked in with this entourage of has-beens that he used to take care of, Joe Louis and José Greco or whoever. He was about half blitzed. He says, 'I don't have to tell anyone here about Israel. I pledge fifty thousand dollars.' And then he looked over at his buddies and began saying, 'I pledge another two thousand dollars for Joe Louis, and another two thousand dollars for José Greco.' It wound up costing him another seventeen thousand dollars. What a night. There were biggies in this town in those days."

The last of the biggies is Moe Dalitz, once alleged to be an important underworld figure and a partner of Meyer Lansky's. Today he is an old man, full of good works, who spends his days dozing at a gin rummy table in one of the local country clubs. I asked Countess about Dalitz, expecting to hear a disclaimer, and got a testimonial instead.

"He just gave half a million bucks to build a new Reform temple out here. Half a million for a temple," Countess said, shaking his head in wonderment. "And it was Mr. Dalitz who set up the annual Temple Men's Club Gin Rummy Tournament at the Desert Inn. Believe me, out here Moe Dalitz is the Zeyde . . . you know, like the Godfather, only not Italian."

I had come to Las Vegas to give a lecture at one of the local synagogues and, as he said good-bye, Jerry Countess grimaced convincingly and explained that he would be unable to attend my talk because of a bad back. The move was well executed, and I imagined that he must have used it before; there is a limit, after all, to how many lectures a federation director can reasonably be expected to attend. He told me that I would be having dinner with several community leaders, pointed me in the direction of the Riviera casino, wished me good luck, and said good-bye.

My hosts that night turned out to be a charming, attractive widow in late middle age, now devoting her life to Jewish causes; and a rumpled, personable physician in his forties who had moved to Las Vegas from Cleveland. Neither seemed likely to have any connection with the Strip, and I didn't want to offend them by implying that they did. To find out about Jewish life in the American Gomorrah, I adopted a strategy of wily indirection.

"I know that the Jews in Las Vegas are mostly business people or professionals, and I'm sure the community has nothing to do with the gambling casinos and nightclubs," I said. But do you have any, ah, occasional contact with any of the people on the Strip?" I asked.

The lady chewed a shrimp from her salad in silence, and for a moment I thought I had offended her. Then she brightened. "Well, I have an example of what you might mean. A number of years ago, we had a rabbi whom some of the congregation didn't care for and wanted to replace. They scheduled a meeting to vote on renewing his contract, and a number of us who supported him decided to do a little campaigning.

"Several of the girls from the sisterhood and I went over to the Strip and talked to some of the Jewish men there who belonged to the temple but weren't really very active. We thought they might make a difference." Her eyes sparkled at the recollection of this Machiavellian move, and she took a dainty sip of water before continuing.

"Well, they promised to come and vote for the rabbi, but on the night of the meeting, none of them did. The rabbi lost and we were terribly disappointed. The next day I went to one of the casinos to find out what had happened, but no one seemed to know where any of the men were. Finally somebody said, 'Didn't you read the papers yesterday? Frank Costello got shot in New York.' "

I was waiting for the rest of the story, but the lady seemed to have finished. "Sorry," I said, "but I don't see the connection."

"Oh," she said, as if addressing a slow child. "You see, it wasn't their fault. If somebody hit Costello in New York, naturally they had to go underground for a while."

My delight in the story was obvious, and it precipitated a flood of local folklore. The doctor, who had led the temple building drive, spoke of Moe Dalitz's generosity in the respectful tone of a Detroit physician talking about Lee Iacocca. The widow, giggling, mentioned that a local Jewish madam had given a talk to a B'nai B'rith meeting. Prostitution is legal in Nevada, and the madam, a Jewish lady named Beverly Hurel, is a highly regarded business-woman.

As the dinner progressed, the Las Vegas Respectables talked knowledgeably and naturally about the gaming business. They rarely gamble—that is a sucker's game, and suckers don't last long in Las Vegas—but the city's economy depends on the casinos, and keeping abreast of developments there is nothing more than informed citizenship.

"I have several friends who are gambling people," the physician said. "Dealers, pit bosses, middle-level management. Of course, I don't see them much, because they work irregular hours. And if the casino is losing money, they change the shifts around, you know, to change the luck." He explained this as if he were discussing an established scientific principle.

The widow, who had lived in Las Vegas for many years, had some vivid recollections of the Golden Era, when the casinos had been run by Jews. "Jack Entratter, for example, was very active in the community," she said. "He was president of the Sands Hotel and Temple Beth Sholom at the same time, and he would donate his facilities for our sisterhood meetings. Jack was a wonderful man. He first came out here as a dealer, I think, or perhaps he was muscle, I can't remember. That was in the days when the Rat Pack used to frequent the Sands. It was a different town in those days."

The federated Jews of Las Vegas know that life is not all sevens and elevens, and living in the city imposes certain obligations. "In the old days," said the widow, "if a Jew came to town and got tapped out, he could always get one of the downtown businessmen to loan him enough to get back home. My husband, may he rest in peace, was always bringing people home for the night.'' Nowadays, emergency assistance is handled by the Jewish Family Service, which provides a meal, a place to spend the night, and in extreme cases bus fare back home. People who require such aid are viewed as imprudent, but the Jews of Las Vegas, sophisticated about human nature, do not make judgments. ''Sometimes you just get a bad run,'' the doctor explained with a philosophical shrug.

Dinner broke up and we went to the synagogue, where about two hundred people were gathered to hear a lecture on Israeli politics. Sammy Davis was at the Holiday Inn Casino that night, Kris Kristofferson was playing the Hilton Showroom, and Don Rickles was working the Sands, but the synagogue-going Jews of Las Vegas weren't interested. Here, on the inside of the great American pinball machine, they gathered to hear a little news from Eretz Israel.

From the platform, they looked like a typical American Jewish audience, middle-class, middle-aged, and intelligent. But when I began by saying that I was happy to be in Las Vegas because I was already seventy dollars up, they burst into a loud cheer. There probably isn't another synagogue in the United States where such a boast would be met by anything but chilly disapproval. But I was supporting the local economy, and even the most straitlaced sisterhood lady could have no objection to that. And besides, I could almost hear them thinking, Israel can use the money.

CHAPTER FOUR

JEWS WITH THE BLUES

O ne autumn Friday night I took a sentimental journey to my old temple in Pontiac, Michigan. Predictably, the visit was a disappointment—everything was smaller, shabbier, and less familiar than I had imagined. The people I had grown up with were gone, and the congregation that night was made up of strangers.

Only the rabbi's sermon was the same. He was a new man, but his talk that night was a set piece right out of my boyhood. It was divided into two parts. The first was its American message—that the prophets had all been liberal Democrats who would have supported the ERA, gun control, school busing, and a cutoff of aid to the contras. In my day, the prophets were Hubert Humphrey men; twenty years later, they were with Mario Cuomo and Michael Dukakis.

With the real—i.e., American—business out of the way, the rabbi turned to the obligatory ''Jewish'' part of his sermon. ''We Jews have been persecuted throughout our history,'' he told the congregation. ''Titus, the Spanish inquisitors, Hitler—all have sought to destroy us; but they are gone, and we are still here. Adversity has kept the Jewish people alive.''

If Jewish survival depends on adversity, the Jews of America are in trouble: There isn't a single Torquemada or Titus on the horizon. But the congregation, familiar with the standard rabbinical rhetoric about oppression, seemed untroubled. Invocations of the horrors of the Jewish past are stylized bows to tradition; the Jews in a place like Pontiac have no personal experience of persecution.

Seen from the inside, their suburban world is a warm, secure place. But below Eight Mile Road, in the inner city of Detroit, where most Jews no longer live or even visit, there is a tiny pocket of people who were left behind during the exodus of 1967. Fundraising to them means finding the rent money. They don't go to Israel because they don't have the bus fare.

A few years ago the federation opened a branch of the Jewish Vocational Service on Woodward Avenue. Woodward Avenue was once the grand thoroughfare of Detroit, a street lined with gracious public buildings, impressive Gothic churches, and fine stores. That was before 1967. Today it lies in the center of the city like a knife wound, raw and sore—a tawdry strip of two-hour motels and porno shops, tottering winos, drug addicts, and underemployed muggers.

Putting the Jewish Vocational Service on Woodward Avenue sent a clear message—it was there to serve the urban, non-Jewish poor. The federation wanted to do something to alleviate Detroit's poverty problem, get a little good publicity, and provide some jobs for Jewish social workers. But when the doors opened, the staff was astonished to find dozens, and ultimately hundreds of Jews turning up for help. Some were mentally ill, others old and sick. A few were men and women on the skids, Jewish bums hiding out in flophouses, unable to face the pressures of suburban respectability.

One person who was not surprised by the appearance of these forgotten Jews was Rabbi Noah Gamze. Gamze had been dealing with them for years at the Downtown Synagogue, the funkiest congregation in the city of Detroit.

The Downtown is located right where it ought to be, in the center of Detroit's once-bustling but now almost deserted business district. When I dropped by, on a weekday afternoon, the sidewalk in front of the small building was empty and there were parking spots right on the street. I rang the bell, and after being inspected through a speakeasylike peephole, I heard the clicking of multiple locks and Noah Gamze swung the door halfway open to let me in.

Rabbi Gamze ushered me into his office, a cluttered room barely large enough to hold a desk, shelves of books, and a threadbare couch. The Downtown Synagogue was founded in the days when hundreds of Jewish merchants worked in the city and sometimes needed a place to say Kaddish or to discharge some religious obligation. In those flush times the synagogue had been solvent, even prosperous. But most of the Jewish merchants left and it has become a struggle to keep things going. The Downtown still provides a daily minyan for businessmen, but Gamze has broadened his mandate; slowly, without intending to, he has become the chief rabbi of Detroit's outsiders.

At first glance Noah Gamze seemed wildly miscast for the role. He is an almost comically mild-mannered little man with wire-rim glasses perched professorily on his nose and a black silk yarmulke resting on thinning white hair. I guessed he must be close to sixty, although his formal, stilted language, high-pitched monotone voice, and didactic conversational style made him seem much older.

My first indication that appearances might be deceiving came when Gamze offered me a drink. Rabbinical refreshments generally run to tea and cookies, but he lugged out a bottle of whisky and shyly asked if I'd join him in a l'chayim toast. I got the feeling that Gamze doesn't get much drop-in trade.

"Isn't it a little rough for you down here sometimes?" I asked. He shook his head mildly. "I've had some experience along those lines in the past," he said. "For one thing, when I was a young rabbi in Chicago I was acquainted with Jacob Guzik. I even had the honor of presiding at his funeral."

It took me a minute. "Jacob Guzik? You mean 'Greasy Thumb' Guzik from the Capone mob?" Gamze smiled modestly. "You were his rabbi?"

"Well, yes I was. And I must say, I always found Mr. Guzik to be a generous and charitable individual. Of course he wasn't a strict observer of the Sabbath, but how many of my congregants are?" Gamze sighed theatrically. I wasn't sure but I thought I detected a twinkle behind his thick spectacles.

There was a knock on the office door, and a tall, stooped man came in. He was dressed in a mismatched plaid jacket and trousers of indeterminate chemical composition, and, like Gamze, wore a black silk yarmulke. With great formality Rabbi Gamze introduced him as Sam Glass, janitor of the synagogue.

Sam Glass is the kind of Jew that people in the suburbs don't believe exists. In his mid-fifties, he has spent his whole life in Detroit on the wrong side of the tracks; currently, he was living in the back of a burned-out store in the barrio. He had no connection with other Jews until a couple years ago when Rabbi Gamze found him selling newspapers in front of the Coney Island on Lafayette Street. Gamze took him in, and Glass has been with him ever since.

"This is Mr. Chafets, Sam," said the rabbi. "He is a writer from Israel."

"Uh, rabbi, you mean he came, uh, all the way from Israel?" gulped Sam in a hollow, Deputy Dawg baritone, a look of the utmost concentration on his face.

"Yes, that is correct," piped Gamze. "He is a resident of Jerusalem, which as you know is the capital of Israel." Sam nodded in affirmation, the pupil of a wise and learned master.

Rabbi Gamze was eager to talk about the media coverage of Israel, and he courteously included Sam in the conversation.

"Sam, Mr. Chafets has delved into the question of journalistic attitudes toward Israel. Perhaps you have seen some of his work on this most important subject?"

Glass let this nicely pass and waited.

"Mr. Chafets has examined the work of many prominent American journalists who are Jewish, such as Mike Wallace, Barbara Walters, Ted Koppel . . ."

Sam lunged forward in amazement. "Uh, wait a minute there, rabbi, are you, uh, saying that Ted Koppel is *Jewish?*"

"That is correct."

"Gosh, I can't believe it. Jewish! I always thought he was *Danish.*"

The doorbell rang and Sam, still shaking his head and muttering in astonishment, went to answer it. The afternoon minyan was beginning to arrive. It has been increasingly difficult to find a quorum in recent years. This, more than anything, is what prompted Noah Gamze to venture out into the inner city to search for new recruits. Combing the Cass Corridor, a greasy stretch of flophouses not far from Wayne State University, he discovered several dozen down-on-their-luck Jews.

"They don't always attend our services, of course, but occasionally some of them drop by. They have the status of paid guest worshipers," Gamze told me.

"How much do they get paid?" I asked.

"Two bucks a shot," he said benignly.

There were a couple guest worshipers in the congregation that afternoon. Gamze introduced me to Willie "The Barber" Schwartz, a nonunion man with a patch over one eye and a suspicious glare in the other. Curtis Dennis introduced himself. A thin black man in his fifties, he was dressed in a war surplus leather bomber jacket, work pants, and a Detroit Tigers baseball cap. Curtis Dennis is a convert to Judaism and a major player in Gamze's game plan for achieving a daily minyan.

The day before, in a ghetto neighborhood not far from the synagogue, an eleven-year-old boy had been murdered by a fourteen-year-old in an argument over an imitation silk shirt. Dennis took me aside and confided that the victim had been his cousin. He also mentioned that he needed ten dollars to send the bereaved family a wreath. "I hope you come up with the money," I told him, and he gave me a baleful look. A few minutes later I saw him talking earnestly to Rabbi Gamze, who listened respectfully, took out his wallet, and handed him a bill.

We went upstairs to the chapel. "Come on, rabbi, we're running late," said one of the businessmen, anxious not to get trapped downtown after dark. Mayor Coleman Young, in his ongoing cold war against the suburbs, had just erected a monument to Joe Louis—a giant black fist that extends over one of the city's main freeway exit ramps. Most white merchants like to pass that statue heading north by sundown.

Gamze picked up his prayerbook and began to read. From the row behind me I felt a tap on my shoulder and Curtis Dennis, in a deep ghetto accent, said, "mincha, page one hundret and eleven."

After services, Rabbi Gamze walked me to the door. "Tell me something, did you believe Dennis's story about that kid being Dennis's cousin?" I asked. The former spiritual advisor of Greasy Thumb Guzik looked at me closely, perhaps wondering if he had overestimated my sophistication. "Of course not."

"Then why did you give him the ten?"

Gamze's expression changed to one of gentle reproach. "Lying is a sin. But poverty is a worse sin. When a fellow Jew needs help, you help." He turned to Sam Glass, standing at his elbow. "That is known as *tzedaka*. Are you familiar with that term, Sam?" Sam nodded vigorously. "Uh, yes rabbi, I, uh, learned it from you."

Over two millennia Jews have been accustomed to turning to each other in times of crisis. In America, where the crises are few and far between, this tendency has been blunted—but not abandoned. When Jews are in real distress, they still turn inward, as if by instinct. That is true in the inner city of Detroit, and it is equally true at Temple Sha'ar Zahav in San Francisco—a gay synagogue in the midst of a deadly epidemic.

There are homosexual congregations in almost every large city in the United States. But San Francisco is the capital of gay America and Sha'ar Zahav, with 250 members, is the most visible and influential gay synagogue in the country. I first heard about the congregation from a reporter on the *Northern California Jewish Bulletin* with the wonderfully unlikely name of Winston Pickett. I assumed that it might be difficult to make contact with Sha'ar Zahav but Pickett assured me that it would be easy, and it was. I simply called Rabbi Yoel Kahn from Sacramento, where I had gone to give a lecture, introduced myself and my project, and asked for an appointment. Kahn was more than agreeable; he suggested that we spend part of a day together, so that I could get a firsthand look at the inner workings of the temple.

Kahn's openness stemmed from the fact that San Francisco takes Sha'ar Zahav in stride. The city is a liberal, tolerant place where Jews have long been accepted as members of the local establishment. Many of the old-line Jewish families, like Caspar Weinberger's, have converted to Christianity, and the intermarriage rate is among the highest in the country. At the time San Francisco had a Jewish mayor, Dianne Feinstein, who was reportedly taken aback to learn, during a visit to Israel, that her Christian mother disqualified her as a Jew in the eyes of the Israeli rabbinical establishment.

This kind of Talmudic distinction is not taken seriously in San Francisco. Orthodox rabbis in the Bay Area maintain cordial relations with their Reform and Conservative colleagues, and even the local Chabad representative is said to be soft on heresy. Aquarian minyans and other New Age worship groups dot the city. San Francisco is probably the only place in the country where a gay synagogue could become a part of the Jewish establishment.

I took a bus from Sacramento, sharing the ride with commuters too smart to drive and travelers too poor to fly. As we boarded the Greyhound, the terminal's loudspeaker boomed, "All aboard for San Francisco. Cigarette smoking is permitted in the last six rows of the coach. Please, no cigar, pipe, or marijuana smoking on board." It was seven-fifteen in the morning. I laughed out loud and a businessman in a dark pinstripe suit standing behind me said, "California."

Temple Sha'ar Zahav, which was once a Mormon church, turned out to be a disarmingly plain two-story white frame building located on a quiet residential street in the Upper Market area. Its ground floor is an unadorned chapel that seats several hundred on spare wooden benches. Upstairs there is an equally functional social hall and the rabbi's modest office. I had expected something garish and lurid—a strobe *ner tamid*, sorcerers' moons, and astrological signs on the ark—and I was a bit disappointed by the austere decor.

To an Israeli, the notion of a gay synagogue is as incongruous as kosher pork chops. The religious establishment in Israel takes the Scriptural view that homosexuality is an abomination, and even the nonreligious Jews tend to see it as a perversion or a sickness. There are a few gay bars and clubs in Tel Aviv, but homosexuality is far from accepted, and it takes considerable courage to come out of the closet. I entered Sha'ar Zahav full of wonder that there could be a synagogue for homosexuals, or that so many would be willing to publicly affiliate with it.

Rabbi Kahn was as disarming as his temple. A sturdy, apple-cheeked man in his late twenties, he was dressed in a ski sweater, blue corduroys, and loafers. And, although he is a Reform rabbi, he was wearing a yarmulke. The synagogue is a member of the Union of American Hebrew Congregations (UAHC), but many of its members come from Conservative or Orthodox backgrounds, and ritually it tends in some ways to be a right-wing Reform temple.

Kahn's study had all the standard rabbinical equipment—a UAHC diploma on the wall, shelves of Hebrew and English books, a complete set of the Babylonian Talmud, and another of the Encyclopedia Judaica. Kahn's library is of limited use, however; traditional Judaism offers little precedent to the rabbi of a homosexual congregation in the midst of an AIDS panic.

At the time of my visit, five of Temple Sha'ar Zahav's members had already died of the disease, and Kahn told me that a number of others—he wouldn't say how many—were ill. "Judaism becomes harder and stronger for people like ours during an AIDS epidemic," Kahn said. "It raises questions about God and mortality, questions people wouldn't normally consider. A lot of people wonder if they are being punished, and there's a strong sense of guilt. That's one of the main issues we have to deal with here."

On the high holidays, when the rabbis of suburban America were discussing South African divestment, environmental protection, or Middle Eastern politics, Yoel Kahn preached to more than one thousand people about life and death, God and suffering.

"We enter this New Year with uncertainty," he told his congregation. "Some of us are ill and others will become ill. Some of us are going to die—whether from complications of AIDS or of some other cause. We cannot undo actions we took years ago, before we understood what we understand today. Let us each forgive our pasts, which cannot be changed, and look to the future, which is in our power to alter."

There was an almost Jobian sense of doom in the sermon, a call for faith in the face of inexplicable suffering. Kahn then led the congregation in a meshaberach, or special prayer, for the victims of AIDS. There is a Talmudic injunction against praying for the impossible, and since there is no known cure for the disease, Kahn had labored over a prayer that was theologically acceptable. "Source of mercy, spread Your mercy on the ill among us and our loved ones, and protect with a special love those who are struggling with AIDS . . . and may we all see the day of healing, amen."

For the gay Jews of San Francisco, the synagogue is a refuge.

An average of 150 people come to services on Friday nights—the biggest Sabbath eve attendance in the city. They come because they need comfort; and because they want that comfort from their own people and their own religion.

In the shadow of the epidemic, the Jews of Sha'ar Zahav, once the avant-garde of the Age of Aquarius, have become almost as tribal as their ancestors in Poland or Russia. "A lot of our members come from back East, but they stay out here when they get ill," Kahn told me. "Often their families don't want to have to deal with them or admit that they are sick. Their real family is here, within the congregation." The dead are shipped home for burial, but Sha'ar Zahav has developed its own one-day ritual to replace the traditional shivah, or week of mourning. There is also a Bikur Holim committee that carries out the commandment to comfort the sick by providing around-the-clock care for the terminally ill.

No one knows exactly how many Jewish homosexuals and lesbians there are in San Francisco. Kahn estimated that there may be as many as ten thousand, a figure based on his assumption that one person in ten is gay. That number may be high, but obviously there are thousands of gay Jews in the Bay Area. The San Francisco Jewish Federation was the first in the country to take on a full-time social worker to deal with AIDS patients.

"People out here are a little more sympathetic than in other parts of the country, but there's still a conspiracy of silence," Kahn said sadly. "Jews are liberal in the abstract, but a lot of them don't want to admit that they know any gays. Being homosexual remains a stigma in the Jewish mainstream."

Kahn himself seemed comfortable talking about AIDS, but anxious to emphasize that Sha'ar Zahav is a synagogue, not just a crisis center. "Obviously AIDS is our first priority, but we're going full speed ahead with the rest of our program, too," he said. "You know, in a lot of ways this is just like any other congregation. People worry about their parents' welfare, they grapple with the meaningful nature of life, the usual concerns. When I first got here I expected a lot of questions about coming out, but actually there have been very few. By the time people get to Sha'ar Zahav, they're already out of the closet."

That is a considerable understatement. The congregation is

explicitly, even aggressively gay. Its statement of purpose defines it as ''A progressive Jewish congregation with a special outreach to lesbians and gay men. At Sha'ar Zahav, we as lesbian and gay Jews, with lovers, friends and families, both Jewish and non-Jewish, have a supportive environment in which to express our spiritual, cultural and ethical values. Sha'ar Zahav enables us to integrate our Jewish heritages (sic) with our gay and lesbian lifestyles. . . .''

In some ways, this integration is straightforward. Sha'ar Zahav is active in the usual pursuits of the Jewish community—aid for Ethiopian Jewry, demonstrations on behalf of Soviet refuseniks, Chanukah book fairs, and outreach programs for the city's Jewish elderly. The congregation has a relatively high percentage of leftists, many of whom are critical of Israel, but most of its members are, according to Kahn, mainstream Zionists of the AIPAC variety.

But along with Sha'ar Zahav's traditional Jewish concerns and activities, the congregation is in the process of developing a unique Jewish homosexual religious culture. The temple bulletin, known as the *Gaily Forward* (a play on the Yiddish *Daily Forward*), advertises, ''Out of Our Kitchen Closets: The San Francisco Gay Jewish Cookbook''—a new subcategory of Jewish cuisine. The bulletin lists anniversaries (Peter and Jeff, Marilyn and Marta) in straightfaced imitation of the middle-class style of the average suburban temple newsletter. And it announces special events not ordinarily associated with synagogues, such as Irene and Rosalinda's lesbian hot tub Havdalah service.

As the spiritual leader of a largely experimental congregation, Yoel Kahn is customarily called upon to deal with issues not normally within the rabbinic sphere. His first appointment that day was with a lesbian couple who had recently had a baby boy through artificial insemination. The biological mother was Edith, a powerfully built blond in a lumberjack shirt. A Christian, she appeared at first to be a bit intimidated by Rabbi Kahn and his synagogue, but as the meeting progressed she grew more relaxed, informally flopping a breast out of her shirt to feed her baby.

Edith's lover, Sally, was a Jew from New York, the daughter of old-time socialists. She had kinky black hair and wore jeans and a soiled red T-shirt. It was Sally who had initiated the meeting. She wanted their uncircumcised son to have a baby-naming ceremony in the temple. The baby was to be named Moshe, in memory of her father.

Kahn was agreeable in principle and he ran through their options. He seemed oblivious to the more unusual aspects of the situation and dealt with the two lesbians in a matter-of-fact style well beyond tolerance. But when Sally said that she wanted him to mention from the pulpit that Moshe's parents came from two traditions, Kahn suddenly balked with the stubbornness of a Chasidic rebbe examining a badly slaughtered chicken.

"Either the child is a Jew or he is not," he told the women. "If you want the ceremony in temple there can't be any question of a dual identity." Edith shrugged indifferently, but Sally was protective of her lover, and she and Kahn negotiated. Finally it was decided that Edith would be mentioned as the other parent, but that Kahn would make no reference to her religion.

"A couple like that puts me in a dilemma," he told me after they left. "I want to help them, but obviously I can't allow them to say in shul that the baby belongs to two traditions."

I didn't understand why this was obvious. Since Kahn makes up his rules as he goes along; every decision is a judgment call. Unlike many other Reform rabbis, he will not perform intermarriages; but he routinely officiates at "ceremonies of affirmation" —homosexual weddings—for gay men and lesbians. Similarly, Kahn was dismayed that baby Moshe had not had a ritual circumcision, but he didn't insist on one as a condition for the naming ceremony. "An uncircumcised Jewish baby has an unfulfilled *mitzvah*. But that's the parents' fault, not his, and there's no reason I should refuse to do the ceremony," he explained.

Child rearing and education are traditional Jewish preoccupations, and Kahn proudly pointed out that his congregation has an increasing number of children. Some belong to homosexual men; others are the offspring of lesbian mothers, many of whom were artificially inseminated. Kahn told me that within a year or two there would be enough kids for a religious school, although it wouldn't necessarily be gay. "The heterosexual-homosexual ratio among the children of gays is the same as in the general population," he explained. "One reason that lesbian couples join Sha'ar Zahav is to expose their boys to male figures active in the temple."

In Sha'ar Zahav's early years there was considerable friction between the men and the women, but lately they had reached a modus vivendi. "The problem," said Kahn, "was mostly the fault of the men. We basically weren't sensitive enough to feminist thinking." Under its constitution, Sha'ar Zahav alternates male and female presidents; and in general there is an effort to seek accommodation rather than confrontation. "After all, we're all Jews. And we don't have tough women in leather on one side, and decorator faggots on the other," Kahn said reasonably.

The female-male issue has also surfaced in liturgical discussions. "We don't say 'Lord' or 'he' when we refer to God," the rabbi explained, "and we use 'human' instead of the generic 'man.' But it's interesting; most people don't want to make the same changes in Hebrew. We do say, 'avinu malcainu, elohenu malcatenu'—our Father our king, our God our queen—but we haven't made many other changes. Personally, I'm torn. I'm rooted in the traditional liturgy, but intellectually I'm committed to a change of language."

Prayer is taken seriously at Sha'ar Zahav—both because of the AIDS panic and because many of Kahn's congregants see prayer as a means to self-discovery and realization. The members of Sha'ar Zahav insist on participating in every aspect of worship, a demand Kahn enthusiastically endorses. He has veto power and occasionally he uses it—he recently banned the use of a Bob Dylan song from the singer's born-again Christian period—but usually he goes along with experimental forms of worship.

That morning Kahn had a telephone appointment with a lesbian lawyer who was scheduled to lead services a few weeks hence. In the course of the conversation it emerged that the lawyer intended to turn the service into a public examination of her own spirituality. Kahn listened, feet on the desk and the earpiece cradled against his shoulder, as she outlined her main points. "I feel I don't have enough spiritual content in my life, and I want to learn to find God in daily life, not just at temple. And I want to be better able to communicate with God, to use him as a resource in my life. . . ."

Kahn interrupted her in the patient voice of someone who had been through this before. "That's very interesting," Kahn interrupted in a diplomatic tone, "but perhaps it's *slightly* self-reflective. Maybe when you tell the congregation how you feel you should pause, take a breath, let them reflect along with you.'' They talked in this vein for a few more minutes, the rabbi swimming patiently upstream against the flow of the lawyer's self-absorption. Kahn asked her to work on her ideas a little more and to call him later in the week.

''You have to understand that the people here are sometimes intoxicated by the chance to express themselves freely in a Jewish context,'' Kahn said, defending the lawyer. ''Mainstream congregations have no place for homosexuals, certainly not for avowed homosexuals. And a lot of the people here grew up afraid to come out of the closet.

''One man told me that when he was a teenager he went to his rabbi and admitted he was a homosexual. The rabbi told him to join the temple youth group and meet some nice girls. Well, naturally that didn't help, and a couple months later he went back to the rabbi and tried to talk to him again. And the rabbi told him again to meet some nice girls. Obviously the rabbi didn't want to hear what he was being told; here, we listen.''

There was a knock on the door and we were joined by Jerry Rosenstein, the temple treasurer. A thin, fastidious man in designer jeans and a well-tended winter tan, he was spending the day trying to get a handle on the temple's shaky finances.

''Forty percent of our members are at or near the poverty line,'' he said. ''We have a lot of single-parent families. And a lot of our people do mostly volunteer work or have low-paying jobs in social services. Economically we're like an old urban synagogue—we don't attract the upwardly mobile boutique owners.'' He sighed in mock sorrow but I had the feeling that he wasn't sorry. Ironically, Sha'ar Zahav is a family-style temple; high-rollers from Boutique Row would upset the community's equilibrium.

As we talked, I noticed that Rosenstein had a slight German accent. ''Jerry is a concentration camp survivor,'' Kahn told me when I mentioned it. ''He was in Auschwitz.'' Kahn is aware that many people consider him a freak rabbi at the head of a freak congregation. The presence of a Holocaust survivor somehow validates the temple, makes it unquestionably Jewish.

The Holocaust has a special significance in the collective consciousness of Sha'ar Zahav. ''Under Hitler, hundreds of thousands of homosexuals were rounded up by the Nazis,'' said

Rosenstein. "Gay Jews were forced to wear a Jewish star that was half yellow and half pink. Some of our people wear that symbol today in public, at demonstrations or community events." The congregation also says a special prayer, before the mourners' Kaddish, commemorating the "homosexual and lesbian martyrs of history."

Rosenstein and Kahn are close friends and collaborators but they disagree on one important issue. The treasurer is a devout environmentalist who believes that cremation is the only ecologically responsible way to go. Kahn is opposed. "It's not just that cremation is frowned on in Jewish tradition," he told Rosenstein. "I also admit that I'm squeamish about seeing it performed on a survivor of Auschwitz."

"Yes, I know it's a problem," agreed Rosenstein, with clinical detachment. "But I have to be true to my convictions."

It was a chilling discussion, made more so by the friendly courtesy with which the two men allowed me to listen. I was reminded of Gaston Hirsch, the last Jew in Donaldsonville; there was a blatant practicality to both men's attitudes toward the future. It was a relief when the conversation ended and the treasurer went back to his ledgers.

Sitting in the rabbi's office I realized how much my attitude had changed in only a few hours. I had come to Sha'ar Zahav expecting a grotesque parody; instead I encountered Jews in distress—men and women coping with problems of identity and morality—turning, as Jews always have, to their religion and their fellow Jews for help and comfort.

Norristown, Pennsylvania, is about as far as you can get from the Upper Market district of San Francisco. Norristown is Bruce Springsteen country, a bleak industrial city about forty minutes from Philadelphia. When I arrived, at eight o'clock on a freezing January morning, downtown Norristown was practically deserted and the only place to get breakfast was the Woolworth's on the main drag. The store smelled like an old-fashioned five-and-dime, the essence of Double Bubble overwhelming the aroma of weak coffee that rose from the counter along the wall.

I took a seat next to a red-faced man with a wool cap pulled over his ears and a set of industrial keys dangling from a belt loop. He regarded me with curiosity, but left the small town interrogation to the grandmotherly waitress. "New around here?" she asked, refilling my cup.

I shook my head. "Just here for the day," I said, and on an impulse added, "I'm going out to Graterford." She smiled sympathetically. Graterford is the site of a state penitentiary for bad men—violent, dangerous criminals doing long, hard time.

"You got somebody out there, hon?" she asked, and I sensed that the man in the cap was listening, too. I shook my head, dropped a dollar on the counter, and went outside to wait for David Maharam, chief rabbi of the JCAG Synagogue—the Jewish community at Graterford.

Maharam came by a few minutes later in a battered compact car. He is a Conservative rabbi in his mid-thirties with a genial manner, receding red hair, and a red beard. His main pulpit is a Conservative congregation in Norristown, but twice a week he drives out to the prison to conduct services for the prison's thirty or so Jewish inmates.

There is no accurate census of Jewish prisoners in the United States, but experts put their number at about two thousand. Most of them are white collar types, but a few—like the men of Graterford—are hard-core criminals. "They're nice guys," Maharam told me on the way out to the prison, "but I wouldn't necessarily want to meet one of them in a dark alley."

As we drove, I told Rabbi Maharam about a meeting I had in Detroit a few weeks earlier with Maxie Silk, one of the last of the old-time Jewish gangsters. Nearing eighty, Maxie runs the Left Field Deli, a diner located near Tiger Stadium. Dressed in his counterman's outfit, he seems a sweet-faced old guy with a white mustache, a prominent nose, and a George C. Scott overbite. But he has the powerful body of a much younger man, and hawklike brown eyes that sparkle when he recalls the good old days.

Although Maxie has gone straight, in his time he served three prison terms, one of them a ten-year stretch for armed hijacking. He talks about his previous career without evident remorse, in a language straight out of Damon Runyon. Italians are "luckshen" (the Yiddish word for noodles), women are "flanken" (beef), and good-looking women are "shtarke flanken"—strong beef. Any place with four walls and a roof is a joint.

"After I got out of the can on the hijack beef I opened up a joint called The Shamrock," he recalled with a laugh. "Talk about a tough spot, we had a guy working full time just repairing the chairs." From The Shamrock Maxie went on to other joints—The Lothrup ("A good buck but I got tired of beating up hillbillies every Saturday night") and his favorite, a "combination kosher deli and rib joint" next to the old Flame Show Bar whose customers included Joe Louis and Dinah Washington, Hank Greenberg and Della Reese. "Now there was a joint with some real action," he said with a faraway look.

Maxie first came to Detroit from Cleveland during prohibition. "I was eighteen when I left," he said, "and the wise guys back home were giving three-to-one I wouldn't make nineteen." It was the heyday of the Jewish gangster—people like Dutch Schultz, Bugsy Siegel, Meyer Lansky, Abner "Longy" Zwillman, and Louis "Lepke" Buchalter. Maxie, who had met some of the ex-yeshiva boys of Murder Incorporated during a short-lived stint as a rabbinical student in the Brownsville neighborhood of Brooklyn, came to the Motor City looking to break into the big time.

In Detroit, the Jewish mob was the Purple Gang, which controlled a good part of the liquor business, numbers, extortion and in Maxie's fond phrase, "twenty square blocks of the best red-light district in the Middle West." They did business with other Jewish gangs around the country and with old man Bronfman, the Canadian liquor supplier whose fortune later enabled his grandson Edgar to finance Israel Singer's theft of the World Jewish Congress.

Maxie is modest about his own affiliations; when I asked him if he had been a member of the Purple Gang, he just grinned and waved one hand in dismissal. "The Purple Gang? That name was a kind of joke. See, there was this fella by the name of Sammy Purple. Couldn't fight his way out of a paper bag, but one time he pulled a rod on a cop and got himself a little reputation. He was harmless, but after that every Jewish kid was automatically a member of the Purple Gang . . . y'know, Sammy's brother is still alive," Maxie said thoughtfully. "He's a Shriner if I'm not mistaken."

In the old days, Maxie and his friends were active in Democratic politics on behalf of Governor Frank Murphy ("He really knew how to keep a state running smooth") and they avidly supported the local sports teams. One of the Purples, a Russian Jew nicknamed Patsy O'Toole, was famous as the most obnoxious rooter in the American League.

"The Tigers used to take him on road trips, that's how *shtark* he was," said Maxie. "One time in Washington Roosevelt comes to the park and this really inspires him, see, I mean Patsy, not Roosevelt. Patsy hollered so loud they kicked him out of the game." Maxie shook his head, grinning.

But there was another, more violent side to the Jewish mob scene. One of the worst incidents came in a clash between the Purples and the Little Jewish Navy, a group of Chicago hoods who ran a flotilla of rum-running ships on the Great Lakes. Their rivalry ended in the Collingwood Massacre, the Motor City equivalent of the St. Valentine's Day Massacre.

"See, the original Little Jewish Navy was a Detroit outfit, used to hang around Third and Seldon," Maxie explained. "The main guys in that were Sleepy Louie Goldman and Shmulkie Solomon. And then these other bums from Chicago muscled in, Hymie Paul, Nigger Joe Levkowitz and the leader of that Chicago bunch . . ." I was taking notes, and Maxie paused to make sure I was getting things right. "Take down the name of the leader, Izzie 'The Rat' Sutker. Izzie the Rat. You know what kind of a bum you gotta be, get a nickname like that?

"Anyways, these guys were shaking down whorehouses, and Raymond Bernstein, who was the leader of the Purples or whatever, got this guy Milton Levine to set up a meet over at the Collingwood Apartment House. And Bernstein, Irving Millburn, and this one other guy—I won't mention his name 'cause he's still alive—they took out them Chicago bums. They went to the joint for thirty years on a murder rap."

Not long afterward, Maxie himself went to prison. "We caught this thief who was stealing our booze, see. So we smacked him around a little and he goes and tells a cop he was held up. They had some rough judges in those days, and I was out on a bond at the time, see I had been picked up before on a b & e, and I had a previous in Cleveland . . ."

Maxie wound up doing ten years. "I went in 1930 and came out 1940—I missed the whole depression. When I got out I was empty, but the boys took care of me. And it wasn't so bad in the joint, I was able to move around pretty good, know what I mean?"

I asked Maxie if there had been a synagogue in prison, and he shook his head. "We weren't that organized. But we had respect for religion. Before I went in the can, I remember the rabbis used to come around to see us at the Sugar House over on Oakland Avenue. They never came away empty either. We did the right thing."

Maxie suddenly slapped the counter. "You know I almost forgot, but for a few years there we did have our own shul on the holidays. Not in the can, right here in Detroit. Not many people know this, but we used to rent the ballroom of a hotel and bring in our own rabbi. There was Sleep Out Louie Lefkowitz—we called him that because he didn't like to go home much—Uncle Abe Ackerman the bail bondsman, and a couple of knock-around guys, Shorty the Bum and Marshall Abrams, we called him Bad Abe. They were the heads of the shul. We got a lot of people on the holidays, especially bookies, we must have had fifty of them." Maxie smiled his sweet smile once again, remembering. "I'll tell you one thing about that shul. Nobody stiffed us on their dues . . ."

By the time I finished telling Rabbi Maharam about Maxie Silk, we were almost at the prison. He cautioned me against expecting anything as exotic as the wiseguys' shul. There are no mobsters with colorful nicknames or fabulous wealth at Graterford; just a collection of losers who have committed crimes for reasons they themselves sometimes fail to understand. "If you're looking for something romantic, you're going to be disappointed," Maharam told me.

The prison itself was certainly prosaic—bleak, blunt concrete walls surrounded by barbed wire and adorned with guard towers. Inside, dispirited visitors sat on scarred benches in a drafty hall, waiting as the guards processed them one at a time. Rabbi Maharam, a regular, was admitted immediately. He waved me through as well, but on the other side of the large steel door I was stopped and asked to empty my pockets for inspection. When the guards were satisfied, I was given an infrared plastic I.D. bracelet. A second set of steel doors swung open, and Maharam and I entered the prison.

The synagogue at Graterford is at the end of the main corridor; to get there we walked, unescorted, the length of the prison through a gauntlet of inmates who regarded us with unfriendly curiosity. On both sides of the yellow brick hallway were long, metallic-looking cell blocks. From time to time raucous laughter wafted our way, but most of the noise came from machinery in the prison's shops and from the murmured conversations of men who loitered in the hall. Almost ninety percent of the inmates at Graterford are black, and I had the sense of walking down the hall of a very tough ghetto high school.

The temple is located directly over a Muslim mosque whose entrance is dominated by a mural of Jerusalem's Dome of the Rock. The temple's decor is less flamboyant. It consists of two carpeted, connected rooms: a chapel with the standard ark, eternal light, and folding chairs; and an adjacent meeting room dominated by a long table. Shelves along one wall hold Jewish books and a large television/VCR console. Behind a partition there is a small area with an electric coffee urn and plastic cups, knives, forks, and spoons—the temple kitchen. In another setting it would have been an unremarkable room; here, amid the thick, sweating walls and iron bars, it seemed like an oasis of civility and safety.

Although the Jews at Graterford are in jail for the same violent offenses as the men in the corridor, I felt a real sense of relief as we entered the synagogue. Jews have been conditioned for hundreds of years to fear physical violence from gentiles, but not from each other. This has changed to some extent in Israel, but in America it persists—Jews simply do not consider other Jews to be dangerous.

Certainly there was nothing aggressive or physically threatening about the inmates as they greeted Rabbi Maharam. They could have been a temple softball team or a B'nai B'rith lodge. Most were in their twenties and thirties, although one weatherbeaten man looked close to seventy. They wore civilian shirts or sweaters, gray institutional trousers with GRATERFORD STATE PENITENTIARY stamped across the upper leg, and jogging shoes. In the general prison population they go hatless, but here in the synagogue they wore yarmulkes or baseball caps.

Rabbi Maharam introduced me as a writer from Israel, and the men immediately became solicitous, even obsequious. One darted off to bring me coffee, another offered me a chair, a third leaped up to light my cigarette. Several convicts around my age called me "sir." They had all heard stories about inmates sprung by sympathetic writers; and while they had no reason to suppose that I might be influential, or even friendly, they had nothing to lose. Besides, new people are always a break from the monotony of prison life.

After coffee we adjourned to the chapel for morning prayers. "Only about half of the congregation are full Jews," Maharam had told me on the ride out to the prison. "The others have one Jewish parent, or maybe a Jewish spouse, some form of Jewish identity. It doesn't matter, though, as long as they feel Jewish. In jail that's what really counts."

Whatever their credentials, the members of JCAG are among the most observant Jews in the country. Their lives revolve around the synagogue in ways that would seem excessive to most people on the outside. For one thing, they have time—for daily prayers, Hebrew lessons, Bible classes, Jewish books, or just sitting around the synagogue shmoozing with their fellow Jews. They have time to celebrate holidays—the fast of Tisha B'av and Lag B'Omer —that are normally observed in America only by Orthodox Jews.

The men of JCAG have motive as well as opportunity. Outside the synagogue is a prison full of angry convicts and casually brutal guards. There have been occasional clashes with Louis Farrakhan's Nation of Islam toughs, and almost all the Jewish inmates have been involved in random violence. The synagogue is the only place they can create what their temple bulletin, *Davar*, calls "a sanctuary of civilization in an otherwise barbaric environment." It offers the same illusion of control and protection that Eastern European Jews found in their village shuls in the days of pogroms.

David Maharam is a Conservative rabbi, but the congregation is officially Reform, a member of the Union of American Hebrew Congregations. The affiliation is a matter of great pride to its members. "Being in the UAHC means we're legit," one of them told me happily. Several of the prisoners grumbled that they should have joined the Conservative movement instead, but they were shouted down. Convicts, like theologians, have the leisure for arcane ecclesiastical dispute.

The morning service began with Rabbi Maharam reading from "Gates of Prayer." He implored God "to open blind eyes, to bring out of prison the captive and from their dungeons those who sit in darkness." The prayer ended in a chorus of heartfelt amens. As the service progressed, the congregation participated in loud, practiced voices. When the time came to remove the Torah from the ark they kissed the fringes of their prayer shawls and touched it reverently.

The Torah portion that morning was Exodus 10:23, the story of the ten plagues. Rabbi Maharam read the text and explained each of the plagues and its significance.

"Now, darkness is an unusual plague," he told his congregation. "Unlike the others, it isn't physically threatening or especially dangerous. But that can be deceptive. Have any of you been in the hole recently?" A titter went up from the group, and a dark, powerful-looking man raised his hand sheepishly. "Alex, what's it like in the hole?" Maharam asked. "Uh, it's dark as hell down there, Rabbi," he said. There was another chorus of laughs, but Rabbi Maharam was pleased. "Exactly. Sometimes darkness can be a very effective punishment."

The example elicited a stream of questions from the floor. Tom, who once spent two years in Israel and now serves as the Hebrew teacher, cited the Hertz Prayerbook's speculation that the darkness might have been caused by an eclipse of the sun. "You have to realize that Rabbi Hertz was a polemicist who looked for rational arguments to support the Torah," Maharam explained. "He thought that scientific explanations would convince skeptics."

Tom nodded thoughtfully, but he was unwilling to abandon Hertz. "His explanation sounds at least interesting," he said with the dispassion of a biblical scholar.

"Yeah, well the darkness lasted three days, didn't it?" someone else called out. "Who ever heard of a three-day eclipse of the sun?" Tom was ready for this, too; he argued that since the sun was Egypt's chief god, the Egyptians may easily have exaggerated the length of its disappearance. This gave rise to a series of loud protests as the congregation chose sides.

After a minute or two, Maharam rapped the rostrum for order and returned to the service. He raced through the Hebrew prayers, led the congregation in singing "Ain K'Eloheinu," and then slipped off his tallis and joined his flock for coffee in the meeting room.

The main topic of conversation that morning was Jewish solidarity. The prison has no Jewish neighborhood—there are Jews in every one of the five cell blocks, including the one reserved for the hardest cases. "This is the worst prison in the state of Pennsylvania," one man said, with a connoisseur's certainty. "The prisoners run this jail. That's why it's so important for us to stick together."

An example of Jewish unity had recently appeared in an article written for the temple bulletin by Nolan Gelman. Entitled "A New Man," it described the author's arrival at Graterford:

"I was processed in and sent to E Block, the quarantine block for newcomers. It is not unlike bedlam; cacophonous, grossly overcrowded, hostile and bewildering. . . .

"A number of individuals came by and asked if I would like to attend the Jewish congregation. I was surprised . . . [and] I accepted the invitation out of curiosity. . . . I was introduced to all the members and warmly welcomed. I was offered a care package containing every conceivable item an inmate might need, all donated by the members themselves. . . .

"My stay here has turned into a time of spiritual awakening and learning. This oasis created amidst the barren concrete of Graterford is testimony and monument to the spirit and resourcefulness of the Jewish inmates here."

Gelman's sentiments were echoed that morning by his fellow inmates. Tom, the argumentative Hebrew teacher, spoke for the group. "When you see the animals here, it's nice to see good people at temple." A tall, impressive man of forty with Clark Kent good looks, he projected a crisp moral authority that made me wonder if his incarceration might be a mistake. Later I learned that he was serving a sentence for sex crimes against minors.

"Per capita we're the best-behaved prisoners at Graterford. We almost never get a misconduct. And we're the most learned," said Jules, a young man with sleepy brown eyes and a sensuous face. He was raised in suburban New Jersey, belonged to a Reform temple, and was an honor student in high school. He could have been a third-year law student getting ready to join a big New York firm; instead, he was doing life.

"What are you in for?" I asked him. Prison etiquette discourages such direct questions. On the way to Graterford Rabbi Maharam had cautioned me about being too inquisitive—"In jail everybody's always innocent anyway," he had said—but my curiosity overcame good manners.

Jules flushed at the question and hesitated. He couldn't lie— the others knew what he had done—but he couldn't quite bring himself to tell the truth, either. "I, ah, was at a party with this girl and it, ah, got a little out of hand," he mumbled.

At the end of the table a squat man with a biker's tattoo on his forearm and a ponytail burst into mocking laughter. Jules shot him a threatening look. "What're *you* laughing at, asshole?" he demanded, and the ponytail held up a conciliatory hand.

Many, perhaps most, of the members of Temple JCAG are in for drug-related offenses. Some committed crimes under the influence, others were caught dealing. The addicts all claimed to have been cured, and they talked about their rehabilitation with the cool impersonality of social workers discussing other people's problems.

"Hey, a Jewish doctor from Philly came in here the other day," said Alex, the man who had been in the hole. "He heard I'm about to get out, and he offered me a place in his house for a few months. And this doctor, he doesn't know me from a can of paint. He said, 'You're a Jew, and that's enough for me.' " Alex, who was born in Brazil to Russian parents, was the only immigrant in the group. He was raised from early boyhood in Philadelphia and was happy to be going home.

"Hey, I'm gonna keep my nose clean, stay away from drugs, just be a mensch," he said, and shammes Jay Schama, the head of the congregation, smiled approvingly. "Al is our rehabilitated guy here," he said, affection mixing with regret. The position of shammes—the lay leader of the temple—is an elective one. Schama, like any politician, was sorry to be losing a supporter.

The shammes stands at the top of Temple JCAG's hierarchy, which also includes a treasurer, secretary, and men's club president. The job carries considerable influence and prestige, and abuses of power are not unknown. Several years ago, for example, one of Schama's predecessors, entrusted with ordering special food for Passover, was caught trying to import several dozen tins of forbidden oysters and shrimp for the Seder.

In most synagogues the first duty of a shammes is finding ten men for a minyan. But this is not a major problem at Temple JCAG; unlike Sammy Davidson of Meridian, Mississippi, for example, Schama has a captive congregation. He is occupied primarily with foreign affairs—maintaining contacts with the Jewish community on the outside, and with the prison authorities. He is also in charge of the annual congregational dinner, a gala event that is the high point of the JCAG social calendar. A couple years ago former governor Milton Shapp gave the main address—a coup by the founding shammes, Victor Hassine.

Hassine was a charismatic lifer, an attorney by profession and Jewish activist by temperament. He was unpopular with the prison officials—particularly after he initiated a lawsuit over living conditions—and he stirred passions among his fellow Jews as well. After winning a hotly contested election for shammes, he received several anonymous death threats that he attributed to a rival faction. Then one day someone caught him off guard and threw a bucket of bleach on him. Hassine was transferred to another prison for his own protection, and a new shammes was installed. Congregational politics at Temple JCAG are definitely hardball.

Schama, the incumbent, is a far less controversial figure. A short, stocky man in his late twenties, he was raised in Philadelphia, dropped out of school after the seventh grade, and worked around town in a series of dead-end jobs. He also developed a drug habit that he tried unsuccessfully to support by armed robbery. Caught during a stickup, he was sentenced to five years; he still had two and a half left to do. Schama was already preparing for his release—he recently completed his high school equivalency exam—but he was determined not to leave a leadership vacuum. "Right now I'm grooming Jules," he said. "He's a perfect choice, you know, 'cause he's in for life."

If Jules does take over, the congregation is due for a hawkish administration. On the day I visited Graterford, Shiites in Beirut had just taken several American hostages and were demanding that Israel release imprisoned terrorists as the price for their return. "Do you think Israel will agree?" Tom asked me. I said I didn't think so.

Jules snorted. "That's what the Israelis said last time, and then the next thing you see is about a thousand Arabs in jogging suits getting on buses. That's bullshit. What they should do is clear all the Americans out of Beirut, bring in the Sixth Fleet, and just flatten the place."

Stan, a wrinkled old man in a gray work shirt who hadn't said a word all day, suddenly interrupted. "Do that and you start World War III," he said, and a debate on Middle Eastern policy was under way. The men at Graterford take a keen interest in Israel; they even have a UJA drive that raises money to support an orphan in Netanya. Only Tom had been there, but several others said they would like to visit. Alex, the rehabilitated guy, wondered if the law of return applied to ex-cons. Another man asked if I could get them a copy of the Israeli film *Beyond the Walls,* which depicts life in an Israeli prison. "Be nice to see what it's like being a majority," he said wistfully.

In Israel, the early pioneers once boasted about Jewish criminals, seeing them as a sign of national normality. Today the country has its share of crooks, and there are several thousand Jews behind bars. They exist because Israel is a real country with the usual human continuum from good citizenship to criminality. But in America, Jews have no such continuum. They are expected to go to college, acquire a profession, raise a family, and become model citizens.

The men at Graterford are freaks and they know it. Sitting around their little shul, they speak in the vocabulary of the Jewish world: Israel, the Holocaust, affiliation with the UAHC, the need to be a mensch. They know the tones and cadences of American Jewish temple talk, and they used it with me, an outsider; but it is their second tongue. For all their Chanukah parties and Hebrew lessons, they are far closer to the harsh realities of their fellow prisoners than to the mellow, domesticated Jewish middle class.

"Don't be fooled by these guys," a prison official told me later. "They're no different than anybody else in jail." I recalled their sober vows of rehabilitation, their hatred of the coarseness and brutality of the penitentiary; somehow they didn't seem to be real criminals. But the official was adamant. "You think because they're Jews that makes them different? Forget it. Most of these guys, when they get released, they'll be back. A lot of them belong in here.''

I didn't doubt that he was right, but I resented him for saying so. My visit to the congregation at Graterford was a lesson in the emotional pull of Jewish solidarity. The final, irreducible point was that this minyan of murderers, sex fiends, and strong-arm men were members of my tribe. I didn't know them, in Alex's phrase, from a can of paint; but in some way they seemed as familiar as cousins.

It was getting toward noon when a guard came into the synagogue and reminded the congregants that they had to get to work. Rabbi Maharam and I said good-bye and began the long, long walk up the cinder block corridor to the gate. This time, though, we had an escort—half a dozen of the guys from the shul. Jay the shammes led the way, along with sleepy-eyed Jules, the ponytailed biker, Tom the Hebrew teacher, and a wiry man in a Mets cap named Jerry who was the congregational treasurer. As we walked we continued to talk, and I was so absorbed in the conversation that I was surprised when the group stopped. "This is as far as we can go," Jay said with an apologetic smile, pointing to the heavy steel door at the exit.

Embarrassed, I began to shake hands with each of the men, wishing them luck. When I got to Jerry he quietly said, "I think you've forgotten something," and then reached up and plucked a black silk yarmulke off my head.

"It belongs to the synagogue," he said.

"Sorry, I wasn't trying to rip you off," I joked, and he gave me a skeptical grin. In prison, everyone's always innocent.

There is a Horatio Alger quality to the Jews of America. In three generations they have gone from rags to riches and in the process have made great contributions to the culture, science, and economy of their new country. The rewards for their success have been prosperity, security, and an unprecedented social acceptance. Many Americans see Jews as a new, improved variety of WASP— Episcopalians with a touch of spice.

In New York, the capital of Jewish America, the situation is a little different. There, too, the great majority of Jews have reached the middle class and beyond. But unlike other American cities, New York also has a significant Jewish poverty class. A recent poll conducted by the UJA revealed eighty thousand Jewish families in the city with an annual income of less than $10,000, and another one hundred and ten thousand households with an income of less than $20,000 a year. Experts believe that there are three hundred thousand Jews in the New York area who qualify as poor—roughly fifteen percent of the total Jewish population.

Many of the poor Jews are Chasidim with huge families and little secular education. Others are old men and women on fixed incomes, or people out of work—perhaps as many as one hundred thousand in the metropolitan area, according to Jewish poverty workers.

At the bottom of the barrel are an estimated fifteen hundred homeless Jews, street people who sleep in the open and carry their belongings with them in shopping bags or on their backs. Warren Feierstein, who runs the Metropolitan New York Coordinating Council on Poverty for the Jewish Federation, has spent his professional life dealing with these people. A soft-spoken man in his mid-thirties, Feierstein is a realist who grew up on New York's Lower East Side. To him, Jewish poverty is both natural and inevitable.

"You have Jewish hookers and Jewish beggars in Israel, why shouldn't we have them here?" he asked reasonably when we met at the Stratford Arms Hotel. "Jews are just people like everybody else. There are strong ones and weak ones. Our job is to help the ones who can't help themselves."

Despite the logic of this approach, poor Jews are something of an embarrassment to the establishment. For years it was difficult to convince the federation to face the issue of Jewish poverty with any seriousness. This changed when Mayor Ed Koch, himself a Jew, publicly berated the community for its indifference. "The third floor of the Stratford Arms is our answer to Koch," Feierstein said.

Nestled between the brownstones on West 70th between Columbus and Broadway, the Stratford Arms looks like a typical Upper West Side residential hotel. But when we went inside that morning it was immediately obvious that the hotel specializes in people with nowhere else to go. The lobby was bare of furniture, and patrons sat on the uncarpeted floor, drinking steaming coffee from white styrofoam cups. Others leaned aimlessly against peeling walls and stared into space. From time to time an unshaven man erupted into barks of unprompted laughter. At the desk, a red-nosed clerk regarded the scene with utter disinterest. Even the candy bars in the lobby's vending machine were crumpled and stale, chocolate-covered reminders of the pervasiveness of poverty.

The Stratford Arms's clientele is made up of people of all races and religions, but the third floor is its Jewish neighborhood. The floor has been taken over by the Metropolitan Council on Poverty, and it serves as a shelter for a shifting collection of misfits and losers. "We had a family of six—a couple with four kids—who drove all the way up here from Florida," Warren told me, as we ascended in the rickety elevator. "He was a factory worker out of a job, and they didn't know what else to do. Poor people have always migrated to New York from the South, why shouldn't Jews?"

The corridor of the third floor reeked of industrial cleanser, stale whisky, and stale cigarettes. A woman in a tattered bathrobe passed us in the hall without looking up, but otherwise the floor was deserted. "It's too early for a lot of them; they're still sleeping," Warren told me. I looked at my watch and saw it was ten-thirty.

Warren Feierstein is a former yeshiva boy who wears a skullcap and considers himself Orthodox, but he is undogmatic about identifying poor Jews. "We can usually tell by the name or by the accent—a lot of our clients are from Eastern Europe," he said. "But basically, if someone claims to be Jewish, we take their word for it. It doesn't really make much sense to go into people's backgrounds. By the time they get here, they need help no matter who they are."

Occasionally Feierstein does find out about a client's background, but the information isn't always helpful. "We had a woman here not long ago, the daughter of a prominent Chasidic rabbi in Brooklyn," Warren told me. "She was a really pretty girl in her late teens. Her parents were extremely strict and she wanted to wear makeup, tight jeans, that sort of thing. So she ran away from home or her parents threw her out, I'm not sure which.

Anyway, she wound up on the streets, and she came to us for help. We got her a job as a margin clerk at the stock market and gave her a room here. Then, about six weeks later, she disappeared. I didn't hear from her until I got a call from the police; she had been picked up on Times Square for hooking.''

"What did you do?" I asked. Warren shrugged. "There isn't much you can do. I wish there was. We do what we can. It isn't very much fun to be poor, but at least Jews have a place to turn. That's something. And believe me, there are an awful lot of poor Jews in New York, young and old, religious and not religious, immigrants and native-born, black and white. . . .''

"Blacks? You mean like Chasidim?" In Israel, ultra-Orthodox Jews are sometimes called "blacks" because of their dark hats and coats.

"Them too. But I'm talking about black blacks. You'd be surprised how many black Jews there are in this city. They even have some congregations. I'm not sure where but I could try to find out if you're interested," he said.

I was, but Feierstein, despite his extensive network of contacts, proved unable to find a black synagogue. My curiosity was aroused, and I tried several other Jewish organizations, but none of them knew what I was talking about. Clearly, if there was a black congregation in New York it was very far out of the Jewish mainstream.

Unwilling to let go, I called *The New York Amsterdam News* in Harlem and spoke to the religion editor. In a Caribbean accent he told me he had heard of black Jewish congregations but didn't know of any personally. "We have a Jewish woman on our switchboard," he said. "Why don't I ring you through and you can ask her." I introduced myself to the operator and asked if she knew the whereabouts of a black synagogue. She was noncommittal but she took my number and said she'd see what she could do.

That evening I got a call from a man named Zakiahu Levy, who invited me to attend Sabbath morning services at Beth Elohim, his shul on Linden Boulevard in St. Albans, Queens. "When you get there just tell the shammes you talked to me and it'll be cool," he said.

Feeling foolish, I asked him if a jacket and tie were the appropriate dress. "Yeah," he said. "Jacket and tie are fine. We dress western, we're a Talmudic congregation. Just be sure you bring your *kippah* [the Hebrew word for skullcap]. You got a kippah, dontcha?" I assured him that I did, and thanked him for his help. "Happy to do it," he said. "Shabbat shalom."

I went out to Queens expecting to find a sect. Israel has a group of "Black Hebrews" from America, led by a charismatic preacher named Ben Ami Carter, who claims that the original Hebrews of the Bible were black, and that modern blacks are, ipso facto, the real Jews. This philosophy has not won him many Israeli supporters; and the Black Hebrews, who entered the country illegally as tourists, live a separate communal life in a couple of Israel's less attractive desert towns.

The Black Hebrews of Israel do not practice Judaism. Their religion consists of homemade rules and rituals—polygamy, vegetarianism, and strict abstinence from alcohol, drugs, and tobacco. The men dress in white, the women wear long robes and cover their heads with turbans. The members all have Hebrew names bestowed by Ben Ami Carter that are said to express each person's personality and character traits. The sect has only one holiday— Appreciation Day ("You just invite anyone you appreciate," a member of the group once told me). Ben Ami Carter, who considers himself the Messiah and tools around in a large Cadillac surrounded by admiring Hebrew sisters, is the most appreciated man in the group.

That's more or less what I expected to find on Linden Boulevard. Instead I entered a storefront synagogue that reminded me of the small shuls that dot Jerusalem's downtown. Beth Elohim (the House of God) is a one-room chapel arranged in the Orthodox way—men's section in front, women's in the rear. Wooden pews face a small platform. On the far wall is a simple ark, and above it an eternal light. A door on the side of the chapel opens to a flight of stairs leading to some basement classrooms. On the door is a sign that reads TALMUD TORAH.

Although it was past ten when I arrived, the chapel was almost empty. A dark-suited usher wished me "Shabbat shalom," discreetly peeked at my head to make sure I was wearing a yarmulke, and then showed me to a seat in the front row. I told him I had been invited by Zakiahu Levy and he nodded his recognition.

"You're welcome here," he said reassuringly, and he left me alone on the hard wooden bench.

I heard a rustling in back of me and turned to see three stout ladies sitting in the women's section. All three wore pastel print dresses, held prayer books in white-gloved hands, and covered their heads with bonnetlike hats. Although the women's section was otherwise empty, they sat shoulder to shoulder, as if they were joined together. I smiled at them. They smiled and called out, "Shabbat shalom."

Gradually members of the congregation began straggling in. The men wore dark business suits, prayer shawls, and knitted yarmulkes or hats; the women covered their heads with hats or scarves and wore festive dresses. The only whites other than myself were a woman who accompanied her husband and teenage daughters and an old lady who looked like she had wandered in to get out of the cold.

While we waited for the service to begin, I leafed through the prayerbook that had been laying on my seat. Beth Elohim uses the Chasidic edition published by Mercaz L'Inyonei Chinuch, Inc., of Brooklyn. The book contained the standard Orthodox service in Hebrew, along with an English translation.

A few minutes before eleven, Rabbi Levi Ben Levi and Cantor Nathaniel Davis entered the room and took their places on the platform. Ben Levi is a dark-skinned, rotund man with a studious, somewhat stiff demeanor. He wore a black robe and white tallis, and he nodded to the congregation in solemn greeting. Ben Levi, I later learned, is the spiritual leader not only of Beth Elohim but of its sister congregation in Harlem.

The rabbi began by sternly admonishing his flock to come on time in the future ("We on CPT in this shul," whispered a man sitting next to me. "You know—Colored People's Time"); then the cantor, Nathaniel Davis, began to chant the service in a warm, thick baritone. Like Ben Levi he wore a black robe and white tallis, but instead of a regular yarmulke he had on a high black hat like the ones worn by Eastern European cantors.

Davis's melodies were heavily tinged with gospel influence, and they went remarkably well with the ancient Hebrew prayers. He studied cantorial music with the renowned Josef Malovany of the Fifth Avenue Synagogue in New York, and he is familiar with traditional liturgical music. "I can *doven* [pray] Ashkenazi style," he told me after the service, "but our people prefer the down-home sound." Down home for the Jews of Linden Boulevard is Mississippi, not Minsk.

Beth Elohim has about 250 members and, judging from the people at services that morning, almost all of them can read Hebrew. They joined in the responsive readings and mumbled along with the cantor like old pros in any shul in the world. But from time to time someone shouted "Hallelujah!" and once or twice a lady in back loudly sighed, "Amen, ain't my Lord somethin'!"

It was a kind of soul Yiddishkeit that reminded me of the fervor of Chasidic synagogues. Later, Davis complained that it had been a quiet morning. Rabbi Ben Levi's son, who plays the piano, was away at Yale, and several of the women who normally beat on tambourines weren't at services. "You wanna hear something, you come by on Simchas Torah. Man, we really rock the shul," the cantor said proudly.

The story of black Jews in America is shrouded in mystery, confusion, and self-interested inaccuracy. A few claim descent from Jewish slave masters. Some are converts or the children of converts. And others have simply decided, more or less on their own, that they are Jews.

Some black Jews belong to mainstream synagogues, but most are members of various black congregations, which are divided along doctrinal lines. "Eastern" black Jews, such as the Ben Ami Carter group in Israel, are sects that believe all blacks are Hebrews. They usually dress in African or Arab garb, use Hebrew in their prayers, mix Christian, Moslem, and Jewish theology and ritual, celebrate holidays with self-ordained customs, and feel no connection to white Jews.

Beth Elohim, on the other hand, calls itself a Talmudic synagogue, which means it practices traditional Judaism. It is not strictly Orthodox—its members ride to synagogue on the Sabbath, and at the service a collection plate is passed around—but ritually it is unmistakably Jewish. The only specific nod to race is the rabbi's prayer, given before his sermon, for the peace of "Eretz Yisrael, Eretz Africa, and Eretz America—the lands of Israel, Africa, and America."

And yet, emotionally the congregation is very much within the holiness tradition of the black church. Its members are poor people, working class and lucky to be. They come to synagogue for only one reason—they need spiritual fortification to get through very hard lives. Black religion is God-oriented, and black Judaism is no exception.

In his sermon that morning, Rabbi Ben Levi spoke about the need for purity and obedience to God's law. "To be a good Jew, you got to do three things. You got to *eat* right—I'm talking about kosher food now. You got to *think* right—I'm talking about Torah thoughts, the word of God—can I get an amen? And you got to *do* right—I'm talking about the commandments of the 'kodosh boruchu,' God almighty."

A murmured amen followed each one of Ben Levi's three principles and he beamed avuncularly at the congregation. "Now, I know that there are people here this morning whose lives aren't going just like they want them to. There are people here today who are in pain, people suffering physically, mentally, emotionally. But I want you to know one thing—you do right and God's gonna do right, too. You take a step toward him and he's going to take two steps toward you. If you eat right and think right and do right, God's going to see to it that your bank book is balanced at the end of the month! God's going to keep you on your job! God's going to help you find the strength to carry on, to take care of your families, and meet your obligations, yes he is, say amen!"

A few weeks earlier, in Jacksonville, Florida, I had met a young Reform rabbi named Michael Matuson, who claimed to detect a new spiritual hunger among his congregants. "People here have everything," he told me. "Materially they can't even think of things to want anymore. But a lot of them are desperate for awe. At services on Friday nights I invite them up to the Torah. I tell them, 'If you've had an experience during the week that needs spiritual transformation, touch the Torah and meditate on it.' You'd be surprised how many people are moved by it.

"The people in a congregation like this want to believe in a myth," Matuson said. "The problem is, most of them don't believe in God. And to tell you the truth, most rabbis don't believe in God, either—at least not the second grade notion of some old man sitting on a cloud."

Rabbi Ben Levi and his congregation believe. Their God can balance your checkbook, cares what you eat for dinner, rewards the righteous and punishes the sinner. It is a primitive kind of religion, close to the roots of Judaism. "American Jews don't feel comfortable with verbal affirmations of God's glory," Ben Waldman, Pat Robertson's advisor, had told me in Washington. "We're a more subtle religion than that." But in synagogues filled with poor people, God is more than just an abstraction. The Jews of Beth Elohim reminded me of people I had seen at the Western Wall in Jerusalem, slipping prayers between the cracks with tears in their eyes.

After his sermon, Rabbi Ben Levi introduced me as a visitor from Israel and invited me to say a few words. I stood facing the congregation, which had grown to about sixty during the service, and was greeted by shouts of "Praise God!" and "Jerusalem!" For a brief, adrenaline-crazed moment I was tempted to launch into an imitation of Prophet Jones, a holiness preacher who was a boyhood idol of mine in Detroit. Instead, I told them how comfortable I felt in their synagogue and mentioned that I was writing a book about American Jews that would certainly include them. Several people shouted "Praise God," but Rabbi Ben Levi seemed a bit disconcerted. "You are very welcome among us," he intoned, and then somewhat cryptically added, "my life is an open book."

Cantor Davis ended the service with a chillingly beautiful rendition of "Yerushalaim Shel Zahav (Jerusalem of Gold)," an anthem of the Six-Day War. In Israel the song is a cliché, the kind of thing small children sing in talent shows; but Davis's version— half Yossele Rosenblatt, half Sam Cooke—had the whole synagogue swaying and clapping.

After services one of the women I had seen when I first came in approached me. "You're from Israel," she said, "maybe you know my son Shlomo? He's at the Tel Aviv University." I told her I didn't, but promised to call and say hello when I got back home. The lady smiled, took my hand in hers, fingers curved as if she were holding a golf club, and pumped my arm. "Shabbat shalom to you," she said. A few handshakes later I realized that the grip is part of the Beth Elohim ritual.

I wanted to talk to some of the members of the congregation, but although they were uniformly friendly, shaking my hand until it hurt and wishing me "Shabbat shalom," none was willing to be interviewed. "You better ask Rabbi about that," was the standard answer, and Rabbi Ben Levi didn't want to talk.

"I'd like to have a discussion, but I can't do it on the Shabbat. I restrict myself to holy thoughts on the Shabbat," he said as we stood on the street in front of the synagogue, surrounded by a small knot of worshippers. He told me to call him at his office for an appointment (I did, but he never returned my calls), gave me a Beth Elohim handshake, and headed down Linden Boulevard.

Rabbi Ben Levi's departure left me standing on the sidewalk with Marshall and Gladys, a mixed couple. Gladys comes from a Jewish family in Kew Gardens and teaches Hebrew school at Beth Elohim. Her husband works for the city in a capacity he declined to specify. A light-skinned man with serious eyes and an earnest manner, he had appeared, in the synagogue, to be elegantly dressed. Now, in the sunlight of Linden Boulevard, I saw that his overcoat was threadbare and his shoes were slightly cracked. He wore a porkpie hat, and he noticed I was bareheaded.

"Ah, excuse my question, but you from Israel. That means you a Jew, right?" I acknowledged that I was. "Well, not meaning any disrespect, why is it that your head is uncovered?"

It seemed a strange question—there are hundreds of thousands of bare-headed Jews in New York. Maybe, I thought, they don't look Jewish to Marshall.

"I'm a secular Jew," I told him. "I'm not religious."

Marshall gazed at me in frank appraisal. "Now, when you say you not religious, you keep the laws of kashrut, don't you? Don't be telling me you eat pork products in Jerusalem?"

It sounded pretty bad when he put it that way and suddenly I felt defensive. "I do sometimes, yes. It's not all that easy to find them, of course, and usually I don't, but . . ."

As I talked I saw the expression on Marshall's face change from friendly curiosity to alarm. It was there in his eyes: This man don't *eat* right, which means he don't *think* right, and he probably don't *do* right. He cast a nervous glance at his teenage daughters.

I wanted to reassure him, tell him there are plenty of good Jews in the world who do right even though they don't keep every commandment or even believe in God. I had examples; it's an old argument. But I left it alone. Marshall and the other members of Beth Elohim aren't interested in Jewish sociology. They are poor people, Jews with the blues. God is a necessity, not a debating point. So I gave Marshall the secret handshake, wished him and his wife a Shabbat shalom, and headed toward the subway and Manhattan.

CHAPTER FIVE

HARD CORE

A few days after my visit to Beth Elohim I took a train down to the Lower East Side of Manhattan to see Warren Feierstein again. I had been on the road for months by now, and had met a bewildering array of Jews—crawfish eaters and politicians, yuppies and welfare cases—all the way from the Succah in the Sky to the lesbian Havdalah hot tub. They had only one thing in common—they seemed like Jewish Americans. Now I wanted to meet American Jews, the hard core who still cling to the old Eastern European attitudes and traditions. Feierstein, who grew up on the Lower East Side, suggested I start in his neighborhood.

When I found him in his office at the Metropolitan Council on Poverty, his desk was stacked high with official-looking papers, and a walkie-talkie crackled from a shelf. Feierstein gestured at the receiver. "I'm a member of Hatzollah," he said proudly. "And we're always on duty."

If you have the misfortune to need an ambulance in New York City, it could take as much as forty-five minutes for one to reach you. But if you are Jewish and live on the Lower East Side or in certain neighborhoods of Brooklyn, Queens, or the Bronx, you can do a lot better than that. Call the right number, ask for help—in Yiddish, Hebrew, or English—and Hatzollah, the Jewish volunteer ambulance corps, will be at your door within ten minutes. "We're like the Red Magen David," Warren said, naming Israel's national emergency first aid service. "Except, with all due respect, I think we're a little more efficient."

Hatzollah was not established only for the sake of efficiency, however. "There are a lot of people in our community who don't know English well, and they have a hard time communicating with paramedics," Feierstein explained. "And let's face it, a lot of them, when they need help, they want to see a Jewish face, to feel like they're with their own people."

This is the essence of the Lower East Side mentality. There are about thirty thousand Jews left in the neighborhood—shopkeepers and blue collar workers, teachers and social workers, gentle Hebraists and karate-chopping Jewish Defense League militants—and they are indivisibly Jewish. They don't need trips to Israel or UJA sensitivity sessions to tell them they are different from their fellow Americans. To them assimilation is a dirty word and the opportunities of the United States a mixed blessing.

Warren strapped on his walkie-talkie and took me out for a tour of his neighborhood. We walked along East Broadway, a street lined with kosher restaurants, religious bookstores, and more synagogues per capita than any other place in America. On one block, between Clinton and Montgomery, I counted twenty shuls and yeshivot—all of them Orthodox. Feierstein told me there isn't a single Reform or Conservative congregation in the neighborhood, a claim not even the Chasidic strongholds of Borough Park and Crown Heights can make.

By far the most influential religious institution on the block is the Mesivtha Tifereth Jerusalem Yeshiva, which was the home base of the late Rabbi Moshe Feinstein. Reb Moshe was the most respected rabbi of his generation, and on the Lower East Side his word was law. It was he, for example, who protected kosher butchers by outlawing self-service meat markets, and although he died a few years ago, the edict has survived. There aren't many spiritual leaders in America of any denomination with that kind of posthumous clout.

Not even Reb Moshe was able to preserve the ethnic homogeneity of the Lower East Side, however. The *Forvitz* Building, once the home of America's most influential Yiddish newspaper, is now the Ling Liang Building. Israel's Bank Leumi's sign is written in Hebrew and Mandarin. Not long ago, a small shul on the corner of Clinton and East Broadway was prevented by rabbinical court decree from selling out to a Buddhist shrine. But despite these incursions, the Lower East Side remains Jewish turf, an island of grass roots tradition and community.

If the rabbis hold the religious reins in the neighborhood, its corporeal power center is the Harry S. Truman Regular Democratic Club on East Broadway. Fittingly, its clubhouse is located in the basement of a Talmudic academy. At sundown the round-shouldered yeshiva boys go home and the little building is taken over by a more worldly group of men.

The leader of the HST Regulars is Whitey Warnetsky, a pink-faced fellow of indeterminate middle age. Whitey is central casting's notion of a Lower East Side politico, from his flashing diamond pinky ring to his aromatic J&R alternative Honduran corona. He has been district leader since the early 1970s, and in the most recent election he had been returned to office unanimously. It takes a pretty good politician to run uncontested anyplace west of Rumania and I figured that he would have some interesting insights into the nature of power in a district of eight thousand mostly Orthodox Jewish voters.

On the way to the HST clubhouse it began to snow heavily. Given the inclement weather and Warnetsky's recent landslide, I wondered if he would show up. But reliability is one of the leader's secrets; when I arrived I found him and two associates seated behind a cheesecloth-covered card table on heraldic chairs that looked like they came from the set of *Camelot*. The three men were there to receive members of the voting public, a twice-weekly ritual that keeps Warnetsky in touch with the people of his district.

Warnetsky welcomed me warmly and introduced me to his colleagues—fellow cigar-smoker Dave Weinberger, a powerfully built young man in a yarmulke who serves as the HST sergeant-at-arms ("I throw people out if they need it," he explained genially); and treasurer Harry Tuerack, a Kent smoker with the worried expression of a man who handles audited money. The public, less intrepid than its servants, had stayed home that night, and so I had the three statesmen all to myself.

"We have problems down here that other districts don't encounter—Jewish problems, if you see what I mean," Warnetsky said, puffing easily on his corona. "For example, let's say with the traffic department. People who can't drive on the Sabbath have a problem with alternate side parking." He lowered his voice and adopted a tone of utmost piety. "This isn't a parking issue, it's a spiritual issue. We have some extremely religious people in this district. And, luckily, we've been able to help them out."

Whitey regards himself as a big brother to his constituents. "I've helped many a young person down here get a position in life, but I never remind them of it. I don't say, 'Hey, look what I've done for you.' Why not? I'll be truthful with you, it doesn't do any good. People aren't grateful—that's human nature."

Harry the treasurer shook his head sorrowfully, contemplating the ingratitude. "You gotta have a strong stomach, some of the things you gotta put up with in this business," he said.

Warnetsky and his fellow HST Regulars are careful to keep their beneficence on a strictly nonpartisan and nonsectarian basis. "I live by our law, the law of the Talmud," he said. "People are hungry, feed them—that's not hard to remember, know what I mean?" The HST organization passes out Passover bundles every year and distributes food and goodies before other Jewish holidays. "And that's without reference to religion, race, or party affiliation," said Dave Weinberger reverently.

There are quite a few gentiles on the Lower East Side, but it is not so easy to find Republicans. In Milwaukee, the boys at A.B. Data had said that Jews are genetically Democrats; and that certainly seems true in the cradle of American Jewry. According to Whitey, in the 1986 election, Democratic Assemblyman Sheldon Silver, a former yeshiva basketball star, carried the district ten to one. "We got a pretty smooth working organization down here," Warnetsky said with modest understatement.

The leader has a couple of simple principles that enable him to keep things functioning on an even keel. "First, as it is written, do your good deeds in private. Our sage, Rabbi Maimonides, taught that." Hallmark greeting cards provide the other pillar of his philosophy: "Second, it's nice to be important, but it's important to be nice. Those two things, in a nutshell, are what I believe," said Whitey.

But politics on the Lower East Side aren't all philosophy. Whitey is a practical man, and he has some more mundane rules for success. For one thing, he never discusses his work with his wife. And he is careful to respect other people's privacy. "Let's say you're having dinner with a guy in a restaurant, and another guy comes over to the table. In that situation, I always get up and go to the bathroom. See, he might be offering the other guy something, see what I mean? And this is something I might be better off not knowing. So I walk away. It helps your longevity in my profession."

Unlike Nassau County's Ninth District, where the Berman-Skelos state senate race turned on foreign policy, people on the Lower East Side are concerned primarily with domestic issues. Support for Israel is a given; Lower East Siders are concerned more with the small services that help them live as their parents and grandparents did before them. The HST Regulars are there to provide those services. But that doesn't mean they are indifferent to international affairs, which roughly speaking begin a block or two above East Broadway.

"You look at Jimmy Carter and his sweet mother," said Harry, his voice dripping with sarcasm. "I don't like to say anything about a dead woman, but she and her son weren't too wild about Jews, that's for sure." The others nodded in agreement.

Anti-Semitism has pretty much been licked on the Lower East Side, but the district leaders keep a wary eye on the rest of the country. For the next few minutes they traded horror stories, gleaned mostly from the Orthodox *Jewish Press* of Brooklyn, about Ku Klux Klan atrocities in Alabama, Connecticut, and other such godless precincts. They pronounced the names with distaste, shaking their heads at the mere mention of these exotic regions— places where you couldn't fix alternate side parking even for Yom Kippur and people wouldn't know what to do with a Passover bundle if you put one on their table.

In some ways the Lower East Side is Manhattan; in others, it resembles the smallest hick towns of Whitey Warnetsky's nightmares. It has, for example, a general store—Bistritzky's Kosher Specialties. The shop is a community institution, and when Warren Feierstein and I dropped in late the next afternoon, it was crowded with neighbors who were there to gossip and look over the fancy new kosher products now the vogue among modern Orthodox Jews.

There are other delicatessens in the area, but none has the crackerbarrel appeal of Bistritzky's. Its owner, Leibel Bistritzky, is a genial Chasid with a white Santa beard. He and Warren are old friends, and he greeted us warmly, leading us to an aromatic little office in the rear of the shop. Bistritzky is a dispatcher for Hatzollah, and his shortwave radio crackled from time to time as he told us about himself and his neighborhood.

Leibel Bistritzky was born in Germany, and although he came to the United States as a boy, he still has a thick Yiddish accent. He started out raising chickens in Vineland, New Jersey, in the Jewish farm belt, and later he peddled eggs from door to door. But he needed more money to feed his ten children, so in the 1960s he and his wife opened up their shop. In those days Jews were still leaving the neighborhood for the suburbs; but in recent years, thanks to new middle-income housing, the community has stabilized.

Naturally this has been good for business, but Leibel Bistritzky considers himself more than just a businessman. Every day he closes his shop for an hour or so, invites fellow merchants to drop by, and leads them in afternoon prayers. The daily minyan, a neighborhood tradition, is not universally popular. As we were standing near the frozen food section, Leibel was accosted by a dissenter, a young man in a flannel shirt with a black yarmulke on his head.

"It's a *shonda* what you're doing, Bistritzky," he said in a loud, aggressive tone. "A minyan belongs in shul, not with salami. You're taking Jews out of shul. It's a *shonda*!"

The man had a small cart of goodies, and Leibel listened to his tirade without comment; after all, the customer is always right. But after he left, Bistritzky cautioned me not to take him seriously. "The man's a 'ba'al tshuva' [newly Orthodox]," he said. "I think he's what they call 'faced out.' "

The shelves of Bistritzky's are stocked with products not usually available at your local A&P—Dagim white-chunk fancy tuna, Kemach Oreo cookies, and yellow and pink kosher El Bubble bubblegum cigars. There is also an assortment of gourmet kosher cheeses and health food products. The main customers for these delicacies are the "ba'ali tshuva" who live in the neighborhood.

The "ba'ali tshuva" movement is a much-discussed phenomenon in American Jewish life; not long after my visit to Bistritzky's, it was elevated to the status of social phenomenon by *New York Magazine,* which reported on the trendy life-styles of young formerly assimilated Jews who have become observant. Many of them attend the uptown Lincoln Square Synagogue, the last word in designer Orthodoxy. Some rabbis and sociologists point to the movement as proof that young American-born Jews are returning to traditional Judaism. Similar claims were made a generation ago by Reform and Conservative thinkers about the Chavura movement. The truth is that these "trends" aren't as important as their supporters would like them to be; the numbers in both cases are small. Still, "ba'ali tshuva" are good customers, and Leibel Bistritzky has become something of an expert on their habits.

"These people want kosher gourmet food because they miss certain tastes they got used to," he explained, pulling a jar of Mrs. Adler's Kosher Bacon Bits off the shelf. "Like, for example, a person used to eat, God forbid, chazer—pork products. So I give him some of this. They put it on their fried eggs and it tastes to them the same as chazer. Try some." He shook some brown flakes into my hand and looked at me expectantly. They were made of vegetable and meant to simulate bacon, but the scientists who invented Mrs. Adler's Kosher Bacon Bits must have been Orthodox Jews unacquainted with the real thing.

"Nu?" said Leibel, beaming. "How about that? Not bad, eh?"

He seemed so proud that I hated to disillusion him. "Tell me, Mr. Bistritzky, have you ever eaten bacon?" I asked, and he reacted as if I had thrown a snake into the frozen food section.

"*Me. Eat chazer?* God forbid!"

"Then how do you know that this tastes like bacon? I hate to say it, but it tastes like fish food," I said.

"How do I know. People tell me. They come back for more. And besides, so what if it doesn't taste like chazer—people can't live without the taste of chazer?"

There are people who can and people who can't. Mrs. Adler takes care of the latter. So do Miriam Mizakura and Rabbi Meyer Leifer, who cater to Orthodox Jews who want a little tempura and a few laughs without violating half a dozen commandments. Miriam is the proprietor of Shalom Japan, the only *glatt* kosher sushi joint and Jewish-Japanese nightclub in New York. Leifer is her rabbi.

Miriam Mizakura is a slim, attractive Japanese-born woman whose parents converted to Judaism for obscure reasons following World War II, shortly before she was born. In Japan she was an aspiring entertainer, and she came to the United States to break into show business. She didn't have much success, though, until the day she went to visit a friend in the hospital and met Rabbi Meyer Leifer, spiritual leader of the 23rd Street Synagogue.

Leifer was intrigued by the young Japanese woman with the Jewish star dangling from her neck, and the two struck up a conversation that blossomed into a kind of partnership. Leifer encouraged her to open a kosher Japanese restaurant–supper club, and provided her with the rabbinical guidance to do it. Mizakura reciprocated by allowing Leifer, a frustrated crooner, to sing in her nightclub.

The first week it opened, Shalom Japan got more than one hundred telephone calls. "They all wanted to know one thing," Leifer told me as we sat in the restaurant eating California rolls. " 'Where do you get your meat?' Naturally the restaurant is kosher, and when they heard the answer, people started pouring in. For the first three months you couldn't get a reservation."

Some people come to Shalom Japan for the food, others for the floor show that takes place every Saturday night in the nightclub adjacent to the restaurant. The club's decor is *glatt kitsch*—art posters from Tel Aviv and Tokyo, large wall fans, a mezuzah on the door, and a huge hand-painted kabuki set on the wall in back of the small stage. The entertainment, provided by Miriam and occasionally by Leifer, is pure schmaltz.

The rabbi took me into the deserted nightclub to hear Miriam rehearse. She has a pleasant voice and a one-joke comedy routine based on her dual identity. We sat at a little table and listened to a sample of her patter.

"How do you do?" she said in a thick oriental accent. "Welcome. I am a real JAP. Do you hear the one about Mr. Yakki who built a succah? Ah yes, people came to eat sukiyaki in Yakki's succah." This is a big laugh line on Saturday nights, when men in dark suits and yarmulkes bring their modestly dressed wives in from Kew Gardens, Borough Park, and Paramus for a night of eclectic dining (the menu offers tempura, sake no nikogori, sushi, cholent, corned beef on rye, and matzoh ball soup) and good clean fun.

Sometimes, when he is in the mood, Meyer Leifer takes the stage and does a little singing. I asked for a demonstration and he grabbed the mike, nodded to Miriam at the piano, and launched into a Tony Bennett-style rendition of the Hebrew standard, "Lila Lila." He dipped his shoulder, closed his eyes on the high notes, and whipped the microphone cord around with professional ease. Miriam joined him on the chorus, singing the "lilas" with a distinct Japanese r where the l should have been.

"I love to sing," Leifer said superfluously, putting down the microphone with reluctance. "I was a child prodigy cantor, I used to appear in synagogues all over the country. I don't sing love songs, but Hebrew and Yiddish favorites are all right. There's no reason that a rabbi shouldn't sing in public. Singing is something that makes people happy."

Shalom Japan is one of a growing number of kosher nightspots in New York that offer American entertainment to modern Orthodox patrons. American—but not too American. Even the most liberal brand of Orthodoxy requires its adherents to adopt a lifestyle based on values, attitudes, and behavior that are specifically Jewish. A kosher Japanese place without matzoh ball soup on the menu, or with a singer who sings in Japanese instead of Yiddish would be too much like the real thing. Mizakura and Rabbi Leifer have created a parody of a Japanese nightclub, and it is perfect because it spoofs America for its Orthodox patrons while allowing them, in Leibel Bistritzky's admirable phrase, "a taste of chazer."

There is a new sense of ascendency and self-confidence among modern Orthodox Jews in America. When they first came to the

United States, most Eastern European Jews were "Orthodox." But in a process of assimilation and secularization, the majority drifted into other, more easygoing denominations or dropped out of the Jewish community altogether. Alarmists predicted that Orthodox Judaism might disappear altogether in America.

But the pessimists underestimated the hold of tradition. Through gradual self-selection, a core of perhaps one million Orthodox Jews has crystallized in America. A minority of them are Chasidim, but the great majority—perhaps ninety percent—are modern Orthodox. They are college educated, speak English as their first language, read the sports page, and follow the stock market. They get married young, to other Orthodox Jews; have large families; and send their children to day schools where they are inculcated with a sense of being different from other Americans—and other American Jews. They have apparently found a way to live in America without losing their religion or their identity; and this discovery has given them a new feeling of control and optimism.

But if the modern Orthodox have found an American modus vivendi, they have yet to resolve their problem with Israel. Other Jews feel no compulsion to move to Israel; American Zionism takes a fan-club approach to the Jewish state. But the Orthodox have no such luxury. Three times a day they face Jerusalem and pray of their longing for Zion. They are required by their own ideology to acknowledge the centrality of Israel and to admit that Jewish life in Jerusalem has a greater validity than in New York. After all, one of their greatest rabbis, Abraham Isaac Kook, taught that "the commandment to live in Israel is as important as all the other commandments combined."

Many modern Orthodox Jews have spent a year or two in an Israeli yeshiva or university. Most have contemplated living there permanently. All of them feel guilty about staying in America. But they stay, because they can make more money, pay less taxes, avoid military duty. They stay because life is easier.

There are various rationalizations for this violation of the commandment to live in Israel: Old people want to be near their grandchildren; yuppies say they can't make a living; many claim that their *aliyah* to Jerusalem is just a matter of time. But none of the rationalizations really work; Israel is the worm in the shiny red apple of modern American Orthodoxy.

*   *   *

The balancing act between the American dream and the demands of the Torah may be a problem in places like the Lower East Side. But across the bridge in Brooklyn there are people who have never heard of sukiyaki, Mrs. Adler's Kosher Bacon Bits, or kosher El Bubble chewing gum, and who consider living in the state of Israel unnecessary or even blasphemous. They are the Chasidim, the black-garbed ultras of Williamsburg, Borough Park, and Crown Heights.

A generation ago, there were about thirty thousand Chasidic Jews in Brooklyn; today they have more than tripled, to an estimated one hundred thousand. While the rest of American Jewry puzzles over demographic reports and watches its numbers dwindle, the Chasidim have tripled their size, mostly through natural increase.

The two superpowers of the Chasidic world are Lubavitch, located in Crown Heights, and Satmar, based in Williamsburg. To the untrained eye their members look as identical as snowflakes, but this is an optical illusion. The Lubavitcher (also known as "Chabad") Chasidim are Jewish Jesuits—adventurous, relatively sophisticated, pseudointellectual, and extroverted. They regard nonreligious Jews as opportunities, and they approach them with the friendly enthusiasm of aluminum siding salesmen.

Satmar Chasidim, on the other hand, are grumps. They are the hardest kernel of the hard core—introverted, self-absorbed, antiintellectual, and militantly opposed to Americanization, Reform Judaism, Conservative Judaism, Zionism, the State of Israel, most other Chasidic sects, and the twentieth century. They would no more go to Shalom Japan than they would attend a bullfight or the Miss Universe pageant.

While I was in New York, the Satmar Chasidim were involved in an illuminating controversy. They send their children to parochial schools, of course, but for some reason a group of Satmar girls were enrolled in a public school remedial education program. Satmar doesn't allow its women to mingle freely with men, Jewish or otherwise, and the group's leaders demanded that a screen be erected down the middle of the classroom to keep the girls separated from the rest of the students.

This demand was immediately and vocally rejected by the parents of the other children, most of whom were blacks and Puerto Ricans. For years there had been tensions between the communities, mostly over street crime and competition for public housing; the classroom controversy brought things to a head. A Puerto Rican spokesman claimed that the Chasidim were elitist and racist, a charge the Satmar spokesman blandly denied. "They think we look down on them," he told reporters, "but they are mistaken. We don't see them at all."

Since that same attitude applies to writers, secular Jews, and Israelis, it was not easy finding a Satmar Chasid who would talk to me. After several abortive approaches, I was finally introduced to one by a mutual acquaintance. The Chasid agreed to meet me on the condition that I wouldn't publish his name. This seemed like an unnecessary precaution—the Satmar Chasidim read only holy texts—but he insisted. "Just call me Mendel," he said.

At thirty-four, Mendel is a short, stocky man with a beard, side locks, and a crewcut. He is a craftsman, and we met in his workshop, a small building located not far from the main shopping district of Williamsburg. Every time a customer came in, Mendel interrupted our conversation and pointedly ignored me. Speaking to strangers is frowned upon by the Satmar community, and he didn't want to be caught in an act that could be construed as disloyal.

In the world of Satmar, the most talented young men spend their lives studying Talmud on a community dole. The merely clever go into business, and many can be found in the Diamond District around 47th Street in Manhattan. Neighborhood merchants and artisans like Mendel are at the bottom of the status ladder.

As a boy Mendel studied Talmud like everyone else. His secular education consisted of one hour a day—arithmetic, spelling, and grammar—for four years. "I was born in Williamsburg, but I din't know Hinglish till I was a big boy," he said, sounding as if he had just gotten off the boat from Europe.

As we talked, I saw that Mendel had two walkie-talkies strapped to his belt. One was for Hatzollah, the ambulance service. The other connected him to the *shomrim* network, a kind of Satmar Conelrad system of early warning against undesirable strangers in the neighborhood.

"Shomrim" is the Hebrew word for "guardians," and Mendel is one of the unit's senior members. A few years ago, street crime began to be a problem in Williamsburg. At first the Chasidim staged mass demonstrations at City Hall. They stormed the local police station after a woman was raped. Finally, unable to get satisfactory protection from the authorities, they created their own private vigilante force.

"We protect the people from the *chayas*, the animals on the street," Mendel said in a soft voice. "Believe me, this is no expression, they are really *chayas*. We're surrounded here by animals." People in the neighborhood know the *shomrim* number, and they can call for help any time of the day or night. "We have a two-minute response time," he said proudly.

"Two minutes for what kind of response?" I asked. Mendel looked around the shop, although there was no one there. "Two minutes for a *chopsim*," he said, looking down at his workbench.

Chopsim, pronounced with a throat-clearing "ch," is Yiddish for "grab 'em." The phrase became a battle cry a few years ago when an elderly rabbi was mugged by a couple of street thugs. "*Yidden, chopsim!*" the old man managed to shout, and dozens of yeshiva boys came charging out of a nearby Talmudic academy in hot pursuit. Within seconds the thugs were a bloody pile on the sidewalk, and a new battle cry was born.

Since that night, the *shomrim* have become an organized force. Only married men can belong ("We see sometimes on the street things a boy shouldn't see," Mendel explained), and they patrol armed with walkie-talkies, clubs, blackjacks, and brass knuckles. "We are the eyes and ears of the police department on the street. We don't bother nobody, but we keep the animals out of the neighborhood," he said.

Before going out to Williamsburg, I had been briefed by a New York police officer who specializes in the Chasidic community. The officer, himself an observant Jew, clearly had mixed feelings about the Satmar approach to law and order. "All together, you got fifty-five different Chasidic groups out there," he said, gesturing in the general direction of Brooklyn. "Most of them are pretty small and quiet. Of the big groups, your Lubavitchers rarely take to the streets. But your Satmar, when they get angry—look out, they don't fool around."

I asked the policeman about rumors that a rapist had once been beaten to death by an outraged group of Chasidim. "I never heard that one," he said, "but nothing's impossible. These are very dangerous people. A lot of them are Holocaust survivors and they want to be left in peace. They don't start trouble but they aren't about to be molested, either. I don't know, maybe they've got the right idea after all."

Much of the sect's violence is directed against other Chasidic groups, or rivals within the group itself. For years, Satmar was controlled by a venerable old rebbe, Moshe Teitelbaum. When he died a power struggle broke out between his widow and her son, the official heir. Psychological warfare raged between the two camps, with the widow's forces claiming that the young rabbi's wife was insufficiently pious. The campaign came to a head when a group of Chasidim broke into the son's house and smashed all the mirrors in protest against his wife's alleged narcissism.

A few years ago a form of gang warfare broke out between the Satmar Chasidim and the rival Belz group. Satmar refuses to recognize the state of Israel on the grounds that only the Messiah can reestablish Jewish sovereignty in the Holy Land. Belz takes a softer line, and its leader, the Belzer rebbe, agreed to accept Israeli government support for his schools in Israel. This decision precipitated a clash between the two groups. Synagogues were trashed and Chasidim fought each other in the streets. The two sects eventually reached a truce, but they still keep a wary eye on each other.

The great rivalry in the Chasidic world is between Satmar and Lubavitch. The police officer who briefed me recalled one time when reserves were needed to save the life of a Chabadnik who had ventured into the Satmar stronghold. "It was one of the holidays, and this fellow came to a synagogue in Williamsburg, got up, and tried to give holiday greetings from the Lubavitcher rebbe," the cop said. "The Satmar people heard about it and I guess they thought it was a power play. They found him on the street and chased him all over the neighborhood. He finally ran into another shul, and in the meantime somebody called the precinct.

"When we got there the place was surrounded. At first he refused to leave with us—he didn't want to violate the law by riding on a holiday. But I explained that his life was in danger, and that riding with us would be 'pikuach nefesh'—saving a life—which is permitted. We finally got him out of there, but if they had got their hands on him he would have been a dead man, believe me.''

I asked Mendel about these incidents, but he had nothing to say. He had already said too much, and I could tell he regretted the meeting. There was no profit in this kind of encounter, nothing the Satmar Chasidim could gain from good publicity. They want to be left alone, to pursue their eighteenth century European lives in the heart of New York. His answers grew shorter and shorter, his silences more impatient.

"Have you ever seen a Charles Bronson movie?'' I asked, closing my notebook and getting ready to leave. He looked at me with incomprehension. "He's an actor,'' I explained. "He makes movies about fighting *chayas*.'' Mendel shook his head. "We don't go to movies, or watch television. It's a waste of time, *goyishe naches* [gentile pleasure],'' he said.

"You mean you've *never* seen a movie?'' I asked.

Mendel hesitated, and then, in a soft voice, confessed. "When I was a boy, I went once. I saw a cowboy by the name Roy Rogers.''

"Did you ever dream about being a cowboy after that?'' I asked, but the mellow moment was past. "That's 'meshuggeh,' '' he said harshly, almost pushing me in the direction of the door. "Only a goy would dream about being a cowboy.''

It is a short drive from Williamsburg to Crown Heights, capital of the Satmar's great rival, Lubavitch. The two sects are more than political enemies; they are ideological foes, exponents of vastly different philosophies of Jewish survival. Satmar is isolationist, but Rabbi Menachem M. Schneerson, the Lubavitcher rebbe, is a man who believes in planting flags all over the world.

There is nothing else like Chabad in Jewish life. It is a cult of personality based on the charismatic leadership of Rabbi Schneerson. His supporters make extravagant claims for his wisdom, holiness, and mystical powers; his detractors consider him an egomaniac or even a false Messiah. But no one disputes that he is a powerful figure, able to command a small army of fanatically dedicated followers in his war against secularism, assimilation, and modernity.

Over the years the rebbe has wrapped himself in a carefully crafted cloak of mystery. He receives important visitors by candlelight in the middle of the night and he almost never leaves his home. "Once, back in 1949, the rebbe was going on vacation," a Chabadnik once told me. "He got a flat tire on the way over the bridge, and he considered it a sign. He hasn't left Brooklyn since."

The rebbe has never visited Israel. Unlike his Satmar rivals, he strongly supports the Jewish state and is a hawk on its defense policies. On the Israeli political scene he is a force in absentia, directing his disciples' lobbying efforts on behalf of an agenda full of theocratic legislation. But the rebbe himself stays at home and has remained silent about his refusal to travel to Jerusalem. "The time isn't ripe yet," his followers say, a mysterious evasion that has given rise to the charge that he has messianic pretensions.

There are thirty thousand Jews in Crown Heights, almost all of them connected with Chabad. The neighborhood itself looks a lot like Williamsburg—unimpressive apartment buildings along a main street, shoddy-looking shops with signs in Yiddish and Hebrew with names like The Shabbos Fish Market, The House of Glatt Butcher Shop, and M. Raskin's Fancy Fruits and Vegetables. On the wall of Jacoff's Drugs I saw a number of notices: an invitation to the Mitzvah Kashrus Tea, where Rivka Shurtzman was scheduled to give a talk titled "Keeping Kosher, My Giant Leap"; an ad for a Hot Shmurgesboard (sic) at the Olei Torah Ballroom; and a sign promising GOOD NEWS, NO MORE MESSY SCHACH for people who suffer from succah drip.

The differences between Crown Heights and Williamsburg are subtle. There are few women drivers in either neighborhood, but in Crown Heights wives sit next to their husbands in the front seat, while in Satmar country they stay in the back. And, not far from Chabad headquarters, there is a bookstore. It is not exactly Scribner's, but in its display window *Kosher Calories* and *King David and the Frog*. shared a shelf with *Brimstone and Fire*. As I stood peering into the shop, two young men in dark raincoats and fedoras came out and smiled at me. The atmosphere in Crown Heights is friendly, hospitable; it is hard to imagine these people out on a *chopsim*.

The heart of the neighborhood is the rebbe's mansion and headquarters at 770 Eastern Parkway. It is from here that young men are dispatched to isolated Jewish communities to act as teachers, kosher butchers, and religious functionaries; orders are drafted for Chabad lobbyists in Israel; and the rebbe's words are disseminated by pamphlet, tape, and videocassette.

I went, uninvited and unannounced, to the headquarters and asked to meet with someone who could tell me about Chabad. One of the yeshiva boys led me through a maze of classrooms and delivered me to the office of a young rabbi named Friedman. He had no idea who I was, and he was obviously busy; but he put everything aside and listened with an encouraging smile as I explained my project. Chabadniks have the missionary's worldliness; unlike the Satmar Chasidim, they are comfortable with non-religious Jews and understand them, up to a point. They are also not averse to publicity. Friedman loaded me down with great piles of press clippings, translations of the rebbe's speeches, and other "background material," with the gentle insistence of a professional flack.

"Is there anything else you need?" he asked helpfully.

"Yes, I'd like to go out with one of your mitzvah tanks," I told him. A mitzvah is, literally, a religious commandment. There are 613, regulating every aspect of life, but the rebbe especially emphasizes one—the commandment to put on tefillin, or prayer phylacteries. Chabad dispatches roving bands of Chasidim who visit businessmen in their offices and implore them to put on the leather straps; others run tefillin stations—known as mitzvah tanks—on street corners of major cities.

Rabbi Friedman picked up the phone with the dispatch of a junior executive and spoke briefly with a subordinate. "We've got a few mitzvah tanks going this week. You can visit any of them but I suggest the one on 47th and Fifth Avenue. That's where the action is," he said with a smile.

That Friday, I found the tank at its appointed spot in midtown Manhattan. Despite its paramilitary name, it proved to be a disappointingly civilian GMC Vandura mobile home, stocked with prayer books and sets of tefillin. The tank crew consisted of seven young men in their late teens or early twenties, all hardened veterans of two years of Chabad missionary work in the Pacific

Northwest. Five were native Brooklynites; the other two were from Oak Park, Michigan, and São Paulo, Brazil.

Mendy ("it's short for Mendel") Kalmanson took charge of me. A smiling, fresh-faced boy in a man's dark suit and fedora, he led me inside the van, offered me a diet Pepsi ("a little nosh," he said shyly), and explained the operation. The crew is divided into two teams—outside men who stop passersby, strike up a conversation, and try to convince them to put on tefillin; and inside men, who wait in the tank and show the volunteers how to do it.

At headquarters, Rabbi Friedman had explained that the Chabad emphasis on tefillin stems from the Six-Day War, when the rebbe ordered his followers to convince fellow Jews to wear them in order to demonstrate Jewish power and solidarity. Rabbi Friedman strongly implied that Israel's victory had been a result of that order—rebbe-centered explanations of historical events and natural phenomena are common among his disciples. But Mendy didn't know the background of the tefillin campaign, and he seemed surprised that I would wonder about it. "It's a *commandment*," he told me with boyish conviction. "It's straight outta the Torah. What more do you need?"

As we were talking, the door of the van opened and a young man in a business suit entered, followed by one of the outside men who blocked his retreat. The man, a Russian immigrant, looked around nervously. "We must make this quick, all right?" he said, but his concern was unnecessary; Mendy was already working with a practiced dispatch, rolling up the man's sleeve and winding the leather straps around his arm. "We'll have you out of here in a jiffy," he said cheerfully as the man looked on with a dubious expression. Mendy handed him a prayerbook, led him in what was obviously an unfamiliar benediction, unwound the straps, and wished him a good Shabbes. The whole operation took about three minutes.

Thousands of people passed the mitzvah tank in the next hour, but only seven more came in—two more Russians, a Moroccan Jew from Montreal, an Israeli who lives in Queens, two Mexican tourists, and a Turkish businessman. There wasn't a single American customer. I pointed this out to Mendy, but he simply shrugged. "It's like anything else, you get your good days and your bad days. Besides, a Jew's a Jew and a mitzvah's a mitzvah."

Curious to see what was happening on the street, I left the van and joined the outside men on the corner of 47th and 5th. Each one had a stack of pamphlets he offered to passersby, asking likely candidates, "Are you Jewish?" People rushed past without looking up, or shook their heads briefly. No one stopped.

"If a person says no right away, that means he isn't Jewish," explained Shaya Harlig, one of the outside men. "So I just say, 'have a nice day.' But if he hesitates before saying no, then he's Jewish. Usually I don't say anything, but sometimes, if he really looks Jewish, I say, 'Come on, gimme a break.' "

"That's right," said another one of the boys. "But you know, sometimes people have funny reactions. Like one time a man came over to me and said, 'Last week you asked if I was Jewish and I said no. I haven't been able to sleep all week. So, yes, I'm Jewish.' "

"Did you get him into the tank?" I asked. The boy shook his head. "He said he was too busy. But at least it was a start," he said, sighing.

A well-dressed lady stopped to talk. The mitzvah tank crew does not stop women, who have no religious duty to put on tefillin. But, unlike other Chasidic men, Chabadniks are not afraid to talk to them in public. The lady had just seen a production of *The Merchant of Venice*. "Are Jews allowed to charge interest or not?" she asked one of the crew, who answered her politely, as if he had been put on the corner as a municipal Talmudic information service.

One of the boys came up to me with a stack of pamphlets. "Why don't you give it a try?" he offered with a grin. "You almost look like one of us." I realized that he was right. I had a beard, a dark coat, and black trousers, as well as a black silk yarmulke on my head, and I looked like an older version of the tank crew. I accepted the pamphlets and, feeling somewhat foolish, took my place on the corner.

Menachem Begun, the Brazilian Chasid, gave me a little coaching. "Don't try to stop everyone. Let the ones who don't look Jewish go by—you know, blacks, Orientals, Latins. The other ones you should at least ask. You're a beginner, you can't pick out the Jews."

"Can you?" I asked.

He smiled. "Sure. It's easy, just look right here," he said, pointing to his nose.

Even with coaching, I soon realized that stopping Jews on a midtown Manhattan corner is like trying to hit major league fastballs—they go whizzing by faster than they look from the stands. By the time I asked people if they were Jewish I was talking to the backs of their heads. After a couple minutes I was more or less continually mumbling, "Are you Jewish are you Jewish are you Jewish," and attracting some peculiar stares. Menachem and Mendy, standing a few feet away, were immensely amused by the spectacle, but after a while they stepped in to give me some more pointers.

"Stand back and offer the pamphlets from a distance—if you get too close, it scares people off. Ask 'Are you Jewish?' in a loud voice, but polite. And you don't have to ask the whole thing, just, 'Ya Jewish?' like that." Mendy and Menachem made it sound easy, but even with my new stance and abbreviated text, I couldn't get anyone to stop.

A little later, I looked up and saw that I was sharing the corner with a colleague, a funky-looking black man wearing an orange vest over a battered imitation leather jacket. Like me, he was distributing leaflets—but, I noted enviously, with considerably more success.

I sidled up to him. "What *you* got?" I asked, and he handed me a flyer announcing specials on stereo equipment at Sound City. I offered him one of mine, a personal letter from the Lubavitcher rebbe on the importance of tefillin. He took it out of professional courtesy, but when he thought I wasn't looking he let it fall to the pavement.

Discouraged, I headed back to the tank, where some of the boys were talking to a beat cop. At first I thought he might be hassling them, but it turned out they were discussing the policeman's days as a yeshiva boy in Kew Gardens. "As a cop, these guys are a pain in the ass," he told me. "They won't move their van when you tell them to; they play their klezmer music so loud that the storekeepers complain; and when you try to talk to them about it, they won't even listen. But as a Jew, I like what they're doing. I mean, somebody's got to go out and remind people that they're still Jews."

*   *   *

In the mitzvah tank, the Chabadniks are reasonable and friendly, ready for amiable argument. But it is a bogus pose; there is a fanatic's hard edge just under the personable facade. The Chabad Chasidim see themselves as medical missionaries in the midst of an epidemic of assimilation and impiety. The rebbe has prescribed a cure—fundamentalist Judaism—that very few American Jews are prepared to take plain. Chabad's great skill is its ability to sugar-coat the pill.

Nowhere is this more evident than in Hollywood. Chabad and show business were meant for each other. The rebbe—for all his piety and isolation—is a master showman who stages his public appearances carefully and beams them around the world via satellite. And in recent years, Chabad has become expert in the use of another American show biz art form—the telethon.

The Chabad telethon is one of the great media events of the Jewish world. When I was in Los Angeles I watched a tape of one with Marilyn Miller, an old friend who was one of the original writers on *Saturday Night Live*. Marilyn grew up in Pittsburgh, where she was active in the Reform youth movement, and she still takes an interest in Jewish life. Lately she has been trying to establish a sitcom library for the Jerusalem Cinemateque. But none of the old comedy series, or even *Saturday Night Live* in its heyday, ever came up with a more improbable premise or a zanier entertainment than the Chabad special.

The show opened with a group of sweating Chabadniks dancing frenetically to the sound of a klezmer band. The number ended with one of them spinning wildly with a quart bottle of Canada Dry ginger ale balanced on his nose. This feat won loud applause from the host of the show, Jan Murray of *Treasure Hunt* fame, who emceed the evening dressed in a black tuxedo and matching silk yarmulke.

Murray told a couple of borscht belt jokes and then introduced the stars who were there to raise money for the rebbe—Ed Asner, Connie Francis, Shelley Berman, Martin Sheen, James Caan, Tony Randall, Elliot Gould, and dozens more. My personal favorite was a Korean nightclub crooner who sang "Volaré" and "B'Shanah Ha'ba'ah," a Hebrew standard whose words he managed to mispronounce in their entirety. Murray didn't seem to notice.

Performances alternated with film clips of Chabad's philanthropic activities and testimonials from some of Hollywood's most powerful (and least pious) Jewish stars and movie big shots. There was something about them that reminded me of a stoned Elvis appearing at the White House on behalf of Richard Nixon's war against drugs.

The television special, like much of what Chabad does in America, was the product of dedicated and talented emissaries, men who know the world and are willing to reach out to assimilated Jews on their own terms. The effort goes on across the country—in Chabad houses on college campuses, in mitzvah tanks, and anywhere else the missionaries can gather an audience.

In L.A. on Super Bowl Sunday, I attended a Chabad show biz study session at the Westwood home of Rabbi Shlomo Schwartz, one of the rebbe's chief West Coast operatives. I was invited by Roger Simon, a novelist whose Jewish private eye, Moses Wine, was portrayed by Richard Dreyfuss in the movie *The Big Fix*. Simon was working on a new Moses Wine story that involved Jewish mysticism, which is how he began attending the weekly class. His motives were of no great concern to Rabbi Schwartz, however; there is a rabbinical principle that holds that if you start out doing the right things for the wrong reasons, you will eventually do them for the right ones. Chabad believes in mitzvah momentum.

Simon and I arrived at Schwartz's comfortably unpretentious home a few minutes before ten in the morning. A dozen men and women in French designer jogging outfits, Reeboks, and yarmulkes were gathered in the kitchen, sipping coffee. The men discussed the Super Bowl, which was being played that afternoon just down the road in Pasadena. The women debated the respective merits of jogging and speed walking. Most of them were between thirty-five and forty, and I knew from Roger that almost all of them had some connection with show business. He pointed out a high-powered agent, several musicians and movie-score composers, a couple of middle-level studio execs, and a film industry lawyer.

Chabad is not the only Jewish group that cultivates show biz contacts. The film industry is a Jewish business, after all, and many of its leading figures have been active on behalf of Israel or other Jewish causes. In Los Angeles, synagogues recruit Jewish stars as drawing cards. But no one has been as successful as Chabad in attracting and exploiting show biz people.

At exactly ten, Rabbi Schwartz joined the group. He is a short, tubby man in his mid-forties, with a red beard and a genial expression. Steel-rimmed glasses were perched on his nose and he wore paisley suspenders over a white, short-sleeved shirt. He looked like a campus eccentric, a sociology professor from the 1960s about to conduct a graduate seminar.

Schwartz took his place at the head of a long table and the others gathered around. For a few minutes he chatted idly with the group, making ostentatiously hip conversation dotted with references to Magic Johnson, Bob Dylan, and "the Village." The technique was familiar; in Jerusalem, Chabadniks stop young tourists at the Wailing Wall, ask them if they want to turn on—and then hand them copies of the rebbe's sermons, saying, "Turn on with this."

The class came to attention after a few minutes, and Schwartz began with an announcement. Meir Kahane was scheduled to come to Los Angeles, and Schwartz suggested that they attend his lecture. Several people groaned, but the rabbi accepted the reaction with unruffled good nature. "You don't have to agree with the man. But he has an interesting message. You owe it to yourselves to hear him firsthand." This appeal to open-mindedness had an effect; several people wrote down the date of the JDL leader's appearance.

Rabbi Schwartz then passed out a schedule of Chabad House events for the coming month. The group's L.A. operation is a combination of Torah and tinsel. Its two major events for February were "Survivors, an evening with former concentration camp survivors"; and "Hollywood and Hassidism—Bruce Vilanch who wrote all the Donny and Marie Show sequences . . . will cause great diversion with humorous choice tidbits of today's Hollywood."

The flyer also advertised the Chabad House weekly Sabbath service: "Friday Night Live! Have a tequila sunrise at sundown every Friday night at Chabad House. The singing and dancing will break the ice. The horseradish on the gefilte fish will defrost the system. And the jalapeño pepper chicken soup will start the 100 proof juices flowing. Enjoy fascinating new faces that will tickle your Platonic fancy, and get some kosher smarts playing stump the rabbi." And, at the bottom of the flyer, "For Orthodox, Conservative, Reform, non-affiliated and any Jew that moves."

Chabad isn't averse to selling Judaism like a singles bar, but in the est belt of Southern California its strongest card is mysticism. The Chabad House offers a number of courses, including a beginner's seminar that promises "insights into human psychology, depression and ecstasy, divine and animal soul, meditation and self-awareness, male and female energy, spirituality and self-centeredness, 'karma' and free choice, etc."

After the flyers had been distributed, Rabbi Schwartz began the class by describing how he had explained the hidden meaning of the Song of Songs to Carole King (and, having revealed its message, convinced her to sing an excerpt from it on the Chabad telethon). Then he passed around mimeographed copies of the day's study material, "Bosi l'gani," an article written by one of the Lubavitcher rebbe's predecessors. The article is a mystical and linguistic interpretation of a single Hebrew phrase in the Song of Songs.

Schwartz read the phrase aloud in English: "I came into my garden, my sister, my bride." Then he asked the man on his right—a sound track composer—to continue reading. The man cleared his throat and began to recite:

"The midrash explains that shir hashirim is not a simple love story, rather a metaphor describing the relationship between God and the Jewish people. The above verse refers to the time of the destruction of the sanctuary, when the shechinah, The Divine Presence, came into the garden—was revealed in the earth. Developing the concept further, the midrash (on the above verse) emphasizes the phonetic relationship between the Hebrew word for my garden, 'gani,' and the Hebrew word 'ginuni,' meaning 'my bridal chamber' (since the verse uses the term 'gani,' *my* garden, the possessive form, implying a place of privacy, it can be interpreted to mean, 'my bridal chamber,' a private place for the groom and bride [note commentaries on the midrash]. It interprets the above verse as 'I came into my bridal chamber, the place where my essence was originally revealed')." The sound track man put down his mimeographed sheet and several of the others nodded solemnly, as if they had been given a sudden insight into the workings of the universe.

One by one, the class recited from the article. They stumbled over unfamiliar Hebrew terms, sometimes completely losing their places as the text became more and more obscure. An intense young woman with a trained speaking voice and a scarf tied severely around her head grappled with "Normally the Hebrew word for 'walking' would be 'mehalach.' Instead the Torah uses 'mis-halech' (which implies a state of withdrawal), as the midrash comments, 'walking and jumping, walking and jumping.' " When she finished reading, heads once again bobbed in agreement.

Orthodox Jews approach mysticism late, after long years of Torah and Talmudic study, and with a firm grasp of Hebrew. Even then, mystical texts are often inaccessible. Teaching "Bosi l'gani" to people like these was like teaching advanced nuclear physics to students who think that an apple thrown in the air will keep on going. The yuppies in Rabbi Schwartz's living room that morning comprehended what they were reading about as well as a group of Yiddish-speaking Chasidim from Poland would have understood the front page of *Variety*.

If anyone was aware of the absurdity of the scene, however, they didn't let on. Schwartz smiled benignly through the reading, and the students exhibited an adolescent eagerness mixed with the self-confidence of people who have made it in a tough town.

"Shlomo, I want to know if I've got the seven tzaddikim who brought the revelation right," said one woman in a tentative voice. "Let's see, there was Abraham, Isaac, and, ah, was Jacob in there someplace?" The woman managed to make the question sound like an inquiry about the final four at Wimbledon.

Another woman mentioned that she had recently read a midrash that explained how Eve's creation gave forth an unnatural love of men by women. Rabbi Schwartz looked puzzled; he had never heard of any such thing. Suddenly she snapped her fingers and laughed without embarrassment. "Now I remember, it's not a midrash, it's from Milton."

I couldn't help feeling sorry for Rabbi Schwartz. It couldn't have been easy for him to sit around in his paisley suspenders talking Torah to a bunch of Americans who wanted to know if God was sincere. Despite his ersatz American cool, Schwartz comes from a world where Judaism is a way of life, complete and consistent. His students, for all their earnest curiosity, were only visitors in that world.

One of the women in the group took me aside and confided that now that she had become religious, she was planning a pilgrimage to Mount Sinai during the holiday of Shavuot. "Is there, like, I don't know, a Hilton or anything where I can stay nearby?" she asked. I told her there was only desert and a monastery, and she visibly cooled. "Well, in that case, maybe I'll just come to Jerusalem. I know there's a Hilton there," she said. "Jerusalem is just as good as Mount Sinai, I guess."

"Look me up when you get there," I offered, and she smiled.

"Don't worry, I will. Maybe you know some cute guys you could fix me up with."

Not long after I got back to the East Coast, a friend, Arthur Samuelson, suggested that I go up to Boston to meet Rabbi Levi Yitzchak Horowitz, also known as the Bostoner Rebbe. I didn't really want to go—Brooklyn and L.A. had satisfied my appetite for Chasidic encounters. But Arthur, normally a skeptical and irreverent fellow, was persistent. "Forget the stuff you saw in Williamsburg," he said. "And forget all those stone-throwing fanatics in Jerusalem. This guy's the real thing. Besides, how often do you get a chance to meet a genuine Chasidic rebbe?"

He had a point; I was still fascinated by the concept of a wonder-working, miracle-making rebbe, and eager to meet one. More than anyone else, the rebbes—dynastic heads of Chasidic sects—are representatives of the Jewish civilization of Eastern Europe that the Nazis destroyed. They are relics of another age, full of dark shtetel arts and mystical fervor, able to command the unquestioning obedience of followers who behave like subjects.

Most rebbes are ancient men from Europe, but Levi Yitzchak Horowitz, the Bostoner Rebbe, is an exception; the first Chasidic rebbe to be born and raised in the United States. According to one of the group's publications, Horowitz "assumed the leadership of his court" at the age of twenty-three. Not many men born in the Dorchester section of Boston have their own court, and I was intrigued by the opportunity to see one face to face.

When I called the Bostoner synagogue, a woman with a brisk New England accent said, ''New England Chasidic Center, rabbi's study'' in a businesslike tone. I wasn't sure how to make an appointment with a mystic, but it turned out to be as simple as fixing a date with the dentist. The secretary gave me instructions on how to reach the Chasidic Center, requested a number where I could be reached in case of a change in plans, and wished me a good day. After I hung up, I realized she hadn't even asked what I wanted to see the rebbe about.

Rabbi Levi Yitzchak Horowitz claims descent from the Ba'al Shem Tov, the founder of Chasidism, and from a long line of famous rebbes. His father, Pinchas David Horowitz, was born in Jerusalem and came to the United States during World War I; there he became the first Chasidic rebbe in Williamsburg. After a few years, the old man left New York for Boston and founded ''the new dynasty'' at 87 Poplar Street. The current rebbe was born there in 1921. Twenty years later the old man died, and in 1944 Levi Yitzchak took over the Boston court.

The literature of the New England Chasidic Center is refreshingly free of false modesty regarding the accomplishments of the rebbe, ''[a] miracle man of mythical dimensions [who] is the surrogate for his Chasidim. His prayers are an intercession. He pleads as an advocate to heaven.'' According to his pamphleteer, ''This city of loving kindness, Boston, is famous because of the rebbe.''

Despite this claim, the Irish cabbie who drove me out to the rebbe's Beacon Street headquarters in Brookline had never heard of Grand Rabbi Horowitz. He was a fortyish man who told me he grew up in Brockton, ''the city of champions.''

''Today it's Marvin Hagler,'' he said, ''but back when I was in school it was Rocky Marciano. Heavyweight champion of the world. What a guy.''

''Did you know him?'' I asked.

''Yeah, him and his brothers. I knew the whole family. Hey, I took a lot of punches in the head because of the Rock.''

''You fought Rocky Marciano?''

''Naw, nothin' like that. See, Rocky got to be champ when I was in high school. And all of a sudden, everybody in town wanted to be a fighter. People fought all over the place—on the way to school, in school, on the way home from school. Every time you turned around, somebody tried to punch you in the head.'' The cabbie paused, lost in nostalgia, contemplating the prolonged donnybrook.

"I'll tell you one thing, though. He really put Brockton on the map," he said. "Anywhere in the world, you say 'Brockton' and people say, 'home of Rocky Marciano.' ''

"Boston is famous because of the rebbe," I said.

"Yeah? Reggie who?''

The New England Chasidic Center, when we reached it, did not look like the site of a dynastic court. It is a simple brick building that contains a synagogue and study hall and, up two flights of stairs, the rebbe's study. In a large outer office, two modestly dressed secretaries busied themselves with clerical tasks, and a young man with a beard sat typing noiselessly on a personal computer. Through the open door of an adjoining room I caught occasional glimpses of a white-bearded figure who paced back and forth, wrapped in a large white prayer shawl.

After a few minutes the man, now wearing an old-fashioned black frock coat, came into the waiting room. He exchanged a few words with the secretaries, peered briefly at the computer screen, and walked over to me and introduced himself as Rabbi Horowitz. He was an arresting figure, the very picture of a Chasidic rebbe— high forehead, prominent nose, long white beard, and soft, expressive brown eyes—and he radiated presence.

The rebbe ushered me into his study, sat at his desk, and motioned me to a chair across from him. He regarded me with a benign stare that I found surprisingly unsettling—for a moment I imagined he was reading my mind. I was impressed, and annoyed with myself for being impressed.

Twenty years ago, when I first moved to Jerusalem, I had a romantic attraction to Chasidic Jews and the lost world they symbolized. But as their fundamentalist fervor grew, I began to see them as the enemy—people who throw stones at my car on the Sabbath, seek to impose theocratic restraints on my freedom, shirk their duties as citizens, and consider me to be a second-class Jew at best. I came to Boston to see the rebbe out of curiosity; but I never considered the possibility that I might find him impressive.

My discomfort made me go on the offensive. "I'm writing a book about Jews in America," I said, "and I'm curious about what you do. Can you really work miracles?"

The rebbe ignored the unmistakable irony in my voice and gazed at me thoughtfully for a long moment. "I think you have a misconception about the role of a Chasidic rebbe," he said in a dry, analytical tone. "A person doesn't feel good in the world if he or she is all alone. That's why people need a rebbe. A Chasidic rebbe is, in essence, a support system.

"There is a special relationship between a Chasid and his rebbe. But to be satisfactory it can't be based on blind obedience. I want my Chasidim to understand me—why I do certain things, the way I see the world—and then to act on that understanding. A Chasid shouldn't be a robot. His relationship with me, or with any rebbe, should make him more sensitive."

"I thought Chasidic rebbes were supposed to be wonder workers, intercede with God, act as an advocate to heaven," I said.

The rebbe smiled, recognizing the phrase from his brochure. "The role of a rebbe depends upon the needs of his Chasidim," he said. "Those who dealt with more ignorant kinds of Jews went in for fairy tales and legends about the rebbe. Others, like the Lubavitcher, became total authority figures for their Chasidim. To a large extent, a rebbe has to be responsive to the needs and limitations of the people he leads.

"Now in the case of our dynasty, when my father came to Boston he found Chasidim here from various courts. All of them had different ideas about what a rebbe should be. He had to be flexible, appeal to everyone, give each person what he needed. That was my father's way, and it's mine."

"You mean, if somebody expects miracles, then you perform miracles?" I asked, and this time he sighed. "No, I don't perform miracles. No Chasidic rebbe can do the supernatural. A good rebbe is like a top doctor, a specialist. If your family doctor needs some help in dealing with a problem, he refers you to an expert. This expert can't perform miracles, but he can get the most out of his training and knowledge, the most out of the natural. Of course, some experts are quacks," he added dryly.

I found his candor disarming. "To be honest, from my perspective as an Israeli, most of them seem like quacks," I said. "Why are people like the Satmar rebbe so intolerant?"

"I think you may misunderstand him," he said. "I was just in Brooklyn for a visit with the Satmar—our families have a special relationship. And believe me, he's a very fine man. But our world is based on different premises than yours, and it's not always easy to understand one another."

The Bostoner was in a reflective mood that morning, and he turned my interview into a monologue. His topics were seemingly unrelated—the place of women in Judaism, the relationship between faith and science, Massachusetts state politics, town planning in Jerusalem—but somehow he managed to connect them, displaying a subtle intelligence and a surprisingly moderate view of the world.

I was determined not to be seduced, however. "Let me ask you something, rabbi," I said. "Are you a Zionist?"

"A Zionist? Of course I'm a Zionist. I may not agree with every single policy of the Israeli government, but is that a reason to punish Israel?"

"A lot of Chasidim seem to think so," I said, and he sighed again. "Look, I have a lot of followers in Har Nof, in Yerushalaim. The neighborhood where they live is ninety-seven percent Orthodox. But the other three percent here have rights, too. So I told my supporters, don't close the streets to traffic on Shabbes—let those who want to drive, drive. We can make Shabbes here without stopping the traffic." I noticed that when he said "here," he meant Jerusalem.

"You see," he continued, " 'Shabbes' used to be the most beautiful word in the Jewish vocabulary. And the stone throwers have turned it into a curse, a threat. When a Jew hears the word 'Shabbes' he should think of flowers, not stones."

"What about here in America?" I asked. "A lot of American Jews don't even know what the word 'Shabbes' means."

The rebbe nodded in agreement. "We've been doing outreach programs in Boston since 1950. Singing, dancing—you'd think such things are old-fashioned, foreign to American students. But it's surprising—a lot of assimilated students respond to it very strongly. I think Americans may be missing certain things in life, certain spiritual things. We respect them, even if they're not religious. We try to understand them, and to remember that it isn't their fault. They haven't had a chance to learn.

"But the problem is, what will keep them 'yidden' in the future? Most of the liberal Jews who come to Harvard or MIT don't have any Yiddishkeit and they don't want any. The ones who want it will find it, but the majority will marry goyim. It's happening now. And their children won't be Jews. We real Jews, with everything we've got, can't hold on to our Judaism here in America; what chance does the child of a mixed marriage have?" He spoke in a matter-of-fact tone, but there was real pain in his eyes.

There was a knock on the door and the rebbe's secretary came in to remind him that his next appointment was waiting. I looked at my watch and was amazed to see that we had been talking for almost two hours.

"I'd like to tell you something personal," I said. "I'm not religious, and I have a pretty cynical view of what Orthodoxy is in Israel. But talking to you makes me almost wish that I had a rebbe."

Horowitz smiled gently. "Don't be so surprised. Everyone needs a rebbe sometimes."

"Who's your rebbe?" I asked, and for the first time in our conversation I had caught him off guard.

"Good question," he said in a soft voice. "You know once, in Jerusalem, a man had a problem, and he decided to travel to Poland to consult with a famous rebbe. His friend said, 'Why leave Jerusalem? After all, here you have the Kotel, the Wailing Wall.' And the man said, 'I'm going to Poland because I want a rebbe who can answer back when I talk to him.'

"You see, my father's example is always before me. I try to imagine what he would do," the Bostoner said in a wistful tone. "But I don't have a rebbe who can answer back." Suddenly his eyes cleared, and his voice resumed its matter-of-fact tone. "Nu, that's just the way it is. There are occupational hazards in every profession. Even mine."

CHAPTER SIX

OUTSIDE LOOKING IN

O n the door of Cisco's Restaurant, Bakery and Bar on East 6th Street in Austin, Texas, there is a sign, WE DO NOT HAVE A NO SMOKING SECTION. Cisco's is the kind of place you'd expect to find Billy Clyde Puckett eating a chicken-fried steak and listening to a jukebox full of Waylon and Willie. Its walls are festooned with photographs of famous sons of the Lone Star State inscribed to Rudy the owner—pictures of Lyndon Johnson and Chill Wills, Tom Landry and Tex Ritter. I took a seat under the portraits, ordered a cup of coffee, and waited for Kinky Friedman to join me for breakfast.

Fifteen years ago Richard "Kinky" Friedman captured the imagination of country & western fans—and the indignation of the American Jewish establishment—by becoming America's first (and only) Jewish hillbilly singer. Like black country crooner Charlie Pride, Kinky was a novelty act; but unlike Pride, who performs standard songs without reference to his race, Kinky Friedman wrote and sang Jewish country tunes. At rodeos and sawdust-floored gin mills across rural America, on college campuses and at Manhattan's Lone Star Café, he and his band, The Texas Jewboys, played his original compositions: "Ride 'Em Jewboy" about the Holocaust, "They Ain't Making Jews Like Jesus Anymore," and my own personal favorite, "We Reserve the Right (to Refuse Services to You)."

"We Reserve the Right" tells the story of a rebel who isn't welcome at his local synagogue. "Hear O Israel, yes indeed, my book was backwards, I could not read," he complains, and the rabbi demands, "Baruch atah adonai, what the hell you doin' back there, boy?" Finally he gets kicked out and the synagogue fathers explain, "We reserve the right to refuse services to you. Your friends are all on welfare and you call yourself a Jew."

The song, like most of Kinky's songs, is funny. But it is also the best three-minute statement I know concerning the plight of the Jewish misfit in America—someone who wants to be Jewish but can't fit into the normal Jewish community framework. Mutual friends told me that the song described Kinky himself and, curious to meet a Texas Jewboy, I called him from New York and set up this meeting.

There was no picture of Kinky on Cisco's wall, but I recognized him the minute he walked in. He *looked* like a Jewish country singer—cowboy boots, faded jeans, a worn work shirt under a khaki jacket, and, planted squarely on a mountain of black nappy hair, a Borsolino hat. To complete the ensemble he was smoking a very large, very aromatic Jamaican Royale. Cisco's is one of the last places in America where you can stoke up a cigar at breakfast without getting into a screaming argument with a subscriber to *Runner's World*.

With me that morning was Michael Stoff, a professor of history at the University of Texas. Stoff is a forty-year-old transplanted New Yorker who, after half a dozen years in Austin, is still fascinated and bemused by the natives. Although he lives in the cosmopolitan world of Austin academia, he is a close student of Texans and their mannerisms. On the way to Cisco's that morning he explained Stoff's Law of Texas Behavior. "Just remember, Texans can't stand to be beaten at anything by anyone. It's total competitive adaptability. Whatever *you* are, *they* are more," he said.

Despite his analytical tone, I could tell that Stoff was excited about meeting Kinky Friedman; at breakfast he would have the chance to test his theory on one of the Lone Star State's most extreme personalities.

Friedman stood at the door, canvassing the room, and I waved him over. "You look just like I expected," I said, meaning it as a compliment. But he fixed me with a hard, wary stare. Friedman has the eyes of a sensitive badass, a man who's taken abuse for being a Jew among rednecks, and a redneck among Jews. "Yeah, well all you book-writer types look the same, too," he said, pulling up a chair.

We ordered huevos rancheros and tequila sunrises. While we waited for the food, Kinky told the story of his recent unsuccessful campaign for the office of sheriff of Kerrville, Texas, a small hill-country town near the ranch–summer camp owned by his father. "I didn't do all that bad; I got two hundred more votes than the candidate who chopped up his collie with a chain saw," he deadpanned. Kinky went on to describe how he had been hurt by his association with Bob Dylan and other unpopular Yankee show biz types. "Them connections lost me the trailer park vote," he lamented. His habit of addressing the voters as "my fellow Kerrverts" probably hadn't helped, either.

Friedman related his election story in the Texas way, as a set piece. Texans don't tell jokes, they spin elaborate yarns that have a fixed, stylized form. Friedman is a genuinely funny man in a dark sort of way, and later in the day he cut loose with some spontaneous humor. But at breakfast, with a highbrow professor from the university and a possibly unfriendly book-writer, he stuck to safe ground.

I discovered as the day went along that Kinky has several accents—Texas cowpoke, Houston sophisticate, newscaster neutral (for sincere moments), and even a creditable New York imitation. He uses Texas cowpoke to hide behind, and at breakfast he laid it on thick.

"I'm the Jewish ambassador to the fucking rednecks in this country, pardner," he declared belligerently, watching Stoff out of the corner of his eye. Kinky's father, whom he idolizes, is a retired professor of psychology at the University of Texas, and Kinky himself attended college, but he never graduated and he's sensitive about it. His first priority that morning was putting Stoff on the defensive. He and I would be spending the whole day together, and I could be dealt with later.

"The only two Jews these shit kickers ever heard of are Kinky Friedman and Jesus Christ," said Kinky Friedman. Stoff, who sees shit kickers mostly through the windshield of his Japanese car, nodded pleasantly. "I have a close friend who knows you," he said, mentioning the name of a prominent local journalist. Kinky snorted. "I hate to tell you this, boy, but your friend's an asshole. I don't want to hurt your feelings or nothin' but the guy's full of shit." Stoff blinked; in his world people don't go around calling each other's friends "asshole," at least not on the first date.

Friedman, sensitive as a cat, felt the professor's disapproval and moved in for the kill. "Where you from, boychik? I know it ain't from these parts," he demanded in an aggressive voice.

"New York. Long Island, actually," said Stoff. Friedman snorted derisively. "Long Island ain't New York. You know New York City? You ever been to the Carnegie Delicatessen?"

"Sure," said Stoff in a neutral way. "I know it well."

"Yeah, well when you go in there, you don't get linen, I guarantee you that." Stoff looked puzzled. "The regular customers get paper napkins; only superstars like Kinky get linen." Satisfied, he burst into a grin, and Stoff grinned back. "Whatever *you* are, *they* are more," he had told me on the way over. Michael Stoff was at his happiest, an academic in possession of a corroborated hypothesis.

Stoff left for a class, and Kinky watched him go. "You think your friend liked me?" he demanded. "About as much as you seemed to like him," I said, determined not to be intimidated. Friedman surprised me. He softened, and in an almost boyish voice said, "I liked him all right. But guys like him, sometimes they don't appreciate Kinky, ya know?"

We paid for breakfast in a hail of y'all-come-backs and climbed into Friedman's pickup truck. "I'm sorry we met down here in Austin," he said. "I hate this town. It's full of phonies. Next time you're down this way you come out to the ranch and we'll have us some fun, I promise you."

Kinky had just published a detective novel (the hero of which was a Jewish country & western singer named Kinky Friedman) and he asked me a few questions about contracts and agents. Suddenly he caught himself. "How old are you, anyway?" he demanded.

"Thirty-nine."

"Thirty-nine! Shit, I'm forty-two. I don't go to people who are younger than me for wisdom and advice, they come to me. You need any wisdom or advice, you come to Kinky. Don't be shy."

"Yessir, Mr. Friedman," I said. He narrowed his eyes for a moment, and then nodded emphatic approval of my deference to an elder statesman.

Kinky drove to his father's place, a conventional ranch house in one of Austin's better neighborhoods. Tom Friedman was reading by the fire when we arrived, but he put his book down to chat with us. A warm man, as friendly as Kinky is suspicious, he shares his son's cockeyed view of the world. He is originally from Chicago, and when his wife died recently he took the body back there for burial. "Listen to this," Tom said. "I was looking at the tombstones in the cemetery and I saw one with a Yiddish inscription. Know what it said? It said, 'The Cubs stink.' In Yiddish. How about that?"

Tom Friedman once taught for a semester at Tel Aviv University, and he still takes a keen interest in the Middle East. He is a hawk on the Arab-Israeli conflict, and we chatted about various aspects of the problem while Kinky listened fitfully. Kinky is a hawk, too—he once was awarded the Jewish Defense League's prize for cultural contribution—but it is a hard-line attitude that owes more to John Wayne than to Menachem Begin.

There is nothing country about Professor Friedman. He could be any Jewish academic in the United States. His home, where Kinky was born and raised, is not exactly a trailer park. Growing up, Kinky belonged to a Reform temple, attended Jewish summer camps, and generally had an urban, middle-class upbringing. As a redneck, he is a self-made man.

And yet, there is something genuine beyond the posturing. Kinky gets linen at the Carnegie, but he can also out-country the biggest hick in the house when the occasion calls for it. He is a man who belongs to two worlds, and to neither.

After high school and a stint at the University of Texas, Kinky joined the Peace Corps and was sent to Borneo. There he acquired a tattoo on his left arm and, inspired by the Six-Day War, wrote his

favorite song, "Ride 'Em Jewboy." The song is pure Kinky—
lyrics that express a deep Jewish sensibility, a tune from an
equally authentic feeling for Texas music.

When he came home from the Peace Corps Kinky formed his
band, and began touring. He had two audiences—country &
western fans who liked his music and young urban Jews who liked
his attitude. He could be irreverent, even offensive—he once invited
an audience at the Lone Star Café to "save Soviet Jewry and win
valuable prizes"—but he was saying something interesting about
the Jewish condition. He even did a concert in Brooklyn with the
Chasidic singer Rabbi Shlomo Carlebach. "Yeah boy, that was
really something," he said, recalling their evening together. "That
same week I did a show with Merle Haggard. Ain't too many
singers can say that."

Kinky still spends a good deal of his time in New York, where he
has a more or less permanent retinue of admirers. Two of them are
Steve Rambam (his real name), a Jewish private eye from Brooklyn; and Rambam's assistant, Boris Shapiro, a human fireplug who
was once a member of the Soviet combat karate team. In Texas,
Kinky bragged that Boris could kill a man a hundred ways with his
bare hands without leaving a mark. A few weeks later, I met Boris
in New York and asked him to verify it. He pursed his thick lips,
wiggled his hand to indicate the approximate nature of Kinky's
boast, and said, "Von hundred, von hundred and two."

Tom Friedman had a luncheon date, and Kinky and I went out
for a drive in Austin. After an hour or so of aimless cruising I
noticed that something was missing—there was no music. "Don't
you have a tape deck or a radio?" I asked.

"Tell you the truth, I hate the sound of the human voice
singing," he said, and he seemed to mean it. Kinky still appears
on stage from time to time but his musical career had been in a
prolonged slump.

"You know, I've never seen you perform," I admitted.

"Well, you don't know what you missed," he said. "I'm
gonna take you back to Tom's and show you a videotape of a
show I did on *Austin City Limits*. It was a great gig even though
it never got on the air. But I got the tape."

The program featured a western-outfitted Kinky and his band
doing a number of outrageous Friedman compositions, including

"I'm Proud to be an Asshole from El Paso" and a particularly tasteless song about using a picture of Jesus for toilet paper. "That's the reason they never showed this mother on TV," Kinky explained superfluously.

Michael Stoff had invited us to a dinner party that night. Kinky had mentioned the party several times during the day, asking if I thought there would be any good-looking women there. But suddenly, as the time approached, he got cold feet. "I won't know anybody except that asshole buddy of his," he said plaintively. "Why don't I just drop you off?"

"What're you talking about? Everybody in Texas knows Kinky Friedman," I said, and he brightened noticeably. "They do, don't they? Hell yes they do, I'm a goddamned cultural *icon*. Shit, they'll be *honored* to have me. . . ." Continuing in this vein, he changed his work shirt, squared the Borsolino he hadn't removed all day ("That's one thing Jews and cowboys have in common; we both wear our hats in the house"), and we headed for Stoff's.

The party was already under way when we arrived. Most of the guests were faculty colleagues of Michael's in their late thirties or early forties, dressed in tweedy university style. Judging by their names and faces, almost everyone was Jewish. Motown music played softly in the background as people chatted over homemade chili and paper cups of chilled chablis.

The mood was mellow, but Kinky was a study in truculent discomfort. He poured himself an eight-ounce glass of bourbon, stoked up a huge Jamaican Royale, and paced the room restlessly. From time to time he blew a cloud of cigar smoke at the assembled guests, who waved their hands to clear the air. I noticed, though, that no one asked him to put out the cigar.

As he wandered around, I watched the other men watching him. Although there was nothing physically threatening about him they gave him room, moving warily out of his path and stealing looks at him from the corners of their eyes. Despite the fact that he was the son of a colleague, a Jewish guy from Austin just about their own age, he seemed out of place, foreign. He had hung out in trailer camps and sung at the Grand Ole Opry, had gotten drunk and crazy, and bragged about it in public. There was something undomesticated and unpredictable about him, something that made the nice Jewish boys of Austin academia uncomfortable. A gentile country outlaw is one thing; but Friedman, with his hard eyes and defiant attitude, his knock-this-off Borsolino and stubborn insistence that being Jewish matters, was a far more threatening proposition.

Around midnight the party began to break up amid talk of Hebrew school car pools and soccer practices. I was at the door saying good-bye to several of Stoff's guests when Kinky joined us. "I gotta hit the road, pardner. I'll see you up in New York City," he said in a loud, somewhat drunken voice. "We'll have us a time up there, round up some chicks, and party." Then, sure of his audience, he lifted one blue-jeaned leg, exposing a green alligator-skin cowboy boot with the name "Kinky" burned into the leather. "Pretty hip, ain't they?" he demanded. "You ever see a Jew with them kind of boots?" And then he blew a last puff of Jamaican Royale at the guests and sauntered off.

Jewish misfits tend to be loners. Like Kinky Friedman, they stick out in a crowd, especially in the mainstream congregations and community centers of America. But there is one national organization, the Jewish Defense League (JDL), where misfits are not only welcome, they are in control.

The JDL was founded in the sixties by Rabbi Meir Kahane. In its early days it attracted a number of idealistic militants who saw it primarily as a neighborhood patrol group. But Kahane had bigger plans, and he led the organization in the direction of anti-Soviet violence, armed clashes with black nationalists, and loud confrontations with the Jewish establishment.

Kahane eventually moved to Israel, where he was elected to the Knesset in 1984. In America, the JDL splintered into various factions that attracted the increased attention of law enforcement agencies. In some cities, JDL splinters operate openly under various names; in others, they are a subterranean presence. In Detroit, for example, the organization has been officially disbanded, but while I was there I heard rumors about a secret chapter. The notion of a Jewish underground was intriguing, and I asked a reporter friend of mine to look into it. A few days later he called with a cryptic message. "Meet me in the parking lot of the Mexican restaurant

on the corner of Nine Mile and Telegraph," he said. "Three
o'clock. I've got a surprise for you."

When I arrived at the abandoned parking lot I found my friend
slouched in the front seat of his car listening to Martha Jean the
Queen on WQBH. "I've got you a meeting with the former head of
the JDL," he told me proudly. "His code name is 'Dovid'—he
asked me not to tell you his real name."

I looked at the little shopping center across the parking lot and
at the suburban moms whizzing down Telegraph Road in their
station wagons, and I couldn't help laughing. "Is this for real?
Where are we supposed to be, Kiev?" The reporter laughed too.
"Hey, what can I tell you? He thinks he's underground, okay?"

A few minutes later a late-model T-bird cruised through the
lot. "There he is," my friend said as the driver signaled us
to follow. He led us through a maze of ranch-housed streets,
stopped in front of one, left his car, and climbed into the backseat
of ours.

I had been expecting a cigar-chomping, Brooklyn-accented
thug. But Dovid turned out to be a gaunt six-footer with a sensitive, puzzled face, a repertoire of barely controlled tics, and a
nasal Detroit accent. He wore a very small black knit skullcap and
carried a portable tape recorder. "I made a tape for you last
night," he said, handing me the machine. "Before we talk, just
drive out by the lakes and listen to it, okay?"

"Is it going to self-destruct when I get done?" I asked, but
humor was evidently not one of Dovid's strong suits. "Nothing
like that," he assured me solemnly. "It was just easier to organize
my thoughts this way."

For the next half hour or so we cruised aimlessly and listened
to Dovid's rambling recorded account of his life in the Jewish
Defense League. Most of it had to do with the internal politics of
the organization, including a long description of an alleged plot to
kill Meir Kahane, cooked up, according to Dovid, by rivals within
the group. None of it made much sense, and after listening to it I
still had no idea what Dovid had done in the JDL or if he was still
a member.

By this time we were in Novi, a working-class township
outside Detroit. When we drove past O'Shea's Bar I suggested
that we stop for a beer. Dovid agreed with a marked lack of

enthusiasm. Bars are for gentiles and gentiles are the enemy, to be approached with caution and fear.

As we got out of the car he took off his skullcap and put it in his pocket. "It doesn't look nice to sit around drinking with a yarmulke on," he said. Then he removed a nine-millimeter Smith & Wesson pistol from a shoulder holster and locked it in the trunk of the car. "It's illegal to take a firearm into a bar in the state of Michigan," Dovid explained.

"Even a puny little gun like that?" I asked, and he looked wounded. "Hey, the greatest assassins in the world have used this weapon," he said indignantly.

O'Shea's was crowded with workingmen who had just come off the first shift at the Ford plant. We took a table in the back of the room next to the cigarette machine. Dovid, surveying the scene, was plainly uncomfortable. When the waitress came over he cringed as if he expected her to take one look at us and scream, "Kikes!" But she merely stood at gum-chewing attention, waiting to take our order. The reporter and I asked for draught Bud; Dovid, after hesitation, ordered a Coors. "That's what the goyim drink," he said knowingly after she left.

In a semiwhisper, Dovid began to talk about himself and his life in the JDL. He was born and raised in Detroit, in a non-Orthodox home. His wife is the daughter of Holocaust survivors. I knew from the reporter that he was out of work, a condition that Dovid attributed to harassment by the Detroit police department. To keep busy he runs eleven miles a day, practices karate (he has a fourth-degree black belt), and plays with his collection of guns, an arsenal that, according to him, is at the disposal of the Jewish people.

"Look, I'm a caring Jew. Okay, I'm not in the JDL anymore, but I still keep up, I still care. Why did I leave the JDL? The truth is, I left because I couldn't handle Kahane. Every time he came to Detroit all he could talk about was how bad the *Jews* are, what the *Jews* are doing wrong. I mean, there are nine hundred trained Arab terrorists in this city, twelve thousand gun-carrying anti-Semites in the Aryan Nation out in Brighton, not thirty miles from here." He looked around at the men drinking at the bar and lowered his voice to a near whisper.

"Listen, Jews need protection. They say it can't happen here?

What a laugh. But I want to tell you something: Israel's not the answer, either. That's just what they want—to get us all in one place and finish us off at once."

A man approached the cigarette machine and suddenly Dovid raised his voice. "Yeah, she was really a great piece of ass," he practically shouted, giving me a significant look. "She was really great in the sack . . .'' The man didn't seem to notice us at all, but Dovid went on about his imaginary conquest until the spy walked away with his Pall Malls.

"We had all kinds of people," Dovid said, picking up the thread of his narrative. "There was a guy trained by the KGB in Cuba. We had another guy who joined because he wanted to kill all the enemies of the Jews in one day. I own ten pistols, I'm no pussy, but I couldn't go for that, no way. You know what? We had a Jewish policeman in the JDL; hell, we had a *federal marshal*. And a couple of Israelis, including a guy who had once been in the intelligence corps. We've got a camp in Michigan, I can't tell you where, and we do urban warfare and guerrilla training three or four times a week."

"I thought you were out of the JDL," I said. Dovid seemed momentarily confused. "I meant that there used to be a camp," he said finally. "Maybe there still is one, I don't know. Officially the Jewish Defense League doesn't exist in Detroit, that's all I want to say about it."

"Come on, we both know it exists. Are you still in it or not?" asked my friend the reporter, his professional curiosity aroused.

Dovid seemed torn between caution and bravado. "I might know some people . . . look, I can't talk about this. My life might be in danger, from other Jews. I mean, I'm not afraid to take risks. I infiltrated hate groups for the FBI. I'd have no remorse about killing someone who killed a Jew. I've been busted by the Detroit police many times, I've been harassed by the Oak Park and Southfield police departments. But when it comes to the JDL . . . I don't want to say anything else. Period."

At some level, most Jews feel uneasy about living in a world that allowed the Holocaust to take place. But federated Jewry has learned to live with its latent insecurity; the JDL has not. Its members belong to a tiny minority whose anger and anxiety cannot be appeased.

As a result, Dovid, who professes to be ready to lay down his life for his fellow Jews, is a pariah in the Jewish community. "The establishment in this city has called me a fascist, and that hurts more than anything," he said, sipping his Coors. "I joined the JDL, most of us did, to be in a position to protect our fellow Jews. I see the Jews around here, all they care about is money, success. They don't want to admit the dangers. They're just like the Jews in Germany before Hitler. They aren't able to defend themselves, and somebody's got to do it. I'm prepared to die defending them and they call me a fascist, worse than Hitler. I just don't understand them.

"You know, I don't feel comfortable among Jews. I hate to admit that, but it's true. In my opinion liberal American Jews can't face reality. Even the Orthodox are living in a dream world. I consider myself to be an Orthodox Jew, but the Torah was written by God, not by rabbis, you understand what I mean? Nowadays, they even have women rabbis. Now how can a woman be a rabbi? They're unclean. I even heard they've got faggot rabbis now. A faggot rabbi? I don't even consider a man like that Jewish."

Dovid finished his beer and looked at his watch. He may have been underground, but he still had to get home in time for dinner. When we reached the car he retrieved his pistol and put the yarmulke back on his head. Even fully dressed he seemed uneasy, though, and he kept looking out the back window until we were several miles from O'Shea's.

"There's one thing I don't understand," I told him as we neared the suburban tract home where he had left his T-bird. "Since you feel the way you do about America, and being Jewish is so important to you, why don't you just move to Israel?"

"Someday maybe I will. I'd like to," said the former commander of the JDL in Detroit. "But I can't right now. The truth is, my wife won't go. She says it's too dangerous."

That night, in a bar across the city from O'Shea's, I met Marty Gaynor for a drink. Like Dovid, Marty is a Jew with a gun; the difference is that when I found him, sitting at a Formica table sipping a Stroh's, he was wearing his—a standard police-issue revolver. A small man with the powerful sloping shoulders of a linebacker, he sat watching two squealing legal secretaries shoot eight ball, his Detroit Police Department baseball cap perched on his head at a cocky angle.

We had met before, a few days earlier. My reporter friend introduced us over lunch in a restaurant in Greektown, not far from police headquarters. At lunch that day Marty shook my hand and took out a small notebook. "Could you please spell your name?" he said courteously, copying it down in a laborious hand. It was a cop's habit, like sitting with his back to the wall, something I noticed he was doing again that night at the tavern.

I sat down at the Formica table and this time I took out a notebook of my own. Marty, whose fair skin, high cheekbones, and lopsided grin make him look a little like a young Moshe Dayan, regarded it with approval. He has been a cop for almost fifteen years, and he has a civil servant's respect for the written word. The notebook meant I was serious, and he wanted to get something on the record right away.

"There's one thing I want you to do for me," he said. "If you write about me I'd really appreciate it if you'd use my real name, which is Goldfine, G-O-L-D-F-I-N-E. That was my grandfather's name, he was a lawyer here in town, he used to represent the Purple Gang. My father changed it to Gaynor, but I consider myself a Goldfine, not a Gaynor."

Marty, who is in his mid-thirties, grew up in Oak Park, a middle-class Jewish suburb on the outskirts of Detroit. Although he was raised among Jews, he realized from an early age that he was different from his serious-minded, well-behaved classmates. "I was a wild kid back then," he said with rueful pride. "Today I realize how much I missed in school, but in those days nobody could tell me a thing. You know, the older you get, the smarter your parents seem. But when I was a kid, I couldn't see beyond my nose."

In high school Marty was a suburban tough guy, who spent his days getting in and out of trouble at school and his nights drag racing up Woodward Avenue or looking for action in the parking lots of drive-ins along the strip. It was an adolescence that prepared him to become a criminal or a policeman. Marty chose the cops, joining the force shortly after graduating from Oak Park High.

Police work in Detroit is a dangerous profession—in the few weeks I was in the city, two cops were shot to death on duty—but Marty has never been intimidated by the violence. "The streets give me a high. I admit it," he said. In his first few years on the job he was involved in three shooting incidents—one of them fatal. He took out his own notebook and began to diagram the cases, carefully explaining the circumstances, as if he were testifying at a departmental inquest.

"There was this dude named Leroy Larry," he said, writing down the name. "He shot someone and then barricaded himself in an apartment house over by Olympia. He was in there with a rifle and I went in after him. I was carrying a forty-four Magnum and a .357." Once again he wrote in his notebook, jotting down the calibers of his pistols. "We wound up in a shootout, and luckily I got him before he got me."

"How did you feel about it? I mean, a nice Jewish boy killing someone?" I asked.

"Look, he was a criminal and I was doing my job. All the incidents I was involved in were the same way. It's what I get paid to do, apprehend perpetrators. I never felt bad about it. And I'll tell you something, I think I gave Jewish cops a better name after those incidents. I really do."

There aren't many Jewish policemen in Detroit—Marty knew of only seven or eight—a fact to which he attributed his lowly patrolman's rank. "The reason I don't get promoted is that there isn't any affirmative action for Jews. The blacks and the other minorities have it, and the other white guys help each other up. But there's no one to help the Jewish cops."

"How about the Jewish community?" I asked, and he snorted.

"The Jewish community are about the last ones who care about us. When I was walking a beat downtown I kept the streets clean. I did a lot of ass kicking down there. The merchants appreciated it, and a lot of them were Jewish. When the department transferred me they even got up a petition. But in the Jewish community at large, they couldn't have cared less. You'd think they'd want to help a Jewish cop, but Jews in Detroit aren't supposed to *be* cops. We don't exist. That's just the way it is."

Marty Gaynor is married to a Methodist woman from a small town in Ohio. "Before I got married I dated a few Jewish girls, but none of them were really looking to marry a cop. They were intrigued for a date or two, but they were looking for a lawyer or a doctor.'' As a city employee Gaynor is required to live in Detroit, where there is no Jewish neighborhood; but even if it were permitted, he couldn't afford to buy a home in a Jewish suburb on a cop's pay.

When he was stationed downtown, Marty used to drop in on Rabbi Gamze from time to time, sometimes serving as an unpaid guest worshiper. Once, on Rosh Hashanah, he was assigned to guard the Downtown Synagogue and he wore a yarmulke under his helmet as a sign of Jewish solidarity. But since his transfer he no longer goes to a synagogue. He doesn't feel comfortable or welcome among the federated Jews of the suburbs, and he has a cop's unease around civilians in social situations.

Occasionally Gaynor fantasizes about changing his life. ''Sometimes I want to do what nice Jewish boys are supposed to do, quit and make some money. Get a place out in Southfield or West Bloomfield, join a temple, the whole shot. But then I go out with the guys on a picnic, or hit some bars downtown for a drink or two, and I think, what the hell, I'd miss the life too much, miss the job. And so I stay.''

It was getting late. I closed my notebook and we walked together out to the parking lot. When I got to my car, Marty put a restraining hand on my arm. ''Listen, I want you to know that it's a thrill for me to be in a book about Jews. Really. That time I told you about, when I was on guard duty in front of the shul—that meant a lot to me. Know what I mean?''

I did know. Marty Gaynor, who wants to be known as Goldfine, lives in a self-imposed exile from the Jewish community, but not from his own Jewish heart. He was born with a cop's temperament, too restless and perhaps too violent for the middle-class world. But for one memorable day in his life, dressed in police blues, with a yarmulke under his crash helmet, he had been the defender of his people.

The day after I met with Dovid and Marty Gaynor, I flew to Columbus, Ohio, to see my favorite Jewish Buddhist, Harvey Wasserman. Back in the 1960s, Harvey was one of America's most prominent radical intellectuals and activists. Today, at forty, he is still fighting the establishment, but his life has taken some surprising twists. For one thing, he is now the president of the Wasserman Uniform & Shoe Company. For another, he has discovered that he has Jewish karma.

On the verge of middle age, Harvey Wasserman has retained the Peter Pan boyishness of his undergraduate days, when he was a campus rebel at the University of Michigan. He still has long hair combed over his collar, still wears granny glasses perched on his Doonesbury nose, still comes to the office in jeans and running shoes. His biography reads like a short history of the New Left. Back in the sixties, he was an early member of SDS. Later he helped found the Liberation News Service, became a Buddhist in India, stormed the Pentagon, and was one of the leaders of the Clamshell Antinuclear Alliance. Somewhere along the way he found time to write eight books, including *Harvey Wasserman's History of the United States,* which was published when he was in his early twenties.

In 1969 Harvey became a founder of Montague Farm, a rural commune in Massachusetts. He lived there long after the others left, stubbornly clinging to his radical life-style like one of the Japanese soldiers said to be roaming the jungles of Southeast Asia unaware that World War II has ended. But by 1983, even Harvey had to admit that the sixties were over, and he left the commune. Uncertain about what to do next, he came home to Columbus for a visit. And, ensconced in his boyhood bedroom, he began to see his hometown—and his family—in a new way.

"I realized that my folks were getting old, that the business was starting to be too much for them," he said. "I started to get some good old Jewish son–type guilt. It was really kind of weird."

Harvey's father, Sig Wasserman, saw an opportunity. A warm man with a formidable potbelly and a Dorchester honk, he is the kind of father girlfriends think is adorable. He is also one of Harvey's greatest admirers—he expects him to be President of the United States someday—and he could never understand why his son was living on a farm. Now, with Harvey back home, Sig made his move—he asked him to come into the office once or twice a week to help out.

Harvey, who has the aging hippie's fascination with business and efficiency, dropped by the Wasserman Uniform & Shoe Company. He saw a medium-sized firm that needed some modern management, and he decided to stay for a few months and whip things into shape. Four years later, he was still there.

Gentle irony is Harvey's style, and he was aware of the incongruity of his current occupation. Some of his best customers are police departments and sheriff's offices; he has become a supplier to the enemy.

"When I decided to stay, I got in touch with Abbie Hoffman," Harvey told me with a wry grin. "I said, 'Hey, I'm out here selling police equipment and it feels kinda weird, you know?' But Abbie just said, 'That's cool, I like cops these days.' It made me feel a little better, but sometimes it's still a weird thing. And I've got my limits. We carry police holsters, and I gave in to my father on Mace, but I won't sell billy clubs."

A lot of former radicals have gone Wall Street, but Harvey Wasserman is different. He hasn't sold out as much as branched out. As we were leaving his office for a tour of the city, I noticed a wall map behind his desk—blue pins marking Wasserman Uniform & Shoe sales outlets, green pins the nuclear power plants he is fighting.

Harvey Wasserman's tour of Columbus reflected his ambivalence toward the city—half radical iconoclasm, half merchant pride in a booming hometown. "Columbus is the third largest data processing center in the world, after Washington, D.C., and Moscow," he told me. (Americans always quantify civic achievement; a few weeks later in Shreveport, Louisiana, a man boasted to me that his city has America's largest VFW post.) Harvey's pride aroused my long-dormant Michigan patriotism. "Well, Detroit's number one in the country in homicides again. They've even got a murder meter on the Lodge Freeway now," I said. "No shit?" said Harvey, impressed. "Go Blue!" he exclaimed, and we both laughed at the University of Michigan cheer.

As we cruised around, Harvey pointed out the local landmarks. They included a street where a lawyer driving a new Mercedes had recently fallen twenty feet through a hole in the pavement; the state capital building ("The only one in America without a dome"); a statue of former governor James Rhodes ("The Butcher of Kent

State," Harvey reminded me); and a gray fortresslike building where Harvey beat his draft physical.

Surprisingly, the tour ended at the Columbus Jewish Community Center. "I love this place," he told me. "I spend at least two hours a day here. It's fantastic."

"Don't tell me you've become a Jew in your old age," I said, and Harvey laughed. "This place is my kind of Judaism. Wait'll you see it."

For the next half hour Harvey showed me around the health club of the Jewish Center. We visited the swimming pool where he does laps, the handball and basketball courts, the weight room and exercise lounge, the sauna and whirlpool. This is Harvey Wasserman's synagogue, and not just his. Jews in Columbus—and throughout the country—are obsessed with their bodies. The old image of the pasty-faced, round-shouldered scholar is being replaced by a new breed of lean-bodied Jewish businessmen, lawyers, and doctors. Health is the new *halacha* in America; cigarettes have replaced pork as the forbidden substance of choice.

In the hall outside the health club Harvey paused in front of some photographs—the Columbus Jewish Sports Hall of Fame. It is not exactly Cooperstown—most of its members were high school sports stars or played on the varsities of small colleges. Harvey himself was what he calls a "Jewish Jock," meaning that he lettered in tennis in high school. This form of self-mockery is still common among American Jewish men—in Detroit someone described himself as a "Jewish six feet," which, he explained, meant five foot ten. Self-image has yet to catch up to reality.

Despite their fitness craze, American Jews have produced few sports stars in recent years. In the old days there were great Jewish boxers, football players, major league baseball players, and hoopsters. Harvey and I grew up on Sandy Koufax, the last of the macho American Jewish sports heroes. Kids today have been reduced to Rod Carew (his wife is Jewish), Jim Palmer (he's not, but his stepfather is), boxer Hank Rossman (only half; he has an Italian mother), and a few swimmers and tennis players.

"I hear the Browns' quarterback, Bernie Kosar, might be Jewish," Harvey said, staring balefully at the Hall of Famers.

"What makes you think so?"

"The name. It could be a Jewish name," he said.

"Kosar? I've never heard that one before."

"No," he said, a bit sheepishly, "Bernie."

"What the hell do you care if Bernie Kosar is a Jew? You're supposed to be a Buddhist."

Harvey shrugged. "What can I tell you? I've got Jewish sports karma."

"Jewish sports karma?"

"Don't laugh," said Harvey. "You can't escape your karma. My parents are very tribal people. But for me, being a Jew was never all that important. I guess that's changing a little now. I mean, let's face it, Hitler drew the bottom line. If you think you can get out of it, you can't. And I'll admit something that's a little weird—I feel more comfortable around Jews. I know that's strange, considering the life I've led, but it's the truth. I feel more comfortable. I was amazed to discover that I wanted to have children with a Jewish woman. It's completely inconsistent, but that's how I feel. You can fight your parental karma for so long, but you'll never escape it."

Since Harvey was single, I assumed he was speaking hypothetically. But I was wrong. "Listen, I want you to come with me tonight to meet someone. It'll be a surprise. She's a woman I've been seeing named Susan. That's all I want to say about it right now. But you're gonna be blown away."

That night we drove a few blocks through suburban Columbus to Susan's house. Harvey, who is usually annoyingly calm, was nervous, and I was affected by his jitters. "What's the secrecy all about?" I asked, thinking that perhaps we were about to attend some bizarre witchcraft ritual. Harvey was noncommittal. "You'll see when we get there," he said, twisting the steering wheel of the Wasserman Uniformobile in his hands.

Susan met us at the door. She was a strikingly beautiful woman with large dark eyes, high cheekbones, a sensuous face—and a very large stomach. Harvey patted her belly with paternal affection. "Actually it's twins," he said, beaming.

The three of us sat in the kitchen. Susan fixed pasta, and Harvey, who had brought his own health food, made a salad. "Are you a vegetarian too?" I asked her, and she made a face.

"Susan's kosher," Harvey said, shaking his head. "Not only

that, she has a nine-year-old daughter from her first marriage who
goes to an Orthodox school. How's that for being Jewish?''

"I'm not really Orthodox," Susan protested. She is a lawyer, and she has a scrupulous regard for fact. "I do keep kosher
though, and I try to observe Shabbes. It's the way I was raised.''

Susan was born and grew up in Cleveland, the daughter of
Holocaust survivors. While Harvey was playing tennis and chasing
girls at B'nai B'rith conventions in high school, she lived in the
dark, melancholy world of the survivors' community; when he was
storming the Pentagon, she was at Case Western Reserve University, studying law and plotting her escape.

"You ought to interview Susan for your book," Harvey said.
He turned to Susan. "Ze'ev's writing a book on American Jews.''

"In that case, I can't help you," she said. "I'm not an American Jew.''

"What are you, then?" I asked.

"The daughter of survivors. That's something completely different. My parents were 'greeners'—you know, greenhorns. They
lived with other greeners. We had nothing to do with American
Jews,'' she said.

To Susan, American Jews are, first and foremost, Americans—
products of an optimistic, prosperous, and tolerant society. As a
girl she felt uncomfortable around them; her family was poor,
pessimistic, and wracked with pain from the Holocaust.

"When I was in high school I did great with the Catholic
boys," she said. "I liked them better than the immigrant Jewish
kids I knew. You know how queer guys like that are.'' I recalled
what a sociologist once told me—in America, Orthodox Jews
marry Catholics, Reform Jews marry Protestants.

Susan wasn't about to marry any kind of gentile ("My father
would have committed suicide''); instead she married, and later
divorced, a Jewish doctor from a working-class family. Now she
was with Harvey, who considers himself a Buddhist and whom she
considers an American Jew.

At nine o'clock we turned on the TV to catch a talk by the
Lubavitcher rebbe, which was being broadcast live by satellite
from Brooklyn. The rebbe sat on a platform surrounded by black-
garbed disciples. He spoke in Yiddish with an English translation
that Harvey and I needed but Susan didn't. Harvey was visibly

taken with the white-bearded Chasidic mystic, and from time to time he murmured an approving "Far out."

After the broadcast, Harvey peppered us with questions about the Chasidim, which Susan answered with an indulgent fondness. He may have written eight books about America, but he knew very little about the modern history of the Jews. "Sometimes when I watch something like that I feel like a real goy," he admitted cheerfully.

"If you were a goy, you wouldn't be here," said Susan. She turned to me. "You're an Israeli, so I suppose you'll understand this. I wanted another child but I didn't necessarily want to get married again. Neither did Harvey. We haven't decided what to do about that. But I had one absolute condition. The father had to be a Jew. Harvey's great, I love him. But even more important, I could trace his family all the way back to his great-grandparents, and all of them were Jews."

"Why is that so important?" I asked.

Susan's dark eyes flashed, and the softness left her face. "I could never have a child with a gentile, or even someone with gentile blood. You see, somewhere in his genetic history there could be someone who put my family into the gas chamber."

Susan and Harvey were still on my mind when I flew back to Detroit the next day, picked up a car at Metro Airport, and headed east for Grosse Pointe, a WASP suburb with a national reputation for bigotry. I had never been there before; when I was growing up, Grosse Pointe was a kind of forbidden city, enemy territory. In those days, Jews weren't allowed to live in. Today it is still beyond the pale of settlement, and the tiny handful of Jews who live there are making a statement. I was on my way to see one of them, a young lawyer named Jody Kommel, who lives in Grosse Pointe with her Catholic husband and their small son, Scott.

It was Jody's mother, Eve Kommel, who set up the meeting. Eve is a handsome, athletic woman in her fifties who came to America as a refugee from Hitler's Germany in the 1930s. She has achieved minor celebrity in Detroit as the commodore of the Great Lakes Yacht Club, probably the only Jewish yacht club in America. It was founded in the 1950s, when Jews weren't welcome in the city's mainline yachting associations. Now the club faces an unanticipated problem—it has been so successful it is now flooded with Christian applicants.

This situation has split Great Lakes into two factions—those who favor a quota to retain the Jewish nature of the club, and those who oppose it as a form of reverse bigotry. Commodore Kommel favors open membership, and in the course of explaining why, she mentioned, without evident disapproval or dismay, that all three of her children were married to non-Jews and that one, Jody, lived in Grosse Pointe. "Why don't you go out and talk to her about what it's like?" she had suggested, and I readily agreed.

I arrived at Jody's prepared to dislike her. Especially after Susan, the idea of a woman with a refugee mother living out in WASPland and trying to pass offended my Jewish nationalism. My first impression of Jody Kommel did nothing to change my attitude. She was tall, athletic, and blue-eyed, with long red hair and freckles. She greeted me in the direct, friendly manner of the captain of the girls' field hockey team and steered me to a seat in her tastefully tweedy living room.

As she sat down across from me I was amazed to see she had a large Star of David dangling from her neck on a gold chain. She caught me staring, fingered the charm, and smiled.

"When we first moved out here, I was afraid that people wouldn't know I was Jewish, and they'd make anti-Semitic remarks," she said. "I wanted to preempt that, let them know who I was—I guess warn them, in a way. My husband was very much against it. His attitude was, it's better to know if someone's a bigot, then we can avoid them. But I don't think that's fair. So I wear it."

The notion that the charm was to protect the feelings of anti-Semites annoyed me. "It's kind of ironic, isn't it?" I said. "Your grandparents had to wear Jewish Stars in Germany and now you've got yourself one out here in Grosse Pointe."

She nodded slowly, thinking it over. "I guess it is ironic, yes. But, to be honest, we haven't had all that many problems out here. Nobody seems to care one way or the other. Now, sometimes in my law firm people let go with a joke, little remarks about Jews being cheap or sharp in business, something like that. I wonder about people who kid around like that, you know?" There was an angry edge to her voice that surprised me.

"Does it really matter all that much to you?" I asked her.

"Does what matter?"

"What people say about Jews. I mean, you're married to a Catholic, you live out here . . ." I gestured out the window in the general direction of the blond world of Grosse Pointe.

"No, no, no, you don't understand," she said in a soft, emotional voice. "I can't even *tell* you how strongly I feel about this. I'm not here on purpose. I never intended to marry a Christian. It just happened, that's all.

"See, when I was growing up I never dated Jewish boys—I was a jock and they weren't. But I always planned to marry one. In college I dated a gentile boy for four years, and I broke up with him because I couldn't handle his belief in Christianity.

"Then I met Jeff in law school. On our second date I told him, 'I won't love you unless you promise it won't be a problem raising our children Jewish.' He cracked up. 'Why don't we get to know each other first?' he said. I must have sounded like a nut. But it was that important to me."

Before the wedding, Jody took Jeff to Temple Beth El, Detroit's upscale Reform synagogue, for ten weeks of classes on Judaism. The ceremony itself took place in the temple. "I told him that raising our children Jewish was a condition for getting married at Temple Beth El," she recalled with a sour grin. "And then the rabbi told him it wasn't. So I said, 'Sorry, rabbi, I'm going to raise them Jewish anyway.' "

She was torpedoed by her mother on another issue. "Jeff wanted a Christmas tree, and I just couldn't deal with that, I couldn't handle the idea at all. We had a discussion about it that turned into a real argument. And then my mother told us that when I was small, we had a tree at home. That ruined my opposition. So this year we put up Christmas lights and had a tree in the basement. Next year it'll probably be upstairs. But it still makes me uncomfortable.

"Listen, being Jewish is the most important thing in the world to me. I don't know where the feeling comes from, but I feel it in my gut. I sometimes almost get sick. I'll hear something on television about Jews, or maybe meet another person, another Jew I didn't know was Jewish, and I get a hard lump in my chest, a feeling of pride and a feeling that I need to protect this other person.''

Jody took a deep breath, and I looked around her living room. There was nothing there that gave even a hint of her attitude—not a single Jewish book, painting, or ceremonial object. Only the gold star dangling from her neck.

"Where does this feeling come from?" I asked her, and she bit her lip in contemplation.

"It's strange, but I actually don't know. It's just something in me. Sometimes I even lay in bed wondering, would I give up my life to protect Judaism? I don't know. But I'll tell you one thing: I'm going to keep the religion going and defend it. My son will have a bar mitzvah, he'll know all the prayers and our history. He'll be a Jew, I'm absolutely determined about that. When he gets older, we're going to move to a Jewish neighborhood.''

"Why a Jewish neighborhood?" I asked.

"Why?" she said, and her clear blue eyes clouded. "So he can be with his own people. I don't want him to be an outsider.''

CHAPTER SEVEN

'OVERWEIGHT? IMPOSSIBLE!'

On the shore of Lake Kiamesha, in the heart of New York's Catskill Mountains, stands the Concord Hotel. Built in 1937, it is a monument to overstatement, the heavyweight champ of resort spas. The Concord has 1,200 rooms and a capacity of more than 2,000, three golf courses (one, known as "The Monster," is 6,793 yards long), and five nightclubs, including the world's biggest, the 24,000-square-foot Imperial Room.

The Concord's attitude toward food makes Henry VIII seem like Jane Fonda. The main dining room can accommodate 3,500 at one sitting and offers a style of service that the hotel describes as "instantaneous feeding." Patrons annually consume 100,000 pounds of butter, 450 tons of meat, and 4 million fresh eggs, not to mention 10,000 pounds of cream cheese. The Concord is the Alamo of cholesterol, the place where animal fat has chosen to make its last stand.

The hotel's ideology of excess is designed to appeal to people with big appetites. For that reason it is the perfect venue for Singles' Weekend, a Catskills institution that periodically brings together 1,800 of the hungriest-hearted young Jews in America.

The Concord is exceptionally image conscious, and it does not want to be characterized as a Jewish resort. It would much rather be regarded as a plain old all-American Eden, nonsectarian and free of its one-time ethnicity. Its publicity, for example, does not mention the fact that the hotel is strictly kosher and that there are rabbis constantly on the prowl to make sure it stays that way. Instead, it discreetly informs guests that "any prescribed diet for adults or children can be arranged at the Concord." There is a synagogue (but no church) on the premises but the hotel is not anxious to advertise it; its literature neutrally advises patrons to consult the desk for a schedule of religious services.

Hotel personnel are encouraged to play down the Jewish angle, but if pressed they admit that perhaps two-thirds of the Singles' Weekend guests are Jews. In fact, the proportion of Jews at these affairs is pretty close to the percentage of Muslims in downtown Mecca. Gentiles who come to a Concord Singles' Weekend come on its terms—gefilte fish, kosher wine, and all. For them the hotel may be a cheap resort, or a good place to pick up girls. But for the Jewish singles of Queens and Brooklyn, the Bronx and Long Island, it is a kind of secular shrine, a borscht belt Lourdes that offers a cure for the most painful of all American afflictions—loneliness.

To see this shrine in action I made my own pilgrimage to the shores of Lake Kiamesha, arriving on a snowy Friday evening. For weeks I had heard stories about the event from friends, some of whom refused to believe I would drive three hours through winter weather to a hotel full of single women just for the sake of research. "You're not going to believe it," one friend told me. "They jump you in the parking lot. You're going to go wild up there."

I braced myself, but when I got to the lot there were no sex fiends anywhere; just a pimply teenage boy who welcomed me in a friendly way and pointed me in the direction of the lobby.

"Lobby" fails to do justice to the foyer of the Concord. It is roughly the size of the Silverdome, and when I arrived it was the scene of mass chaos. Hundreds of young people stood in line for room assignments and hundreds more milled around the check-in

counter or surged through the room in aimless patterns. I was a
guest of the hotel, and Mike Hall, the Concord's publicity man,
went to the head of the line to get my key. Some of the others saw
this favoritism, but no one objected. Standing in line is a part of
the Concord experience. "It's as good a place as any to meet
people," Hall said. "A lot of couples have found each other
waiting in line for room assignments."

There are various ways to meet members of the opposite sex at
the Concord, and few of them are subtle. On the other hand, there
is no reason for subtlety. The hotel is a three-hour drive from
civilization, and no one just drops in for a drink. People are there
on purpose, and this makes them both bolder and more shy than
they might normally be—torn between a fear of lost opportunity
(not to mention wasted money), and the dread knowledge that if
you make a fool of yourself with someone, you will undoubtedly
keep bumping into each other for the entire weekend.

The most organized way to get acquainted is through the
Meeters' Digest. The *Digest* is the Concord's contribution to
fix-up journalism, a gazette of do-it-yourself personal ads, like the
ones that appear in *New York Magazine* or *The Village Voice*.
Submitted on Friday before dinner, the ads are numbered, collated
by the staff in a frenzied, all-night effort, and distributed in the
form of a thick computer printout in time for Saturday breakfast.

To get in touch with another Meeter, you simply write a note
addressed to his or her number and turn it in at the message center
in the lobby, where it is filed. During the weekend people stop by
every hour or so to check their mail.

The instructions for placing the ad advise not to worry about
cleverness, which is like telling Ronald Reagan not to worry about
Communism. The singles, especially the veterans, know that the
Digest is their one shot at reaching a mass audience, and many of
them had worked on their entries for weeks in advance. Those who
hadn't sat in the lobby chewing pencils in nervous concentration,
or stared helplessly into space in search of inspiration.

Mike Hall invited me to fill out an ad, and I felt a twinge of
competitive pressure. I was supposed to be a writer, after all, and I
didn't want to be outdone by a bunch of amateurs. But when the
Digest came out the next morning, I saw that I was out of my
league—many of the ads would have done credit to a Madison

Avenue copywriter. In my own ad I settled for the truth—"Israeli author looking for information"—a formulation that made me feel virtuously above the fray. In the course of the weekend, however, I learned that "author looking for information" is one of the most shopworn ploys in the catalog of come-ons.

Once the ad was placed, I went to the dining room for an instantaneous feeding. As a guest of the hotel I was seated at a specially reserved table with Mike Hall, a lugubrious widower named Joe who covers the nightclub scene for *Variety,* and a couple of fellow deadheads.

My host, Hall, is a Broadway publicist with nightspots, starlets, popular authors, and fancy restaurants for clients. Hall's is an anachronistic calling, but then the Concord is an anachronistic place. For all its computerized digests and nonsectarian pretensions, the aura of Marjorie Morningstar lies over the hotel like a latke on an empty stomach. Many of the singles began coming to the mountains, to this very resort, as children on family holidays; a number of their own parents met each other at the Concord. To these singles, residents of the great Jewish middle class of the outer boroughs, this is home, familiar turf, their place in the country.

Hall introduced me to Jimmy the Celebrity Waiter, who instantaneously produced matzoh ball soup, gefilte fish, chopped liver, and other deli items. The meal was a shock. The Concord is justly famous for the quantity of its food, but the quality reminded me of holiday dinners in the Israeli army—kosher, bland, and overcooked.

No one seemed to mind the food, though. Throughout the gigantic room, people sat at round tables of eight or ten and tried to eat while looking over each others' shoulders. This kind of rubbernecking is the standard Singles' Weekend posture, used in all conversations and other activities. The unofficial motto of the weekend is "Keep looking, there's always somebody better."

Almost no one is brave enough to come to Singles' Weekend alone. People arrive in pairs or threesomes and at Friday dinner they were still together. They talked among themselves but never stopped scouting the other tables, occasionally nudging one another to point out an interesting prospect.

After dinner, the real action began. Eighteen hundred singles rose en masse and began to surge up and down the long indoor promenade that connects the dining room to the lobby. Some sat on the gray sofas that were arranged, living room style, on either side of the walkway. Young men dressed in expensive sportswear sauntered back and forth in boisterous groups, bottles of Budweiser in hand. The women, quieter but no less intent, cruised the corridor displaying the peripheral vision of NBA guards. It was still early, and people traveled in pairs or groups for protection, but here and there you could already spot couples coming together. Singles' Weekend was now officially under way, a college mixer held in a suburban shopping mall.

People who attend these events have a losers' image, but the singles in the promenade seemed perfectly normal, even attractive. Most of the women were between twenty and thirty, although quite a few were close to forty, and a handful were in their fifties. The median age of the men was a few years older. Both the men and women appeared to be in very good shape; many had been dieting and working out for months to prepare for the weekend.

A few months earlier, in Detroit, I had found out how important physical conditioning is on the Jewish singles circuit. While I was in town a controversy erupted when a disgruntled young woman wrote to a local paper complaining that she had been turned down by Lo-la, a private Jewish dating service, because she was too fat. She claimed to be a victim of weight discrimination and scorned the service's proprietors—two Detroit grandmothers named Millie Rosenbaum and Claire Arm—for caring more about pounds and ounces than personality and character.

Millie Rosenbaum, a kindly woman, was plainly distressed by the affair and eager to explain the realities of the Jewish singles scene. She told me that most of her customers were under thirty. The agency accepts only Jews (using the traditional rabbinical criteria to determine eligibility); and most of them are assimilated, Reform, or Conservative types.

"They want partners who are culturally compatible," Rosenbaum explained. "About half are willing to date people who keep kosher, but no one asks for it. Jewish values don't mean much to them—mostly they're just American yuppies, with a little Jewishness thrown in.

"As far as that overweight girl is concerned, I really feel for her. She's right. Personality, character, those things *should* be important. But today, the big thing—for both men and women—is physical fitness. They say, 'I take care of my body, I want someone who takes care of his.' That's the attitude. The women want a professional, someone who can make a good living. Sometimes the men say they want a smart woman. But believe me, slender is the first requirement.

"I was in Chicago not too long ago," she continued. "I stopped in at the Jewish dating bureau there, just to compare notes. I got to talking with the woman who runs it and I said, 'I want to mention just one word to you, to see your reaction. And that word is 'overweight.' And the woman looked me right in the eye and said, *Overweight? I can answer that with just one word:* Impossible!' "

The emphasis on good looks and good health is a national phenomenon, from the fathers of North Dallas who don't want ugly daughters to the synagogue in L.A. that conducts aerobic Hebrew school classes, and the the crowd at the Concord reflected this preoccupation with fitness. Among the swirling throng it was hard to focus on individuals, but the overall impression was of attractive, robust people. On the other hand, I was surprised to find a large number of smokers. At first I attributed this to the pressure of the weekend, but later I realized that it was a class thing. The singles at the Concord dressed and talked like yuppies, but many were slightly downscale—legal secretaries and social workers, high school teachers and middle-level bureaucrats, optometrists and small-time CPAs. They were night-school graduates or the alumnae of subway colleges. The men sported last year's Zapata mustaches, the women wore too much makeup and had overbites uncorrected by orthodontia.

As I walked along the promenade I was stopped by three swarthy young men, brothers from Brooklyn. "Hey," one of them called to me. "What are you, some kind of professor?" The other two laughed loudly. I could see their point. In a corduroy jacket and jeans, and wearing a beard, I did have a kind of sixties look that seemed incongruous among these people who were dressed sharp as a tack. There was an edge to the question, too, an aggressive challenge I recognized from Israel but hadn't heard from American Jews.

"Aleppo, right?" I guessed, and they looked at me like I was a magician. Actually, it was an easy call. My Israeli eye told me they were Syrian Jews, my American ear that they were from Brooklyn; and Brooklyn is full of Jews from Aleppo. I explained to them that I was from Jerusalem, and was working on a book about Jews in America. "Maybe I'll write about you guys," I said lightly. "We can talk about the Jewish singles scene."

The brothers didn't care for the idea at all, and they huddled closer together as if I had threatened them. "Forget it, we came up here to relax, y'know," said one. He had a half-open shirt that revealed a large Jewish Star and a hairy chest. "We don't have to come all the way to the mountains to get laid, y'understand?" The others nodded emphatically, three cool cats from Brooklyn—Huey, Dewey, and Louie at the Concord. "Go find yourself somebody else, professor, we ain't washing our dirty linens in public."

It was cabaret time, and the crowd began to file into the World's Largest Nightclub for a free show, which consisted of a black singer who did Tom Jones imitations and a stand-up comic named Jackie Eagle. His routine leaned heavily on ethnic jokes ("Anyone here from Brooklyn?" Loud cheers. "Brooklyn, home of the Chasidim. Thirteenth Avenue is called the Rue da la Payes") and anti-Arab material ("Ever notice that the Jews eat prunes? Sure we do. Now, the Arabs, they don't eat any prunes. That's why they're full of shit.")

The crowd laughed at the jokes and sang along with the Tom Jones imitator but their minds were elsewhere. The Concord's PR kit claims that the resort "is to popular entertainment what LaStrada [sic] is to opera," but Singles' Weekend isn't prime time. The hotel assumes that the crowd is more interested in socializing than being entertained, and the acts it books for the singles are mostly "middle-of-the-week" quality.

After the show, the younger women went upstairs and came down wearing dancing outfits—loose-fitting tops over black tights—and joined the younger men in the disco. Next door the thirties crowd gathered in the lounge, which looks like a Manhattan singles bar, and danced to a Motown-style band. Other nightclubs featured a jazz combo that played pre-Elvis fox-trots, a magician-comedian, and a lady who sang Gershwin tunes and accompanied herself on a baby grand.

I stood alone in the foyer trying to decide where to go first when a woman came up and introduced herself. Her name was Carol and, in a manner that was direct and friendly, she invited me to join her for a drink. Often it is the women who make the first move at these events; the men, for all their macho pose, seem shy, even a bit frightened. Carol, who told me she was a clinical psychologist from Long Island, explained the dynamics of the Singles' Weekend.

"People come here expecting a big sex scene," she said. "A lot of guys are afraid of sexual encounters and so they freeze. But once you've been up here a couple of times you realize that there is very little sex. For one thing, people live two or three in a room, and it's not convenient. But mainly, sex is a waste of time. People come to meet other people, to build up a social life back in the city. If you pair off with one person and it doesn't pan out, where are you?"

Put another way, sex at a Singles' Weekend is not cost effective. It involves some preliminary work and perhaps a commitment for the rest of the weekend—and what if somebody better turns up? The system is to keep moving, keep circulating, keep getting names and numbers for real life. If the Concord is a kosher meat market, it is a wholesale one.

Of course, Singles' Weekends are not celibate; sex has been known to take place on the premises. With the AIDS scare, Carol admitted that she had brought condoms, just in case. "I can't believe I did it," she said, laughing. "I mean, the other day I called a girlfriend and asked her how to ask for them in a drugstore. What are you supposed to say, like, 'Gimme a dozen rubbers,' or what? It's such a high school thing, but what choice do you have? Listen, some people are really freaked—I met a woman up here with a doctor's certificate, and she won't even dance with anybody who doesn't have one too. Now that's sick. I mean, who brings a health certificate to the mountains?"

Carol got up to mingle as the band whanged its way into a Junior Walker medley. She was unembarrassed about the defection. "I'll see you around," she promised, "but I want to try to meet as many men as possible tonight. It's good to start weeding them out early."

I went to another table and introduced myself to a very pretty tax lawyer in her early twenties and a young man who told me in simple Hebrew that he teaches special education. The lawyer had curly brown hair and dark almond eyes, and the teacher was obviously taken by her. They had known each other only a couple hours, but they allowed me to interrupt their budding courtship and talked candidly, almost clinically, about their hopes for the weekend and beyond.

"I live on Long Island," the man said. "I have a nice house, a nice car. But I'm lonely. You have no idea how desolate Long Island can be in the winter. I've never been to one of these weekends before, but I want to find someone, a nice Jewish girl, and this is the place." He looked fondly at the lawyer, and she smiled.

"I've been up here five times," she said. "I moved to New York after law school, and I don't have many friends in the city. This is like a whole separate social life up here. I'm not hung up on finding a Jewish man—I want to find the right man, and he could be anything. But the truth is, I'm more comfortable with Jewish guys. It's just that a lot of them are very spoiled. But I'm ready for a family, and I'd like to have a Jewish family. I'd just feel more comfortable, that's all."

It wasn't hard to figure out that they were speaking mostly for each other's benefit, bouncing courtship signals off me like a communications satellite. I made a mental note to look them up again on Sunday, wished them luck, and headed back to the promenade.

There is an intentional sense of timelessness at the Concord; things stay open all night and there are no clocks. By two in the morning, the urinals in the men's rooms were clogged with Budweiser cans and some of the dancers were panting for breath, but hundreds of people still surged up and down the halls. The more impatient ones were already a bit wild-eyed, working up the courage to take direct action but uncertain about what to do.

I decided to call it a night and headed for the elevator. On the way I saw a lurching, almost menacing approach by a man who passed a woman, turned, stared at her for a moment, and then yelled, "Hey." She spun around, five or six paces beyond him, and waited. "What's your name?" he called in an aggrieved voice, as if she had just smashed into his car.

The woman didn't seem to mind the tone. "Mine? Debbie. What's yours?"

"Mine? Howard. Hey, you want to go in and dance or something?" She nodded and they walked together toward the disco, but both of them kept glancing around to make sure they weren't missing anyone better.

On Friday night I didn't see a single book, not even carried as a prop. But at Saturday breakfast, the huge dining hall of the Concord Hotel looked like a college dormitory during finals week. Hundreds of red-eyed singles dressed in jogging suits and leisure outfits sat at the round tables, bent in concentration over their *Digests*. They had pencils in their hands and made notes next to the entries, like handicappers before a big race. Some of the ads were sexually explicit. No. 1208 claimed that "They call me marathon man and I don't like to jog. I'm here for one thing and one thing only—to break my old record of four hours and twenty-six minutes." No. 1166 was terse: "I want good sex. Answer only if you can give it." And No. 653: "Single male seeking dominating female to put me in my place. Leather preferred."

On the distaff side, No. 222 described herself as "An attractive, tall blond looking for strong Jewish man for less than meaningful relationship. Must be into mayonnaise and leather." A balding man at my table broke the silence with a low whistle and read the ad out loud. "You think it's for real?" he asked, scanning the room.

"Even if it's not, imagine what kind of a girl thinks up an ad like that," said the man sitting next to him with a wolfish grin.

The *Digest* is unedited, and its entries appear in random juxtaposition. "Party animal, action packed looking for wild time with right partner" was next to "Sincere, respectful, nice looking seeks shy, quiet, friendly female." Some of the ads were cute in a *New York Magazine* way ("Furrier looking for a fox. Beavers also accepted"); a few alluded to drugs ("Snowloving entrepreneur looking for snowgirl"); but most were middle-of-the-road come-ons aimed at attracting as much weekend business as possible. There were some overtly materialistic pitches—"Knock, knock, who's there? A rich successful businessman who wants you to knock on my door''; or ''Englewood Cliffs JAP with condo in Florida. Daddy is a doctor and very particular about my dates. Be Mr. Right!''—but most advertised physical attributes rather than financial assets.

Many of the singles asked for Jewish partners or listed themselves SJMs or SJWs in the stylized way of the personal columns. A typical entry was, ''Wanted, nice-looking, educated Jewish male, age 24–28, 5'8" to 6'0" tall, for attractive, 5'2" Jewish teacher. Nerds need not apply.'' Or, on the male side, ''Wanted, that special Jewish girl. Down-to-earth person who is willing to share their [sic] special feelings with me.''

''Down-to-earth'' is a phrase I heard all over America from Jewish men. It is what they want Jewish women to be, and claim they rarely are. A man who came all the way from Cleveland to attend the weekend told me he hadn't been able to find a down-to-earth Jewish girl in the entire state of Ohio. ''You take them camping, out in the woods, and all they can say is, 'Ick, I'm freezing out here, when are we going home?' '' he complained.

Jewish women, for their part, complain that Jewish men are nerdy, or spoiled. They have stories of their own, and the phrase ''God's gift to women'' keeps cropping up. Jewish men and women seem both attracted to and angry with one another. Partly this is an expression of the general hostility between the sexes in America; but at least some of the animosity is specifically Jewish and reflects the distorted way Jews often view themselves and each other.

No. 1427: ''JAP princess wanted for immediate session of intense whining and verbal abuse. Just like mama.'' It is American Jewish humorists and writers who have stigmatized their women—mothers, wives, and daughters—as shrill, castrating, shallow, selfish, and spoiled, held them up to ridicule in a hundred films, a thousand comedy routines. In the Philip Roth–Neil Simon–Woody Allen world, Jewish women are always second best, consolation prizes or stopgaps until the Real Woman (blond, blue-eyed, and down-to-earth) comes along.

No. 0039: ''Single female, 30. No nerds, no JAPs, seeks handsome, exciting man with brains.'' What Woody Allen and Philip Roth did to Jewish women, they have done to themselves in spades. They, and an army of lesser writers, routinely depict

Jewish men as neurotics, mama's boys, victims, wimps, or money-mad materialists in gold chains. Jewish men write and produce much of America's cinema, theater, and television. It is they who create these stereotypes. The most enduring and recognizable Jewish character in American popular culture is Woody Allen's bumbling romantic who plays the fool for his Christian girlfriends and, by extension, for a Christian audience.

The striking thing is how little most of the young Jews at the Concord, or indeed anyplace in America, resemble these caricatures. Allen, Roth, and the others belong to an older generation. Their notions of Jews are derived from the ethnic neighborhoods of their boyhoods, and the now middle-aged people who emerged from them. But that first-generation community, still quivering with the traumas, temptations, and timid gratitude of the immigrant's children, is rapidly disappearing. Even at the Concord, bastion of the still-ethnic Eastern Seaboard Jewish middle-middle class, the squirrely little nerds and cloying princesses are mostly a figment of each others' imaginations.

"You want to know who these people are? They're Americans," said Jeanie, a pert blond of about thirty who was sitting at our table. The daughter of Holocaust survivors, she was at the Concord to find a Jewish husband. When Jeanie said "Americans," it didn't sound like a compliment.

"Look at these guys," she said, pointing at two powerfully built young men who sauntered by wearing only red bathing suits and wolfish grins. "They parade around like stallions. I have a real hard time finding Jewish men with what I consider Jewish values. A lot of Jews today believe that how you look or what you do for a living is what you are. That isn't Jewish, that's American."

"What's Jewish?" I asked.

"Jewish is being a mensch. Jewish is caring about tradition. Anyway," she said, gesturing at the room, "it sure as hell isn't about this stuff. . . . The thing is, my parents were in the camps. They're real Jews, and so am I. I wouldn't want my children to have a father who was an outsider."

Jeanie's father, a small businessman in Queens, survived Auschwitz. Her mother was orphaned at seven and spent her childhood hiding from Germans in the Polish woods. Jeanie was educated at a girls' yeshiva in Queens, and at Columbia, where she got an M.A. in social work. No longer Orthodox, she is still militant on the subject of gentiles. "I'm very, very careful about picking non-Jewish friends. That's a statement, I guess, about how little I trust them. When I hear a woman at work talking about rich Jews or whatever, I look at her and think, 'This chick would send me to the gas chamber.' I can't help it, it's just the way I feel."

Jeanie's entry in the *Meeters' Digest*—"hip, cool, healthy woman" —was a fair self-portrait. Her hobby is painting and she knows the Manhattan art scene and the fashionable clubs and restaurants. Her conversational style was funny, direct, and surprisingly candid.

"I'm up here for exposure," she said, dissecting her case with the curious dispassion of many of the singles I talked to. "I turned thirty this year and I'm pushing myself now. I want to get married, and I don't want to get schlepped into any long relationships." She lives at home, for the sake of economy, but that doesn't bother her. "My parents are religious, but they're also practical people. They know what you have to do to get married in America, and they trust me to lead my own life."

A handsome even-featured man in his thirties came over and introduced himself as Frank. This kind of intrusion is considered acceptable Singles' Weekend behavior. Frank had a copy of the *Digest*. "I bet I can guess your ad," he said to Jeanie in a bantering tone. He did not offer to guess mine.

"What do you want to bet?" asked Jeanie, suddenly flirtatious.

"How about a game of tennis? I guess your ad and we play tennis together," said Frank. They shook on it and, after a few broad hints, he found the ad. Jeanie was obviously attracted by Frank's easy manner and taut good looks. Just as obviously, our conversation was over. I had my project, she had hers.

I stopped by the message center to see how my ad was doing, and I was secretly gratified to find a stack of replies tacked to my number on the bulletin board. Suddenly I was a sought-after single, able to choose from Judy ("Let's meet, talk, and see what happens"), Carole ("You sound interesting, give me a call"), Marge ("Hi, author. I'm smart, interesting, tall, blond and love to read"), and an anonymous "Meet by fountain, I'm wearing black sweater."

Faced with such prosperity I chose Jackie, whose note was a cryptic, "Can copy, room K221." I called her from a house phone in the lobby. "This is 1680," I said, feeling foolish. "You know, the author."

"Hi, author," she said in a New Jersey accent. "I'll meet you downstairs at the bar in ten minutes. I'm tall, slim, and dark haired, and I'm wearing a red sweater and black ski pants. Think you can find me?"

I found her easily. She was an attractive woman of forty, with a wise-guy Jersey grin and a Kent going in the ashtray. She also had fingernails bitten to the quick and shifty brown eyes. I got the feeling she didn't enjoy meeting men in bars.

"I might as well tell you right away that I really *am* writing a book," I said. "I live in Jerusalem. So if you don't want to waste your time, I won't be offended if you don't want to talk to me." Jackie took a deep breath. She was relieved rather than put off, and her relief made her voluble.

"If you're really a writer, you're going to fall off your chair when you hear my story," she promised, taking a gulp of her Bloody Mary. "I'm a widow, okay? I mean, can you believe it? Do I look like a widow? One day I'm married, living in Glen Rock, New Jersey, with my husband, who's also my best friend, and two kids. And then, all of a sudden, at forty he drops dead. Just like that, drops dead. Of an *aneurysm*. And there I am, all alone."

It took Jackie months to begin looking for a new man. But despite the fact that she is attractive and financially secure, she hadn't found anyone she liked. "It's a couples world among the Jews in my age bracket," she said. Finally desperate, she decided to come to the Concord.

"Being back in this scene is shit," she said, gesturing broadly at the crowded bar. "I went through all this before, fifteen years ago. I even went to Singles' Weekends up here. Want to know something? Nothing's changed. The people haven't changed, the lines are the same, the only thing that's changed is me. When I came up here fifteen years ago, I was looking for a good time. Now I'm looking for survival."

Survival means a man, and for Jackie, with a split-level home in the suburbs and two children, a man means marriage. "My husband was a real tough act to follow," she said, and her eyes grew moist. "I'm ready to settle for less, that's the truth. I want somebody as tall as me, somebody not ugly—bright, a nice man. Does he have to be Jewish? No, not really. The first time that was a condition, but I've already got my kids; they're Jewish no matter what, so to be honest I'd have to say that it would be nice, but it isn't necessary.''

Jackie and I chatted for a while longer, but she was already distracted, looking around the room and checking her watch. "I'm supposed to be meeting a stockbroker and I don't know what he looks like," she said, unapologetic about having allotted me only half an hour. If I had been a prospect, she would have given me her phone number and told me to call her when we got back to the city; but I was merely an Israeli writer, and what good could that do her?

On the way out of the bar I ran into Huey, Dewey, and Louie, the brothers from Brooklyn. They were sitting on one of the gray couches along the promenade, making rude remarks to the passing women. "Hey, professor," one of them called out. "You're from Israel, you know Arabic, right?''

I smiled, and he made an obscene remark about my mother's anatomy. All three broke into raucous laughter, like the juvenile delinquents in *The Blackboard Jungle*.

I ignored the remark. "How are you guys making out?" I asked, genuinely curious.

The question ruffled them. "Hey, we're up here to relax and have a good time, period. That's it, okay? Don't worry about us.''

I took their advice and headed for the traditional Saturday night cocktail party, a Concord-sized bash with hors d'oeuvres and second-line booze for two thousand people, compliments of the management. The party marks the official beginning of Saturday night, which at Singles' Weekend is a combination of New Year's Eve and the senior prom.

Strangely, there still weren't many couples. Eighteen hundred people is too many to survey in one day, and most of the singles were still reluctant to make a commitment. Arrangements were tentative—"Maybe we'll have dinner together" or "I'll try to look for you at the show tonight," with "unless something better comes along" implicit and acceptable. They were all here for the same reason, and they conducted their transitions with a fine professional courtesy.

At the party I ran into Jeanie. She was alone. "How did it go with Frank?" I asked, and she sighed. "It was going great. We played tennis, we talked, and then he asked me to be his date for tonight."

"And?"

"And then it turns out that he's not Jewish. Of all the guys up here, I have to get a goy. My mazel. He told me how his cousin is married to a Jewish girl, like that makes him half Jewish or something. Shit!"

"What did you tell him?" I asked.

"That's just the problem. I didn't tell him anything," she said. "What was I *supposed* to tell him, that I don't go out with goyim? That sounds totally prejudiced. So I just told him I didn't want to go out with him tonight. I guess it hurt his feelings, but I just didn't know what else to do." She opened her purse and took out a dollar bill. "Listen, do me a favor. You're going back to Jerusalem, give this dollar to *tzedaka*, help me do a mitzvah. I gotta change my luck around here." I took the dollar and a few weeks later I gave it to a panhandler on Jaffa Road in Jerusalem.

At dinner that night I was seated with three still-unattached female social workers from Long Island, a fleshy young man from New Jersey who sold televisions, and the only black woman at the hotel. She told me she worked for a radio station in New York and had been given a free weekend at the resort as a bonus. "Looking for a husband?" I asked, and she laughed. "Not in this crowd, baby. I'm just here for the skiing."

Dinner was an edgy affair, carried on through a hail of aggressively cheerful chatter that couldn't obscure the central fact—no one at our table had found anyone yet. We were in the midst of a derisive analysis of the dining room's Leif Ericsson decor when the oldest of the social workers suddenly burst into tears. "I can't believe I let you talk me into coming," she said bitterly to her friends. "I feel ridiculous. I don't belong here. If my husband and I were still together . . ."

She fled from the table, followed by one of her friends. "No one's said a word to her since we got here," explained the other. I guessed she would spend the rest of the weekend alone in her triple-occupancy room, but I underestimated her resilience; after dinner I spotted her on the promenade, talking to a bald man in a powder-blue sports jacket and from time to time looking over his shoulder.

The show that night was a reverse of Friday's—black comedienne and white singers. The comic's act was a series of jokes about her Jewish husband, and it had the virtue of brevity. The singers were Lenny Coco and the Chimes, a doo-wop group that had a hit with "Once in a While" back in the early 1960s.

The Singles' Weekend entertainment policy seems to have been set sometime around 1962. The Chimes, I was delighted to note, were still in fine voice. They sang standards of the doo-wop repertoire that the audience was, for the most part, too young to remember. But it didn't matter. People applauded loudly, making a display of enthusiasm and high morale.

After the show, crowds once again surged through the hallways and mobbed the bars and lounges. There were fewer bottles of beer tonight, more hard liquor, and the women were drinking too. There was a feel of Las Vegas about the place—the same timeless rush of energy, people running on adrenaline, hope, and alcohol.

The finish line was in sight, but here and there people were beginning to fade. A thin, balding man sat on one of the gray sofas with his head buried in his hands. Nearby, two exhausted young women leaned against each other for support. In the abandoned game room, an overweight woman in a black dance outfit sat alone, glumly playing Pac-Man.

It was past two when I decided to go upstairs. A man about my age took the elevator up with me, his room key already in his hand. We rode in silence, but when we reached our floor he looked at the key, said "Fuck it," and pushed the down button, an inveterate gambler determined to give it one last roll.

On Sunday morning at breakfast, the atmosphere was once again like a college dorm—this time on the day after finals. People sat at the round tables eating as much as they wanted and reading *The New York Times*—the first contact many had had with the outside world since Friday.

I had a date for breakfast, a woman I had picked out of the *Digest*. Her name was Sherri, but I knew her as No. 524: "Blond-haired, blue-eyed Zionist who is tired of short JAPs.'' Hers was the only ad that mentioned Zionism or Israel, and I was intrigued. ''What kind of people answer an ad from a Zionist?'' I asked after we had introduced ourselves.

Sherri shrugged. ''I don't know, you're the only one who answered it,'' she said. ''I mean, there aren't a lot of people around here who even know what a Zionist is.''

I could see her point. There were eighteen hundred Jews at the Concord that weekend, but an outsider wouldn't have guessed it. Most of them could have been any kind of ethnic Eastern Seaboard Americans—Italians, Greeks, even Irish. Their culture was the culture of the New York middle class, their language the dialect of the outer boroughs, their aspirations shaped more by the American dream than by any particular Jewish sensitivity.

They kept their distance like Americans, too. Throughout the weekend I met dozens of people, the men sizing me up as a competitor, the women as a prospect. But only Jeanie and, I realized with surprise, Huey, Dewey, and Louie from Brooklyn had related to me as an Israeli or a Jew. The only Yiddish words I heard all weekend were in Jackie Eagle's stand-up routine; the only Hebrew, a few words spoken by the special education teacher in the nightclub on Friday night. There had been no Jewish songs, no Israeli dancing, not a single Jewish conversation that I hadn't initiated. And there had been no feeling of intimacy, no hint of the peculiar mix of affection, aggravation, and curiosity that Jews normally evoke in one another.

Finding a Zionist among these people was a warming experience. Sherri spoke my language, the language of Jewish obligation and concern, and I was happy to discover a kindred spirit.

''It seems like half the people I know have married goyim,'' she said. ''It's such a tragedy. . . . There won't be any Jews left in this country in another fifty years. After all we lost in the Holocaust, when I hear about people who just drop out like that, it makes me want to break down and cry. . . .''

''Well, at least you won't have to worry about that,'' I said. ''We have a lot of problems in Israel, but intermarriage isn't one of them.''

She looked at me with genuine surprise. ''Oh, I'm not planning to live in Israel,'' she said. ''I work with Young Judea and I think aliyah is very important; and if they ever needed me over there in an emergency, I'd be the first one on the plane. But I can't live there. See, I'm engaged to this man who lives in Denver, and I'll be moving out there in the spring." I had been in Denver a few weeks before; it is the intermarriage capital of America, an estimated seventy percent, the perfect place for an American Zionist to raise her children. We chatted for a few minutes more, and then she wished me *Shalom ve le'hitraot* and went to an aerobics class.

By this time, people were already starting to assemble in the lobby for checkout. It is a part of the Concord's lore that it is never too late—hundreds of couples have reputedly come together while waiting in line to pay their bills. But despite this legend, most of the singles seemed to have stopped trying. The mood was resigned, even mellow. They had given it their best shot, made the effort. The lucky ones had succeeded, but even the wallflowers seemed relieved to be getting back to their comfortable, everyday selves. For the first time all weekend I heard real, unconstrained laughter.

Near the checkout desk I saw Frank the Goy, tweedy and dejected, sitting on his suitcase and waiting for the valet to bring his car around. For a moment I considered going over and telling him the truth—that it was nothing personal, he had just picked the wrong Jewish girl. Statistics were on his side—probably not one woman in ten would have refused a date with a gentile on principle. He looked grimly at his watch, and I imagined that he had decided to take his next vacation in Vermont.

I was still debating whether to go over and cheer him up when I heard familiar voices. "Hey, Professor!" yelled Huey, Dewey, and Louie, and they surrounded me, grinning broadly. "Guess what? We got laid!" They gave each other exuberant high fives.

"Hey, that's great. Who was the lucky girl?" I asked, but they were too flushed with success to take offense. "The boys from Brooklyn strike again. Put that in your book!" one of them said.

Near the door I ran into Carol, my Friday night dancing partner. She was with a dapper man in his early thirties, who held her arm possessively. She introduced us and, perhaps wary of one of the storied last-minute moves, he mentioned pointedly that they would be having dinner together in the city that night. Carol nodded happily and took me aside.

"How did it go?" I asked conspiratorially.

"Big weekend," she said, beaming. "I met half a dozen guys, including Jeffrey. He's perfect—Jewish, lawyer, no kids, the whole shot. We met this morning at breakfast. And that's not all. You hear about that fire last night? There was some kind of little fire in a linen closet on my floor. Well, I even met a guy out in the hall in his underpants. I'm on a roll."

Carol gave me a kiss on the cheek and then wrote her phone number on the back cover of my notebook. "Call me," she said airily and went back to join her new boyfriend, a modern American-Jewish woman with numbers in her book and condoms in her purse.

CHAPTER EIGHT

LIFE CYCLES

In January I did what thousands of American Jews do every winter—I went to Florida. My final destination was Miami, but on the way I stopped at the University of Florida in Gainesville to give a Friday night lecture at the Hillel House. "You're going to love the rabbi," a friend of mine who knew the campus told me. "His name is Gerald Friedman, but everybody calls him Yossil. He used to be a Satmar Chasid. There aren't too many people like him in northern Florida."

That seemed like an understatement; it was hard to imagine a Williamsburg yeshiva bocher among the tan coeds and fraternity boys of one of America's premier party schools.

I met Friedman in his office near campus on Friday around noon. He turned out to be a pudgy man in his late forties whose appearance didn't betray his Chasidic origins. He was clean-shaven except for a neat little mustache, wore black framed glasses, and had a square, even-featured face that made him look a little like Steve Allen. On his head he wore a red knit yarmulke, which he took off when we went out to lunch.

I had been expecting to stay at a hotel, but Friedman wouldn't hear of it. He insisted I spend the night with him and his wife, Dora, a concentration camp survivor. I could, he said, share a room with his twelve-year-old son, Akiva. It didn't seem like the ideal arrangement and I tried to get out of it.

"I wouldn't feel right smoking at your place on Shabbat," I said, but he waved away the problem. "If you don't feel right about doing it, don't do it. But if you want to smoke, smoke. We're not that strict, and I want you to feel comfortable." I couldn't think of any other objections. Cornered, I accepted his invitation.

After lunch, Friedman suggested that we go to his place to "freshen up for Shabbes." Dora was preparing a kosher meal for the more than one hundred people who would be at the Hillel that night, but Yossil had nothing to do until sundown, when he was supposed to lead services. "Friday nights are sweet at our Hillel," he said. "We make a real Shabbes. You'll see."

On the way to Friedman's suburban tract house we talked about Israel, which he knew well. He was diffident and a little shy, and I wondered why my friend had thought I'd love him. To me he seemed like a more or less normal Hillel rabbi—intelligent, serious, and a bit ponderous. It would, I thought, be a long weekend.

When we arrived, Friedman pulled his car into the driveway and got out. The house next door had a basket mounted on its garage. A basketball lay on the lawn. Friedman took off his jacket, exposing a large potbelly, and picked up the ball. "Do you play basketball?" he asked. "I used to," I said, recognizing the moment when the rabbi demonstrates that he is a regular guy by tossing up an awkward shot.

Instead he gave me a long, appraising look, whipped the ball around his back and, tie flying, faked a move to his right, dribbled gracefully to the left, threw a head fake and hit an eighteen-foot jump shot. "Bob Cousy!" he yelled, retrieving the ball.

For the next five minutes I watched, astonished, while Yossil Friedman of Williamsburg put on a show. He moved around the court, sinking jump shots and hooking with both hands, or charging the basket with leaping, grunting aggressiveness. He rarely missed, and although he was sweating heavily he didn't seem at all tired. Finally he invited me to try to guard him.

I got between him and the basket, and he dribbled slowly. Suddenly he faked to the right, switched hands and flashed by me to make a lay-up. "How many Jewish guys you know can go to their left like that?" he crowed.

Friedman brought the ball out again, working toward the basket, with me following. "What are you, five-eleven?" he guessed with expert accuracy. "I'm five-eight. Watch this." He pivoted and threw up a graceful hook that swished through the net. "Guys *six-eleven* can't stop that shot," he said with the pride of a high school letterman.

For half an hour Friedman and I bounded around the court. He played with the happy abandon of a teenager, and seemed disappointed when his son, Akiva, came out to tell us it was time to get dressed for services. He eyed the basket, yelled "Bob Cousy," and hit a twenty-foot set shot. Grinning, he threw an arm over Akiva's skinny shoulder and started walking toward the house. Suddenly he broke away, scooped up the ball, and tossed in a long running shot. "Bob Cousy goes in to dress for Shabbes," he hollered, and broke into a Chasidic melody.

As we were dressing, Friedman, no longer shy, told me about himself and his voyage from Williamsburg to Gainesville. In Brooklyn his father had been a kosher butcher and his uncle, Lipa Friedman, had organized the Satmar sect politically. "He taught them how to vote, how to get poverty money, how to deal with America, the whole shmeer," Friedman said.

Growing up in Brooklyn, Yossil spoke Yiddish at home and attended a neighborhood cheder and, later, Torah V'Das Yeshiva. As a boy he looked and talked like the other Satmar children, but he was different. Unlike Mendel the Chasid, he wasn't satisfied with a single glimpse of Roy Rogers. Yossil Friedman wanted America.

"It all started with basketball," he said. "I was crazy about the game. . . . Well, I guess I still am. But as a kid, I couldn't get enough. I used to skip school and go out to playgrounds in other neighborhoods, dressed in a black suit and white shirt with *tzitzes* hanging down and my *payes* flapping. I might have looked a little strange, but I played on every tough court in New York—Bridge

Park Plaza, Manhattan Beach, Avenue B in Brooklyn—you name it, I played there. In those days, I wanted to be a professional basketball player.''

"What happened?" I asked.

Friedman smiled, knotting his tie and slipping on a dark suit coat. "I didn't become one. I became a Hillel director. Come on, let's go to services. It's Shabbes." On the way to the car, Friedman, dressed in a suit, took an imaginary jump shot at the basket in his neighbor's driveway.

There were more than a hundred people at the Hillel House when we arrived. Friedman threw a tallis over his shoulders with practiced ease and began to chant a Chasidic tune. The congregation of students and faculty joined in and within seconds the sanctuary was full of music. Friedman sang with his eyes closed and a dreamy half smile on his face.

As the service progressed, someone handed me a mimeographed sheet. It had the words to a couple of Chasidic tunes, and several short Chasidic parables that all began, typically, with variations of "One day Reb Moshe was walking in the woods near Vilna . . ." In America, Jewish stories usually take place someplace else.

When the prayers were over, Friedman invited the congregation to the roast chicken and kreplach soup dinner that his wife had prepared. The food was delicious and Dora, a curly-headed, vivacious woman, raced around the room to make sure everyone had enough. Every few minutes, Friedman burst into a melodic chant, keeping time on the table by banging his knife and fork. He seemed almost unaware that he was singing, but people looked over at him and smiled fondly. "Yossil's still a Chasid at heart," Dora said to me as she sailed by with a tray of dark meat and baked potatoes.

After dinner I talked about Israeli politics. It was a speech I had given before, and it seemed to go over well enough. But later that night, after we got back to his house, Friedman took me aside and gently protested.

"You were very good, very *informative*," he said, making the word a pejorative. "But on Shabbes, a Jew needs more than information. A Jew needs something for the 'neshama,' the soul. You can't talk to Jews about Eretz Yisrael and just give them information. To a Jew, Eretz Yisrael is a sweet place, not just another country."

I was stung by the criticism and began to argue that information—and not schmaltz—is exactly what Jews need to hear about Israel. Friedman cut me off gently, putting his hand on my arm. "Listen, I might be right, I might be wrong. Think about it, that's all I'm saying. To another person I might not mention it at all, but I feel I know you. I know more about you than you think. After all, we played ball together."

Dora came in, after supervising the cleanup effort at the Hillel. She is a warm, articulate woman who came to the States as a girl after World War II and was raised in an Orthodox home in Philadelphia. She gave Yossil an affectionate hug, went into the kitchen, and emerged a minute later with three cups of tea.

We sat in the Friedmans' living room, talking quietly about Akiva's upcoming bar mitzvah. Yossil had just received a letter, in Yiddish, from an aunt in Brooklyn, imploring him to make sure that the affair would be kosher. He was amused by the letter—it never would have occurred to him not to have a kosher party—and dismayed that his family has so little confidence in him.

"It must have been hard for you to get out of that world," I said, thinking of Mendel and the *chopsim* patrol of Williamsburg. Yossil laughed and looked at Dora. "It wasn't easy. In those days I lived a schizophrenic existence. By day I was a yeshiva boy, by night I used to get into regular clothes and hang out in the Village. That place was like magic for me back then, all the coffeehouses and the clubs. And then one summer I worked as a bellhop in the Catskills. That was the beginning of the end. I went to the Concord and drank a daiquiri and watched people dancing the cha-cha-cha. I promised myself I'd learn to dance, and when I got back to the city I began to hang around Killer Joe Piro. I got so good that I wound up as a Latin dance instructor at the Dale Institute in Manhattan."

Yossil also studied English literature at Brooklyn College; his first job was teaching English at his old yeshiva, Torah v'Das. By this time, though, he was out of the Satmar community for good.

"I still go home to visit," he said. "People are happy to see me, and I'm happy to see them. They have no idea what a Hillel director does, but they know where I come from and who I really am. Their attitude is, 'You've come for a visit, it's good to see you again.' My family accepts me with love, but they don't understand my world.''

Yossil and Dora want their son to know his Satmar roots, and occasionally they take him to visit Brooklyn. ''Akiva's bar mitzvah has caused us to seriously consider sending him to New York to a Jewish school,'' Yossil said. ''You can't carry Yiddishkeit on the narrow shoulders of a nuclear family. Our son needs hard learning and a Jewish environment. We want him to have that, but we won't send him to Satmar. Even I couldn't survive there anymore. It's very hard to find the proper balance for Akiva.''

Yossil Friedman has no illusions about the power of America. He himself was seduced by Bob Cousy and Killer Joe, and although he has enough residual Jewishness to last a lifetime, he can't be sure even about his own children. He and Dora have created a Jewish home in Gainesville; but, like the mimeographed Chasidic stories at the Hillel, it draws its sustenance from other times and other places.

''You know, I named our Akiva after Rabbi Akiva,'' said Dora. ''He was always a special hero of mine, a real 'ohev israel' [a lover of Israel].''

Friedman looked at her fondly. ''He was a hero of mine, too,'' he said with a smile.

''Yes,'' she replied with gentle insistence, ''but that name was my idea, Yossil.''

Friedman gave her a look of mock disagreement and then broke into a Chasidic song about the famous rabbi. ''I could sing six or eight songs about Rabbi Akiva right now,'' he said, smiling. ''That's a yeshiva thing to do. Not just to know, but to *show* that you know. That's what my kind of education gives you—that, and a feeling of pity for other Jews who don't know what you do, Jews who have traded a place in the Palace for a condominium in Florida.''

We sat up late talking about family things. Strangely, I felt very close to the Friedmans. I grew up as an assimilated kid in the Midwest; in those days I never even met a Chasid or a Holocaust survivor. But after twenty years in Israel, I understood the Friedmans perfectly, and they understood me. That night at their place we talked Jew talk—not Israeli politics or federation business, certainly not religion—just simple conversation among members of the same tribe, people with shared values and a common understanding of the world.

"You know what the saddest thing is?" said Yossil. "People down here don't understand that Judaism isn't just about being—it's about doing. I can teach if I have to, and I can counsel if I need to, but first and foremost I'm not a Hillel director, I'm a Jew. Jews *do*. They lead Jewish lives."

"I went to a conference not long ago," said Dora, "on 'Intermarriage: Prevention and Cure.' There was a whole room full of Conservative rabbis, and not one had any idea what to do. One got up and said, 'The converts I have are better than born Jews.' Imagine that. I've got nothing against converts, but how could he say a thing like that? How much Yiddishkeit can a convert have?"

Friedman sighed. The Jewish students at the University of Florida don't have much Yiddishkeit either. "There's so much alienation here. People don't want to come even to your sweetest programs. They have no Jewish imagination, no Jewish knowledge or growth. They come to college knowing four Jewish songs, and they leave with the same four songs.

"Look, can you call yourself a basketball player if you can't play?" he said. "Jews down here settle for so little. The boy comes home with a girl and the mother says, 'Thank God she's Jewish.' What's that? What does it amount to?" Yossil leaned over and gave Dora a warm, un-self-conscious hug. "They should ask, 'Does she sing like a Jew? Can she make love like a Jew?' "

Dora giggled and ruffled her husband's hair. Yossil seemed suddenly abashed, and he smiled like a little boy. "Don't get excited, I got that last line out of a Marvel Comic," he said, and broke into a Chasidic tune.

"Conversion to Judaism in one day," read the ad in *The Miami Herald*. "Six months of instruction in one eight-hour seminar. Join others in this spiritual adventure." I was in Miami to meet the man behind the ad, Rabbi Dr. Emmet Allen Frank,* founder of

*In December 1987, less than a year after my visit to Miami, Emmet Frank passed away.

the All People's Synagogue of Miami Beach, the Crazy Eddie of American Judaism.

I called the number listed in the paper and got a recorded announcement. It began with a lilting baritone voice (which turned out to be Emmet Frank's) singing the opening line of "Oh What a Beautiful Morning." The recording then invited me to leave my name and number, which I did.

It took a couple of days, but Rabbi Frank eventually returned my call. I introduced myself and asked if he would be willing to explain his brand of Judaism to a puzzled Israeli. At first he was plainly unenthusiastic, a reticence I mistakenly attributed to a bad conscience. Later I learned that Frank had been having trouble with Meir Kahane's toughs, and he was afraid I might be setting him up for a hit.

Frank finally agreed to meet me at his synagogue, which was appropriately located over a branch of Citibank, on the corner of Collins Avenue and 75th, in Miami Beach. It is a Jewish corner, two blocks from the ocean, inhabited mostly by old, discouraged-looking people from New York. A kiosk carries the *New York Post* and *The Jewish Press*. There were challas and bagels for sale at Abraham's Kosher Shomer Shabbat Bakery. At Goldstein and Sons Strictly Kosher Meat Market, butchers in "Kosher Treat" baseball caps cut cheap pieces of brisket and rump for the elderly customers. A station wagon with HEBREW HOME FOR THE AGED on its doors cruised the quiet street like a truant officer looking for delinquents. The midday silence was reproachful; the people on Collins Avenue have no energy to waste on idle noisemaking.

On the door of the All People's Synagogue was a multicolored modernistic mezuzah and a warning: VANDALIZING A CHURCH OR SYNAGOGUE IS PUNISHABLE BY FIVE YEARS IN JAIL AND A $5,000 FINE. I rang the doorbell and after a considerable interval, during which I was inspected through a peephole, I was admitted. Throughout America, Jewish offices and institutions are guarded by sophisticated security precautions—bulletproof screens, closed-circuit television, and rent-a-cop guards. Usually these measures are directed against the threat of Arab terrorism; but at the All People's Synagogue, the danger was from other Jews.

Emmet Frank did not look like the kind of man who lives behind locked doors. In his late fifties, he was a cheerful, open-faced fellow with ginger hair turning gray and a reddish beard. That day he was dressed in a pink, yellow, and blue argyle sweater, matching socks, saddle shoes, and a blue silk racer's jacket. A huge diamond ring shaped like the Ten Commandments extended to the knuckle of his left index finger, and gold chains—one holding a small Chai, another a Star of David—were draped over his chest. The effect was splendid and eclectic, as if he had been dressed in shifts by Liberace, A. J. Foyt, and George Bush.

Rabbi Frank greeted me suspiciously, but after a minute or two of small talk he broke down and took me on a tour of his synagogue—a suite of three spacious rooms linked by connecting doors. The room on the left was dominated by an exhibit of his paintings—large, skillfully rendered oils on Jewish themes, many of them featuring ornate Hebrew calligraphy. Frank's artwork, according to a brochure he gave me, has hung in the Smithsonian Institute and in the lobby of the B'nai B'rith building in Washington. The brochure also listed his other accomplishments: "Artist, Violinist [with the Houston Symphony Orchestra], Singer, Writer [of an unpublished novel, *I Am God's Janitor*], Photographer, Teacher, Minister of God."

The room on the right was the rabbi's study, its walls festooned with plaques and awards. Back in the 1950s, Emmet Frank was considered a talented, promising young rabbi, a political liberal and something of a charismatic figure in the Reform movement. His walls bore witness to his period of respectability: a rabbinical ordination degree and doctor of divinity diploma from the Hebrew Union College, a certificate of appreciation from the Mid-Atlantic Council of the Union of American Hebrew Congregations, a plaque from Israel Bonds, and an award from the American Jewish Congress lauding his achievements as a civil rights pioneer in the state of Virginia.

The pinnacle of his career came in the early 1960s, when Frank served as the rabbi of a large temple in Alexandria, Virginia. Although he was happy there, he decided to go to Seattle, to an even larger pulpit. The move ended in disaster—he couldn't get along with the congregation and was fired.

Emmet Frank moved back East, to a small temple in Pennsylvania. But he didn't last long there, either. Like a former big league ballplayer on the way down, he drifted from one tank town to another, eventually winding up—unemployed—in Miami Beach. "I believe it was God's plan for me to come here. There are thousands of Jewish people who need my help and my services, and I don't think it's a coincidence that I found this place," he told me with a faraway look in his clear blue eyes.

The center room of Frank's synagogue was a miniature chapel with stained glass windows, blond wood pews, a small organ, and an ark covered with what appeared to be a Danish tapestry. The sanctuary resembled a tasteful Las Vegas marriage parlor—the right decor for a rabbi prepared, in his own words, "to marry anybody to anybody, anytime and anyplace."

"I advertise interfaith marriages," he said proudly, displaying his listing in the Greater Miami Yellow Pages: "Intermarriage, conversion, bris, bar mitzvah." There is a rabbi in New Jersey who publishes a kind of tout sheet of colleagues who will perform intermarriages, and under what conditions. Most of them demand that the non-Jewish partner study Judaism, or at least promise to raise the children as Jews. Frank was proud of the fact that he was the only rabbi on the list who has no conditions at all.

"I'll do a wedding in a Catholic or Protestant church, co-officiate with a minister or priest, whatever the couple wants. I sing, I chant, I have a beautiful robe. Believe me, nobody does a wedding like I do," he said. Frank's matrimonial services included a chauffeured ride to the chapel in the rabbi's $90,000 Silver Spirit Rolls Royce, driven by his son and disciple, Loring.

"Rabbis think that by not doing interfaith marriages they're saving Judaism. I suppose they think that if a couple can't find a rabbi, they won't get married," Frank told me, shaking his head at the innocence of his colleagues. "Actually, I'm saving Judaism, not harming it. I increase the number of Jews. If you chase Jews away, all you do is make them non-Jews. Besides, I'm not that different from a lot of other rabbis. They do interfaith marriages in the closet. I advertise, that's all."

It was the advertising that got Emmet Frank thrown out of the Central Conference of American Rabbis, the professional body of the Reform rabbinate. Although Frank had been an embarrassment for years, there were no grounds for his dismissal from membership. But advertising—unlike eight-hour conversions or performing weddings in a church—is a violation of Reform rabbinical ethics and his colleagues used it as an excuse for booting him out.

Rabbi Frank responded with a wounded defiance, stepping up his advertising campaign and sniping at his fellow rabbis on local talk shows. He also founded his own rabbinical association, FAIR (the Free Assembly of Independent Rabbis). Emmet Frank was its only member, but he hoped to attract followers. "Someday I may even open my own rabbinical school," he said grandly.

Emmet Frank was born and raised in the South and educated in Classical Reform congregations. His classmates at the Hebrew Union College remember him as an engaging young man, but an indifferent student. "There are still a lot of things about Judaism I don't know," he admitted. "But really, I don't need to know all that much. I'm a life cycle rabbi."

A life cycle rabbi, according to Emmet Frank, offers services to people who couldn't otherwise get them. Frank himself had no formal congregation—his experiences in Seattle and Harrisburg turned him against organized religion—but he claimed to have several thousand followers in Miami. He led Passover Seders for them at hotels or country clubs, conducts bar mitzvah ceremonies in backyards or on the beach. But most of his life cycle business came from performing weddings, more than one hundred a year, sometimes for couples who have traveled thousands of miles to be married by a rabbi.

The far-flung nature of Frank's ministry and the publicity surrounding it aroused considerable controversy and opposition. One of Frank's most vocal critics was Jewish Defense League chief Meir Kahane, who visited the All People's Synagogue a few months before.

"I invited him in and we talked for a while," Frank recalled. "He was actually quite pleasant. But then I heard a lot of noise downstairs. I looked out the window and saw a bunch of his supporters demonstrating. They were carrying signs that said EM-MET FRANK WOULD MARRY A GOAT TO A SHEEP. You know, they actually had a goat down there, with a yarmulke on its head and a tallis on its back, and they yelled up at me to marry it to a sheep. I hated that. I'm the chaplain for the local humane society, and I felt terribly sorry for the goat."

Frank called the police, and Kahane finally left, but the demonstration marked the beginning of a campaign to harass the spiritual leader of the All People's Synagogue. "I got abusive phone calls in the middle of the night, they put ads in the paper offering free phone sex and listed my home number. I got sent doo-wop records C.O.D. They made my life miserable. That's why I was afraid to meet you. I thought you might be one of them," he said in an apologetic tone.

Naturally Rabbi Frank never married a goat to a sheep. The closest he had come was a wedding he performed for a Jewish elephant trainer with the improbable name of O'Brien and his tightrope-walker bride. The ceremony was carried out in the elephant tent, a venue that allowed the groom's closest friends—three elephants with whom he worked—to take part by holding poles of the bridal canopy in their trunks. The fourth pole was held by a clown in whiteface. Frank showed me pictures of the groom and his extravagantly tattooed bride under the canopy. It was, he said, perhaps his finest hour as a life cycle rabbi.

The wedding business had its satisfactions, but it was in the area of conversions to Judaism that Frank was a pioneer. "I convert people in one day, and that's controversial," he said, "but let's be honest. How long do other rabbis take? Six months? A year at the most. Okay, so let's say a rabbi does a conversion in six months, one hour a week. And during that time, the student is sick once or twice, the rabbi can't make it once or twice, maybe they meet twenty times, something like that. That's, what, twenty hours? Thirty hours at the most. Mine takes eight hours. Now, what's the difference? You know, a lot depends on what kind of a teacher you are.

"I cover all the major holidays, teach them the symbols, the whole life cycle," he said. "I give a special emphasis to the Sabbath blessings. Then we finish up with a ritual baptism, right here." He pointed out the window in the direction of the beach. "I tell them, 'When you step into the ocean, you're stepping into God.' "

Frank estimated he had converted several hundred people since the seminars began. "Look, they don't remember everything. But I tell them, 'If you forget something, just give me a call.' " It was the only conversion program in the country that came with its own warranty.

There was a knock on the door. Rabbi Frank was immediately wary, afraid perhaps that it was more doo-wop records. He looked through the peephole before opening the door and welcoming his son, Loring, who joined us in the rabbi's study.

Loring Frank, a thin, nervous man in his late thirties with the credulous manner of a teenager, introduced himself as a marketing consultant; but his main job was serving as his father's acolyte. Like the sons of other successful men, he was being groomed to take over the family business.

"I'm training Loring to be a rabbi," Frank said blandly. "He's only been at this about six months, but someday I want him to take over my synagogue and FAIR." Loring nodded his enthusiastic approval of this master plan. I asked him if he had much Jewish background before entering upon his rabbinical training.

"Well, I believe in lighting candles on Friday night, and I go to temple once in a while, but I don't say a prayer after going to the bathroom or just go around praying all the time like the Orthodox, if that's what you mean," he said. "And my dad has taught me a lot. But you don't need to know everything. I mean, let's say that somebody wants to know about kosher. Then I'd send him to another rabbi who knows those rules. Personally, I'm macrobiotic, that's my style, but I can respect other people's beliefs, too. I'm just not worried about tiny details."

Loring acquired his knowledge of the big picture by accompanying his father on his rabbinical rounds—getting hands-on experience, like a plumber's apprentice. "We do brises, weddings, everything. I still haven't taught bar mitzvah training yet, but I will soon, won't I, Dad?"

Rabbi Frank nodded, a proud father. "I didn't push my son to become a rabbi. The Lord did."

"Hey, Dad, who was that guy who became a rabbi when he was about my age?" Loring asked.

"That was Rabbi Akiva, son," Frank said, clearly pleased with the boy's erudition. Loring slapped his knee. "Right, well, it's never too late. You know, I don't know why these Orthodox attack us. I mean, we don't attack them for doing their thing. What we want to do is to cater to the people, give them what they want. We don't necessarily expect them to change their whole lives just to be Jewish."

While I pondered this approach, Loring turned again to his father and, in a voice that indicated an oft-repeated routine, asked, "Dad, when was the Hebrew Union College founded?"

"1850, Loring."

"1850!" he exclaimed. "Well, who did ordinations before 1850? I mean, who ordained *Moses*? Or Jesus? Or, ah, Rabbi Hillel? There was no college back then, was there, Dad?"

Emmet Frank feigned surprise at the question. "You know something, you're absolutely right."

"You're not really going to do this, are you?" I asked him, the icy self-control of an afternoon melting fast in the blaze of Loring's enthusiasm. Loring himself must have sensed he had gone too far with the Moses comparison. In a concerned voice he sought reassurance from his father. "Dad, do you have to get a special license in Florida to perform weddings? I mean, if you tell them that I'm a rabbi, isn't that enough?" Frank confirmed this. "In Florida, all you have to do is be inspired by God, and you can be considered a clergyman. And any notary public can perform weddings."

Relieved, Loring turned to me again, this time for help. "You're an Israeli, what does Zipporah mean?" Frank beat me to it. "Zipporah was Moses's wife, son." Suddenly animated, Loring leaped out of his chair. "Hey, I just met this Israeli chick named Zipporah. I'm gonna give her a call, I'll be right back." He bounded out of the room.

Loring's girlfriend reminded Emmet Frank of Israel. "It's my spiritual home," he said. "I've been there a number of times. I'm not an aliyah Zionist, but I tell people in my classes that Israel is the distillation of four thousand years of Jewish history. I make certain that they understand that support for Israel is central to the Jewish experience."

Loring came back into the room and plopped back down in his easy chair. Zipporah was out, and her roommate didn't know when she'd be back. He listened dejectedly as his father explained the other requirements of his one-day conversions.

"I have four things I ask them to do. First, they must recite the Shema. Then I ask them: 'Do you wish to be a Jew? Do you promise to live a Jewish life to the best of your ability? Do you agree to circumcise your children according to Jewish law? Do you cast your lot with the Jewish people?' If they answer yes to all four, then I go ahead with the conversion.''

Loring, dejected no longer, shook his head in admiration. "If you listen to this for every day of your life for thirty-seven years—that's how old I am—do you still have to go to religious school to be a rabbi? I mean, what more do you need?"

"Exactly," said Rabbi Frank without false humility. "My family is related to the Vilna Gaon, and back in the old days, his kind of scholarship made sense. But today? I'm not going to make Loring study Talmud for a whole year when I can pick out the highlights for him. He needs to know the essence of Judaism, how to help people; and believe me, he can learn a lot more watching me than from a bunch of outdated laws.''

Emmet Frank suddenly snapped his fingers. "I just had a great idea. Remember when Loring mentioned Rabbi Hillel. Well, Hillel once converted a man standing on one foot. You know that story. Supposing I put an ad in the paper: 'Come to Rabbi Emmet Frank. He'll convert you while you stand on one foot.' How about that for a slogan?'' Loring shook his head in admiration and Emmet Frank closed his eyes in sweet contemplation of the next big breakthrough in American life cycle Judaism.

Emmet Frank's philosophy, neatly summed up by his son, is that people don't need to change their lives just to be Jewish. But not far away from the corner of Collins and 75th, in the posh oceanfront high-rises and sprawling haciendas of Miami, live a group of people with an opposite view. They are the Hispanic Jews of Florida, and they are determined not to change their Jewish lives just to be American.

There have been Latin Jews in Miami since the late 1950s, when Cuban refugees fled the Castro regime. Lately they have been joined by Jews from South American and Central American countries plagued by political instability. Today there are between five and six thousand Hispanic Jewish families in Miami, roughly half of them Cuban, and experts predict that there may be twenty thousand by the end of the century.

These Latinos differ in two important respects from other immigrants. First, they are very rich; there isn't a taxi driver, street peddler, or short-order cook among them. And second, they have no ambition to become "real Americans." They don't even want to become real American Jews.

"When I first came to this country—to Miami—I went to the Jewish Community Center," said Rafael Russ over dinner at Patrino's. Russ, called "Rafa" by his friends, is an athletic, darkly handsome man in his late twenties, with serious eyes, a well-attended mustache, and the self-confident charm of a Latin American diplomat. He came to America from Guatemala and, using family money, established himself as a successful entrepreneur. At home he had been active in the Jewish community and he naturally gravitated to the Jewish Center in Miami. His reception there left him shocked and angry.

"I met a man, and we played racquetball together," he recalled in careful, precise English. "We played racquetball every Wednesday for many months. But this man did not ask me about myself. He did not ask me about my family. And he told me nothing about himself. We played racquetball and he went home. That, to me, is what an American Jew is—he is a racquetball partner."

Rafa's companion, Valerie Shalom, nodded in agreement. A willowy young woman who looks a little like Jacqueline Bisset, she grew up in Barranquilla, Columbia, and came to the United States to study at Brandeis, and later earned an M.A. in education at Stanford.

"When I first came to Brandeis I experienced a kind of culture shock," she said in nearly accentless English. "At home, we lived in a Jewish world. We lived in Colombia, but we were Jews, not Colombians. I chose Brandeis because it was supposed to be a Jewish university. And then, when I got there, I found kids who were just Americans. They said they were Jews, but there was nothing Jewish about them. It was not at all my idea of what being a Jew is."

The waitress approached, and Valerie ordered for me: *"bistec de palomilla and moros y cristianos."* Her years in America have taught her that gringos like a little folklore with their Latin food, and she automatically translated *moros y cristianos*—a dish made of white rice and black beans—into "Moors and Christians." The waitress assumed that Rafa was also a tourist and asked in English for his order. Offended, he replied emphatically in rapid Spanish.

Both Rafa and Valerie socialize mostly with other Hispanic Jews. Rafa often attends the Cuban theater or goes to Latin nightclubs. Valerie, who loves to dance, frequents the Club International, where they play salsa music. Neither is married, and neither wants to marry an American.

"I have an affinity for Latin men or Israelis," she said. "We seem to have more in common. It is hard for me to understand the American Jewish mentality, even after all these years."

"How about non-Jewish Americans?" I asked.

"Never," she said. "I would never consider marrying someone who isn't Jewish. My identity means too much to me, my obligation to my people."

"I once had an American Jewish girlfriend," recalled Rafa, with a mirthless grin. "We were together for almost a year, but it did not work out. Why? She said that I was too macho, too Latin, ah, too *chauvinist,* although I do not consider myself to be macho. So I believe that I will be happier with a woman from the Hispanic community. And there is another reason. I do not expect to live all my life in America. I believe that it would be very difficult to take an American woman to another place."

"Yes, me too, Rafa," said Valerie. "I myself like America, but I see myself moving to Israel. My eyes are looking to Israel for the future."

"I'm not certain about Israel," said Rafa, "but I cannot see myself remaining in this country permanently, that is certain."

For many Hispanic Jews, the United States has retained something of its "evil giant to the north" image. These Jews were raised in places where Yanquis are resented; many of them came to Miami more out of necessity than choice.

"It is not safe any longer for people like us in Latin America," Valerie explained. "I know a man, a Jewish industrialist, who was kidnapped by the guerrillas and held for four months. His family paid the ransom of one million dollars and he was returned unhurt. Now he has a bulletproof car and bodyguards, and wherever he goes he carries a gun. But these will not protect him, and he knows that. He is just waiting to be kidnapped once again."

"Why does he stay?" I asked. Rafa, who knew similar stories

from Guatemala, shrugged. "This man cannot legally transfer his money outside of the country. And many such people have businesses so large that no private person in the country can buy them. And so they stay."

They stay, but their children are free to leave—and perhaps to take some part of the family fortune with them. They are safe and prosperous in Miami, but they are homesick, too; they miss the close-knit Jewish communities where they were raised.

"At home, on Shabbat, everyone went to the Jewish Center to be together," said Valerie. "Here, except for the Orthodox, Shabbat is just another day. People go to shopping malls, health clubs. The Jewish Center is just a place to go for a workout. None of us is Orthodox, but we need more than that for our Jewish lives. And we need a place to be by ourselves. It's nothing against American Jews, but we're different."

"American Jews think the Hispanic Jews are shit!" said Yosi Teitelbaum, the director of Hebraica, when I went to see him the next day. "The Cuban Jews have been in Miami for twenty-five, twenty-six years, and not one has been on the federation board. Why? Because they think we are shit. The truth is, we Latinos have been rejected by the gringos."

Teitelbaum put his feet up on his cluttered desk and peered out the window at the manicured lawn. Hebraica is located in a former country club in one of Miami's wealthiest residential areas. That day its tree-shaded grounds and spacious clubhouse were undergoing renovations. It is not the kind of place usually associated with persecuted minorities.

Teitelbaum is in his mid-forties, a potbellied man with a ready smile, a brash, bombastic manner, and more than a little charm. By profession he is a social worker, by temperament an activist with a confrontational style. Born in Argentina, he moved to Israel as a young man. The Jewish Agency sent him to Miami to help the Hispanic community organize itself; and he has chosen to interpret this task as a mandate for taking on the local establishment.

"The Cubans, who were the first to arrive, had a religious tradition but no community spirit," he told me, speaking in Hebrew. "They established two synagogues, one Ashkenazi and one

Sephardi. Both of them were Orthodox, of course; Latin Americans had no concept of American Reform or Conservative temples, and they still don't feel comfortable in them. The Cubans were happy just going to their synagogues and living their lives. It was enough for them.

"But then, the other Latinos began to come. They had a community tradition as well as a religious one. Most of them aren't what you'd call Orthodox, but they have good Jewish educations, they know Hebrew, at home they were all wrapped up in the life of the Jewish community. The main thing was that they were taught from birth to feel different from gentiles, from the people surrounding them."

Suddenly Yosi banged his hand on the desk for emphasis. "When the Latinos came to this country, they looked around at the American community and found a system that was a total disaster. Total shit! They want their own children to be Jews and marry Jews, the way it has always been. If the price of America is not being Jewish, or hardly being Jewish, they don't want to pay it. They say, 'Amigos, let us preserve our Judaism.' This is why they founded Hebraica."

Teitelbaum was interrupted by high-pitched children's voices squealing in Spanish. He heaved himself out of his chair and led me into the clubhouse, where, in a side room, a nursery school class was in progress. We opened the door, which bore the legend, "MIS HIJOS ESTÁN EN HEBRAICA . . . Y LOS SUYOS? (MY CHILDREN ARE IN HEBRAICA . . . AND YOURS?)." "These are our children," he said grandly, as if he and the nursery school teacher had produced them all personally.

We walked out to the clubhouse, where workmen were tearing up the dance floor. It is a kind of kosher Club Babaloo, where people like Valerie and Rafa dance to Rubén Blades, Roberto Carlos, and David Broza, sip strong Cuban coffee or rum punches, and feel the warmth of community in a strange land.

"This is an island," Teitelbaum said, gesturing around the clubhouse. "American trends don't affect us, and we don't want them to affect us in the future. We want to be independent. And we will work to insure that independence. Believe me, these people know what it means to be Jews, to live real Jewish lives. It is something they will never surrender."

It was a fine speech, spoiled only by the fact that Teitelbaum and I both understood that he was talking about doing the impossible. Over the coming decades the Hispanic community in Miami will undoubtedly grow in numbers and influence. It will fight with the federated establishment and eventually become a part of it. The Latin Jews will send their children to the Hebraica nursery school, dance to Israeli samba singers, support their synagogues, and stick to themselves. Some will dream of moving to Israel, and a few may even do it.

But no matter how much money they raise, no matter how hard they try to pass on their heritage to their children, no matter how stubbornly they struggle against America, America will win. Slowly, inexorably, their children and grandchildren will become American Jews—and then, Jewish-Americans. Like Jewish immigrants before them, the hijos of Hebraica will be enriched and impoverished by their new country. It is only a matter of time.

Forty minutes from Hebraica, along a palm-studded highway, is Century Village at Pembroke Oaks. Near its entrance is a billboard with the Century Village motto—"Where Life Has No Limits." The village is the kind of place where you can dream of living for a century, although most of its elderly residents would be delighted just to make it to the next one.

Century Village is officially nonsectarian, but more than eighty percent of the people who live there are retired middle-class Jews from New York's outer boroughs or from other large northeastern cities. (Midwestern Jews, by contrast, usually retire to Florida's west coast.) Gentiles, mostly Italian-Americans, comprise a tolerated minority.

The village itself consists of low-rise apartment buildings whose one- or two-bedroom flats are priced to attract retired civil servants, small-time merchants, and widows living on fixed incomes. In early 1987, the population was 3,600, but a recruiting drive aimed at attracting an additional 4,500 people was in full swing.

Public relations director Shirley Klein, an elegant, fiftyish former New Yorker, took a few minutes to explain the Century Village concept. "We try to offer people a great place to retire," she said with obvious sincerity. "Living here is like living at

Grossinger's or the Concord. Retirees have their own activities, their own culture. . . .''

The phone rang. Someone in the New York office wanted to discuss an ad scheduled to run in Jewish newspapers that weekend. Before getting down to business, Shirley took a minute to gloat. "How's the weather up there?" she asked. "Snowing? That's terrible. Down here? Seventy-five today and sunny. Yeah, it's perfect." Climate is the constant preoccupation in Florida, the great justifier. "I couldn't live up there anymore," Shirley said when she got off the phone. "I mean, it's nuts. Who needs that when you can have this?"

The complex at Pembroke Oaks is built for fun in the sun. It has elaborate sports facilities—a golf course, tennis courts, swimming pools, and in the middle of everything the Clubhouse, a multipurpose community center. Shirley pointed out the facilities on a map of the village. "You know why people love it down here so much?" she said. "Simple. This is the sleep-away camp they couldn't afford when they were kids."

Century Village is, indeed, a strikingly juvenile place. Gray-haired men with crooked brown legs wander around in play clothes, carrying golf clubs or tennis rackets. Women (there are four or five for every man) in leisure suits stroll the grounds in pairs, glancing flirtatiously at the geriatric Jewish jocks, or toss Frisbees to each other across the manicured lawn. Unlike the old people on Collins Avenue, the golden-agers of Century Village have energy to spare.

The local newspaper, *The Century Village Voice,* mirrors the obsession with fun. Its pages are full of articles about the acts due to play the Clubhouse nightclub—Keely Smith, Jack Carter, Patrice Munsel, and Freddie Roman—sports news, such as the results of the recent walkathon and exercise tips from the staff.

At first glance, Century Village seems to have everything. But something is missing. In this village of three thousand elderly Jews there are no children—no toddlers, no teenagers, and except for the staff, barely anyone under sixty. Nor are there any bearded elders on benches, gabbing away in Yiddish. The Century Villagers are a new breed of Old Jew—bronzed, vigorous, dedicated to a happy ending. Life without limits, Century Village style; a life without family or the friendships and obligations of a snow-filled lifetime.

"Most people here don't seem to miss their children very much," Shirley Klein confided. "Our society has gotten away from traditional, close-knit family units. Young people go away to college, old people go away to retire. Now, a lot of them *do* miss their grandchildren, but we tell them, 'Don't worry about your grandchildren, they're fine. Do what's right for you.' "

Century Village has a number of rules, but only one commandment: NO CHILDREN IN THE CLUBHOUSE. And since the Clubhouse is the heart of village life, site of the nightclub, theater, sports facilities, and meeting rooms, the rule might just as well be: No children in the village. Sometimes grandchildren do visit, of course; but they are second-class citizens. Considering the traditional Jewish obsession with children, it is an astonishing policy.

But then, the residents of Century Village are not traditional Jews; they are the first generation of *American* Old Jews, people like Laura and Jake.

Laura is a crisp, rosy-cheeked woman of about sixty-five who left Brooklyn after forty years as a union clerk. Jake, a few years older, came down to Florida after selling his small clothing shop in Queens. A ferret-faced chain smoker, he has the teasing patter of a neighborhood retailer. Neither one lives within a thousand miles of their children.

"I came down here not just for the sunshine," Jake said. "I came down for a new life, a brand new start. Sure it's hard at first, but you meet friends, you forget about the street you lived on. As far as kids are concerned, it depends. Lemme tell you, a lot of people here created monsters. Plenty of them don't even come down for a visit."

Laura disagreed. She is a placid woman, and she discussed the issue with the detachment of a pop psychologist on *Donahue*. "It's true to some extent that we created takers. We never taught our children to give, but that's our fault, not theirs. Don't forget," she said, turning to Jake, "our generation was raised the same way. We were brought up on doing our own thing, only they didn't call it that in the old days. Our parents came from Europe and they gave us what they didn't have. They taught us to take care of ourselves first. And that's the way I still feel today. You have your own life. I don't want to live near my kids. I brought them up to feel the same way I do. I love 'em, and I love those grandchildren, but I'll tell you, I don't want them calling me every time the baby has a stomachache.''

It was a perspective I had never considered. The people at Century Village are not Portnoy's mother but Portnoy himself—selfish, individualistic, pleasure-oriented. Their accents are Flatbush or Jersey City, not Minsk or Vilna. Their furniture isn't covered with plastic slip covers. Their kitchens have only one set of dishes (and that rarely used; they prefer to eat the half-price early bird special at the nearby mall). There are no kugel bakers, minyon makers, or cheek pinchers here—just guys and gals having a blast at summer camp.

"These people are in such good shape that you can't even tell how old they are," said Angela Varone, the clubhouse director. But they can easily tell how old you are, and visitors under fifty feel a certain amount of hostility. "They tend to be a little defensive with outsiders, especially younger people," Angela explained. "A lot of people treat the elderly like they were retarded or something. But their attitude here is, 'Hey, I'm no dummy, I've been around. I want some respect.' We try to keep them from feeling inferior just because they're getting older, but sometimes that feeling of inferiority comes out in a basic dislike of younger people."

Age is the great common denominator at Century Village; it creates a sense of solidarity against the outside world. The Italians occasionally complain that the Jews dominate the entertainment schedule, but there is very little friction. "Age gives them more in common than ethnic differences divide them," Angela told me. "And they do have a lot in common. There isn't that much difference between a Jew from Brooklyn and an Italian from Brooklyn. They're all just people. There are even Italians in the Yiddish club."

Lou Steiner confirmed this when he joined Laura, Jake, and me at the clubhouse. A spare, dapper man who still works as a union organizer, Steiner came down to Florida after the death of his wife and immediately began trying to raise Jewish consciousness among his fellow Villagers. One of his pet projects is the weekly Yiddish sing-along. "Sure we have gentiles," he said. "Why not? Most of the Jews down here don't know Yiddish any better than they do."

Steiner led us to the sing-along—sixty or so senior citizens in shorts and alligator shirts sitting on folding chairs in a large rec room. On the stage in front of them, a flabby, middle-aged man with an Israeli accent sat at an upright piano and went over the words of a song. I wasn't surprised that the conductor was Israeli; increasingly, American Jews, even elderly ones, need to import Israelis to help them carry out Jewish activities.

Someone handed me a mimeographed sheet with lyrics written in English transliteration. Laura, who is the head of the Yiddish speakers group, doesn't read the language; most of the group's members can barely speak it. They repeated the words of a Purim song—"Hynt is Purim Brider"—in tentative voices, and then sang the song in powerful American accents.

"Sixty years ago I heard the great Yiddish entertainer Tomaschevsky sing this song," Jake said to me in a loud whisper. "Now listen to it." He waved his hand in disgusted dismissal. "Feh!"

Lou Steiner, who was standing nearby, caught the gesture and waved his own hand. "I've been trying to raise money for a synagogue down here," he said. "You think it's easy? These people don't care about being Jewish anymore. We've got a little Conservative congregation, meets in one of the buildings here, but we need a real place of our own."

"How many people attend services, usually?" I asked. A grim look came over Steiner's face. "I won't even tell you. The truth is, it's a shame before God. You need a minyan here? After all, we got a lot of people need to have a minyan from time to time. You go in the clubhouse, they're playing cards. You even mention a minyan, they say 'Leave me alone.' Sometimes they even tell you, 'I'm not Jewish, I'm Spanish.' " He looked around and lowered his voice to a confidential tone. "You won't believe it, but there are men here, right in this room, who refuse to say Kaddish for their own wives."

Jake stubbed out his cigarette with an angry gesture. "It's just assimilation. That's all it is, nobody's Jewish anymore. Believe me, sometimes I cry at night just to think of it." He nodded at the group, singing now in their flat, broad American accents. "Just listen to them," he said plaintively. "Tomaschevsky is spinning in his grave."

The Century Villagers are the first generation of Eastern European Jews to run all the way through the American experience, from birth to retirement. They have the memories of immigrants' children and these memories matter; but the real influence on their lives has been America—its language and rhythms, culture and ethos. They are charter members of the first Jewish generation taught, in Laura's phrase, "to do its own thing." And here, in Florida, at the end of the cycle, in the twilight of their lives, who can blame them if that thing has turned out to be mixed doubles, early bird dining, and the fox-trot.

CHAPTER NINE

THE PROMISED LAND

S hortly after I began my trip to the United States, Elie Wiesel was awarded the Nobel Peace Prize for his work commemorating the Holocaust. Jews, including Henry Kissinger and Menachem Begin, had won the prize before, of course. But Elie Wiesel is the closest thing America has to a secular chief rabbi, and his selection was a source of pride and excitement to Jews all across the country.

Other Jewish news was less upbeat. Revelations about Kurt Waldheim's Nazi past continued to surface. New York's Cardinal John O'Connor visited Israel, snubbed its leaders on orders from the Vatican, and was given a televised dressing-down by the heads of some Jewish organizations. Susan Miller, a Reform convert from Colorado, won Israeli citizenship in a landmark Supreme Court decision in Jerusalem—and proceeded to leave the country the next day. On the cultural front, borscht-belt comic Jackie Mason scored a Broadway triumph with a one-man show composed largely of Jewish put-downs.

By far the two biggest Jewish news stories of the year were the Boesky scandal and the Pollard affair. Both made headlines far beyond the Jewish community and both were particularly disturbing because they recalled long-discredited anti-Semitic stereotypes.

Ivan Boesky a Wall Street speculator who was caught in an illegal, multimillion-dollar insider trading scam was a former head of the New York Jewish federation. But despite his high profile, the fallout from the Boesky scandal was surprisingly mild. Many of Boesky's fellow Jewish leaders feared that the affair would conjure up old images of crooked Jewish business practices; but the grass roots reacted with a shrug. A generation before, when John Kennedy was assassinated, six million Jews had the same simultaneous thought—*I hope the killer wasn't one of ours.* But Ivan Boesky didn't shoot a president, and American Jews are no longer so insecure.

Not long after Boesky was caught, I spoke at a Hadassah luncheon in Chicago. I shared the dais that day with a sweet, blue-haired lady who gossiped through lunch about her garden, her grandchildren, and her many trips to Israel. But when I mentioned Boesky, she paused with a fork full of Palmer House chef salad halfway to her mouth and fixed me with a flinty look. "If *they* start counting up the Jewish crooks," she said, "*I* start counting up the Jewish Nobel Prize winners . . . and screw 'em."

Of all the Jewish news that broke during my months in America, no story was more dramatic or discomforting than the Pollard affair. Jonathan Jay Pollard was an American naval security officer who was caught stealing and selling U.S. military secrets to Israel and was sentenced to life in prison. Like Boesky, Pollard conjured up an old anti-Semitic charge—that Jews give their first loyalty not to their countries of residence, but to one another.

The Jewish establishment was clearly spooked by the Pollard case. Some of its leaders loudly applauded the harsh sentence, and a delegation came to Jerusalem to publicly denounce Israel for having recruited an American Jew. They had a point; the operation was stupid and irresponsible. But there was also no mistaking an undertone of fear, a hint of the ancient ghetto question: What will the goyim think?

Judging from public opinion polls, they didn't think much about it one way or the other—a *New York Times* survey revealed that eighty-two percent had no idea whom Pollard had been spying for. And, as in the Boesky case, there was surprisingly little concern among the Jewish grass roots. I could almost hear my Hadassah luncheon partner: "If *they* count up the Jewish traitors, then *I* count up the Jewish patriots . . . and screw 'em."

Most Jewish news stories in America have one thing in common—they relate to other times and other places. Since World War II, the energy and imagination of the American Jewish community have been outer-directed—toward Israel, the Holocaust, the plight of Soviet Jewry, and other causes and concerns. During my trip in America, only the Boesky scandal was strictly a domestic matter. The others reflected the centrality of Israel (the Susan Miller case, Cardinal O'Connor's trip to Jerusalem, the Pollard affair) and the Holocaust (the revelations about Waldheim, Wiesel's Nobel Prize).

This obsession with the Holocaust and Israel (and, to a lesser extent, Soviet Jewry) is understandable—they are major historical events. But it also clouds and distorts American Jewish life. Both the Holocaust and the establishment of Israel posed challenges that the American community failed to meet. All the memorials and UJA banquets cannot obscure the central fact: America's Jews did almost nothing to save Hitler's victims, and they haven't shared the real burdens of building the Jewish state.

The Holocaust poses a particularly vexing problem. If an event so unique may be said to have a lesson, it is clearly that anti-Semitism can happen even in a "civilized" Western country. But this notion pits history and logic against the present realities of American life.

Very few American Jews, especially those born since World War II, have personally experienced anti-Semitism more virulent than a curse or a snowball. Tell them that there is a latent hatred of Jews that could turn ugly and you are accused of paranoia or Zionist alarmism. On the other hand, assert that there is no anti-Semitism and these same people seem almost offended. The paradoxical fact is that most American Jews feel both very much at home and not quite safe. This ambivalence was obvious everywhere I went, but nowhere did I encounter it more starkly than in Colchester, Connecticut.

Colchester is the hometown of Jonathan Broder, the former Jerusalem bureau chief of the *Chicago Tribune*. Like most friends who meet in adulthood, he and I swapped stories about our boyhoods, giving them, in the process, a kind of mythical aspect. But even allowing for his formidable dramatic powers, Broder's hometown seemed a unique and intriguing place—a New England Jewish farm shtetel halfway between Chelm and Hartford.

Colchester was incorporated in 1699, and during its first two centuries it was an unremarkable Yankee hamlet whose economy was based on agriculture and the Hayward Rubber Company. But in 1895, the factory closed and Colchester was plunged into a depression. Three years later, a fire wiped out most of the downtown business district and, according to local historian Adam Schwartz, the town's existence was threatened.

Salvation came from an unexpected source. At about this time, hundreds of thousands of Eastern European Jewish immigrants were crowding into New York's Lower East Side. Several enterprising realtors began offering farm properties at bargain prices to Jews who wanted to escape the urban squalor. Within a decade, there were more than a thousand Jews in Colchester, and by World War I they made up about half the town.

In some ways, Jewish Colchester was like any other rural New England hamlet. The grown-ups scratched livings out of thin soil and raised poultry and dairy cattle. The kids won blue ribbons at the Hartford agricultural fair, joined the 4-H Club, and played baseball on the village square. And when America entered World War I, like thousands of other rawboned farmboys, they joined the Army.

But Colchester was different, too. Grange meetings were conducted in Yiddish. The local dry goods store stocked Shabbes candles and prayer shawls along with the usual farm implements and calico. And there weren't too many Yankee farm towns with a mikvah ritual bath, two Orthodox synagogues, and a kosher slaughterhouse.

Among the early Jewish settlers was Aaron Schwartz, who came to Colchester from Russia and established the S&S Leather Company. Today the firm is Colchester's major industry and its owner, Steve Schwartz, Aaron's grandson, is the leading man in town.

There is nothing rustic about Steve Schwartz. He is a sophisticated businessman in his early forties, a Brandeis graduate who met his wife, Carla, in college. A big-city girl from Brooklyn, Carla wanted to live in New York, but Steve was intent upon returning to his hometown. The Schwartz family is to Colchester what the Fords are to Detroit or the DuPonts to Wilmington. Steve had a sense of obligation and so he came home.

It is almost impossible to get to Colchester by bus. I took a Greyhound as far as Hartford, where Steve and Carla met me. We drove half an hour to reach Colchester, and when we arrived—at nine-thirty on a Friday night—the town was already asleep. The only signs of life were at the state police barracks on the road leading into town, and at a small pizza parlor off the main square. "Tomorrow I'll show you the sights," Steve promised.

Steve and Carla live in a large modern house with a swimming pool just outside of town on Route 2. They also have a place in Vermont. In Colchester they keep kosher; in Vermont, they do not. "Some people have two sets of dishes; we have two sets of houses," Steve joked.

The Schwartzes have two sons. The younger one was enrolled in a prep school in Hartford; the older one, Adam, was away at Harvard. Some weekends Steve and Carla drive up to Cambridge in the Jaguar that Carla gave him for his fortieth birthday. But Steve rarely drives the sports car in Colchester. "This is a working-class town," he said. "It's not Aspen or Stowe. We don't want to seem conspicuous. This isn't a Jaguar kind of town."

Before turning in, Carla proudly gave me a paper Adam had written about the town for his freshman history course. I read it in bed that night, and I could hear his father's pride in Colchester in the paper's concluding sentences. "Jewish farmers and their families were welcomed into the town, and eventually became an important part of it," Adam wrote. "Although they no longer make their living off the land, Colchester's Jews are tied to it, as inextricably as the oldest Yankee family, in this quiet New England town."

We got up early the next morning. Although it was Saturday, Steve wanted to go to his office for a few hours, and he volunteered to drop me off at the synagogue. On the way he gave me a tour of the town. Colchester is no longer an isolated hamlet—some of its residents commute to jobs as far away as Hartford—but it has retained its rural feeling. It is so far in the country that TV reception is a problem; so small that Steve and Carla can speedwalk from one end to another in half an hour; and so old-fashioned that the Old Market Ice Cream Parlour is the hottest spot in town.

There are still about eight hundred Jews in Colchester, but most of the old Jewish institutions are now historical landmarks. Steve pointed them out as we drove—a frame building that once housed the mikvah, a sprawling shingle mansion that used to be the Cohen Hotel, and the workshop of Levine & Levine, FAMOUS MAKER OF WOMEN'S SHOES, FOUNDED 1922. Only two synagogues are left; next to the one I attended that morning is Walter's Kosher Bakery, which Steve claimed has the best onion rolls north of Flatbush Avenue. And Walter isn't even Jewish.

The synagogue itself turned out to be a barnlike building, much larger than Colchester's depleted Jewish population now requires. Its fixtures are a written record of the congregation's history—virtually everything in the place is covered with a donor's plaque. These include a CHANDELIER IN MEMORY OF MR. AND MRS. ISAAC HOROWITZ; ETERNAL LIGHT IN MEMORY OF DR. AND MRS. HEYMAN; DOOR IN LOVING MEMORY OF HYMAN ALPERT; and my favorites—AIR CONDITIONER DONATED BY MR. AND MRS. MORRIS SCHULMAN and THE TEN COMMANDMENTS (a statue, not the original) DEDICATED IN MEMORY OF ISIDORE BROUNSTEIN.

It was Succot, the Feast of Tabernacles, and I was interested to see how the Jewish farmers of Colchester celebrated the agricultural festival. But the service that morning was unremarkable. Following the prayers, everyone gathered in a small ceremonial booth outside the synagogue, toasted the holiday with wine, and talked about their coming winter migration to Florida. "There aren't many Jewish farmers left around here anymore," Rabbi Scheindlin told me. "Most of them are retired. It's not easy to make a living in agriculture anymore."

I left the synagogue and walked through the town. Colchester is built around a village green, complete with white steepled church, red brick schoolhouse, and a war memorial. The roster of veterans on the monument tells the story of the town. Its Civil War vets had names like Hawthorne, Styles, and Johnston; but by World War I, the names had changed to Saul Agranovitch and Isador Blatt, Hyman Kravitzky and Julius Cohen. Dozens of Jewish boys served in World War I, World War II, and Korea. Three—Rudy Klein, Morris Heller, and Richard Adler—have stars beside their names.

I stood looking at the monument for a long moment; in Israel, the war memorials list soldiers with similar last names. Then I walked across the green to Tami's Cafe, where Sid Einhorn and old man Steg were chewing the fat.

Mr. Steg sat at the horseshoe-shaped counter sipping weak coffee and tapping a spoon to a Boxcar Willie rendition of "Lonesome Hobo" that was playing on the jukebox. He was born in Europe around the turn of the century and came to town as a young man. Now in his mid-eighties, he is still alert and dapper. For many years, Steg was the town assessor. He also served as president at the local Knights of Pythias chapter and as master of the Colchester Grange with the rank of Ceres.

Sid Einhorn sat across the horseshoe counter and munched a doughnut. Einhorn is a powerfully built fellow with a farmer's sloping shoulders and big weather-hardened hands. His father moved to Colchester around 1910 and worked as a cutter at the S&S Leather Company. Later, just after World War I, he bought a poultry farm, where Sid was born and raised.

"It was Little Israel around here in those days," said Einhorn, and Steg nodded in agreement. "I was six or seven before I spoke anything but Yiddish. I never even saw anyone who wasn't Jewish until the first grade."

"There weren't many goyim around then," Steg observed with the judiciousness of a retired politician, "but the ones there were were fine people."

"Fine people," Einhorn agreed. "A goy's a goy, but they were good people."

Einhorn bought his first farm when he was seventeen, a thirty-acre poultry operation, and he spent the next three decades raising chickens and cattle. But it was impossible to make a living as a small farmer, and after World War II he bought a feed and hardware store to supplement his income.

"When I first started out, chickens were still floor birds," he said. "In those days, one man could take care of seven thousand layers. But nowadays, everything's in cages. One man can take care of seventy thousand or eighty thousand birds. There's no way that small farmers can compete with that. So I gave it up in the mid-sixties. But I still get outdoors plenty. I go trout fishing and deer hunting. It's still great country up here."

"The greatest country in the world," said Steg, and tapped his spoon on his coffee cup for a refill.

As we were talking, Steve Schwartz came in. He greeted Einhorn, whose father used to sleep on the floor of Steve's grandfather's factory when he first came to town. He greeted Mr. Steg, who assessed his father's business. He greeted the waitress, who gave him a cup of coffee without being asked.

Steve Schwartz knows everyone in Colchester and everyone knows him. His factory employs four hundred fifty people—out of a population of eight thousand. The S&S Christmas party is the major social event of the Colchester calendar. The Schwartz family has been in town for almost one hundred years.

Later that afternoon, Jake Mitzengendler and Marcia Schuster dropped in at the Schwartzes' for a visit. Marcia is the daughter of another of Colchester's leading Jewish families; her father, Paul Schuster, started out hauling fruit to market and eventually established the Schuster Trucking Company. Jake is a newcomer by local standards. He came to the United States from the Soviet Union in 1960 and settled in Colchester. His arrival in town was dramatic; on his first day in school he built a large, high-flying paper airplane that, in the post-Sputnik era, impressed and frightened his classmates.

Steve Schwartz and Marcia Schuster began to reminisce about their town and its folklore. They recalled old man Balaban, the cleaner who wore your suit all week before returning it laundered on Friday; the regulars at the shul who always kept a bottle of schnapps hidden under the synagogue stairwell for their morning medicinal shots and referred to the members of the rival synagogue as "the mugwumps"; the time Yank Broder had a tryout with the Boston Red Sox; the days when special trains used to leave Grand Central Station for Colchester, bringing up citified Jews for a week of fresh air at the Cohen Hotel. They told stories about the redneck Yiddish-speaking farmers who would spit tobacco into the gutter as they idled in front of the general stores and ice cream parlors along Merchant's Row, across from the war memorial. There was a timeless quality to the nostalgia. Events from the early days mixed easily with anecdotes from recent years. Colchester folklore comes naturally to Steve Schwartz and Marcia Schuster; it is their birthright.

Toward evening, Marcia and Jake left. Steve and Carla and I sat in the darkening shadows and chatted about the town and its future. Steve hopes that one of his sons will come home after college and take over the family business, making him the fourth generation at S&S.

"I'm not sure that either of them will want to, and we won't get bent out of shape if they don't, but it would be nice," Steve said. "We have a big investment—and not just financial—in this place."

"You'd never consider leaving, would you?" I asked.

"No, I don't think so. But I'll be honest, I'm less sure today than I was a few years ago. Not long ago there was a kind of an anti-Semitic incident here in town. Nothing major, but still, it got us to thinking. That's when we sat down and made a contingency plan."

"What kind of contingency plan?"

"Nothing drastic," Steve said in a matter-of-fact voice. "Just some thoughts about what we'd do if we were ever forced to leave Colchester or the United States in a hurry. I'm sure we'll never need them, but . . ."

Suddenly I remembered the paper their son had written for his Harvard history course. " 'The Jews in Colchester are as firmly rooted in the land as the oldest Yankee families,' " I quoted. "Adam wrote that."

Steve thought for a long moment. "Did he? Well, he's right. We are rooted here. But we're not Yankees. And after Germany, well, you never know. I mean, you never really know."

While American Jewry focuses on the Holocaust and Israel, it has yet to come to terms with the clear and present danger of erosion from within. A generation ago, most Jews married other Jews; today, in many parts of the United States, this is no longer true. Sometimes the non-Jewish partner converts—according to the

UAHC, between four hundred thousand and five hundred thousand American Jews were born Christian. Often, however, this is not the case.

Experts dispute the impact of intermarriage on the number of Jews in America. But there is no doubt that it has drastically altered the ethnic composition and internal dynamics of the Jewish community. Converts, even the most dedicated, have no tradition of Jewish solidarity, no blood ties to other Jews past or present, and no inherited Jewish cultural attitudes or skills. They may be devout believers or active members of their congregations; but it is unlikely that they will ever scrutinize film credits for Jewish names or cry when they see *Fiddler on the Roof.*

Some people view the demise of the old *kosher nostra* kind of ethnicity as a tragedy; but if so, it is an inevitable one. America does not offer the conditions for a distinct Eastern European–like Jewish culture. In most places, Judaism doesn't seem to be about anything. It is a holding operation—an effort to wring one more generation of allegiance from people who are no longer sure what being a Jew is all about. In Israel, the national anthem is "Ha-Tikvah," the hope; in America it is, "We're Here Because We're Here."

When I was in Los Angeles, I discussed the shape of the Jewish future in America over lunch at Factor's Deli with Bruce Phillips, who teaches demography at the Hebrew Union College, and Norman Mirsky, an eccentric sociologist who claims to be able to categorize Jews according to body type.

"There is a definite correlation between weight and affiliation," Mirsky asserted. "The more Orthodox the congregation, the worse the bodies. And vice versa, the more Reform, the better the bodies. Temple Leo Baeck is the most upscale synagogue in L.A., and its bodies are absolutely the best. It's what I'd call a size three congregation."

My sister Julie and her husband Alan were there that day, and they laughed appreciatively. They don't belong to Leo Baeck, but they could. Alan, in his early forties, is a Harvard-educated lawyer with a gentle, ironic manner. Julie is a bright, charmingly kooky suburban mom who works half time as a program director for their Reform temple. They have a split-level house, a Japanese car, a Chevy van, a live-in housekeeper from El Salvador, and two small sons. Not long ago their six-year-old, Benjamin, asked if all Christians speak Spanish.

Julie and Alan care about being Jews. Although he is not Orthodox, Alan puts on a tallis and prays every morning. Julie takes courses at the University of Judaism. They are active in their temple, send their kids to Hebrew school, celebrate the holidays, and on Friday nights gather around the table to light Sabbath candles and sing blessings over the bread and the wine. They live in a safe little island of prosperity and middle-class respectability, like a Jewish Cosby family.

There are families like this all over the country, but they are rapidly becoming exceptional. In L.A., only one Jewish family in four belongs to a synagogue, and less than fifteen percent give money to the local federation. And by the year 2000, half the children under eighteen who consider themselves Jewish in Los Angeles will have a non-Jewish parent. "The numbers out here are a little worse than the rest of the country," said Phillips, "but this is the wave of the future. After all, how often do you meet someone in Michigan or Brooklyn who moved there from L.A.?"

Some demographers have argued that intermarriage is a net gain for Judaism; more people "convert in" than "opt out." Phillips pooh-poohed the notion. "It could be true, in strictly numerical terms. But most Christian partners don't convert. And mixed couples who claim to be raising their kids as Jews rarely belong to synagogues or live in Jewish neighborhoods, so it isn't entirely clear what they mean."

"What can we do?" asked Julie. "I mean, how can we be sure that *our* children will marry Jews and have Jewish children?"

"There are five main factors that influence a decision like that," said Phillips. "First, raise them in a Jewish neighborhood. Second, send them to Jewish camps in the summer. Third, give them an economic status that will allow them to interact with other Jews on a social level. Fourth, set an example of Jewish commitment at home. And fifth, when the time comes, send them to a college with a high percentage of Jewish students."

"And if we do all that, what are the chances of them marrying Jews?" asked Alan.

"Ah, fifty-fifty," said Phillips.

"That's it?" asked Julie. "Fifty percent?"

"Statistically, yes," said Phillips, and Mirsky nodded in confirmation.

"So what you're saying is that the Jews are eventually going to disappear in America," said Julie in a dismayed and somewhat angry voice. "You're saying that we don't have a chance."

"No, I'm not saying that," said Phillips dispassionately. "What you'll have in the future is a very intense core of Jews, surrounded by a thin outer layer. And the inner core will be a visible reminder to the outer core of what Judaism is really all about."

"It's a function of life in America, that's all," Mirsky added. "There's no reason to view people who marry out of the faith, or even leave it, as defectors. That's unfair. The policy goal of the Jewish establishment in America over the past fifty years has been full integration into society—and assimilation and intermarriage are just logical consequences of that policy. Imagine how you would react if some Lutheran group sent out flyers saying: DON'T MARRY JEWS. The whole community would be up in arms. The Jews in the United States today are just getting what they always wanted."

Later, at home, Julie and Alan pondered what they had heard at lunch. They are well-informed and deeply involved in the Jewish community, and yet they reacted to Phillips's and Mirsky's statistics with something like shock. They feel an obligation to pass along their Jewish heritage and they talked about taking measures—parochial schools, a summer in Israel, something . . .

Julie and Alan are concerned Jewish parents. But for them, and tens of thousands like them, their children's Jewish future is not quite the first priority. If they lived in a place with bad schools or unsafe streets, they would move; they are committed to getting their sons, safe and sound, into good colleges and well-paid professions. Preserving their children's Jewish heritage is important to them, too—but not important enough for them to sacrifice their American life-style. Naturally they hope for the best, but they are emotionally reconciled to the possibility—unthinkable even two generations ago—that their own grandchildren may not be Jews.

And yet, beyond the statistics and the projections, beyond the loss of culture and literacy, beyond the evidence of decline and the logic of demise, lies a great imponderable. America has formed the minds and lives of its Jews, but it has not quite changed their hearts.

All across the country I met people with American lives and Jewish hearts—Macy B. Hart, obsessed with the dying Dixie diaspora; Harvey Wasserman, the Buddhist with Jewish parental karma; Jody Kommel, who lives in Grosse Pointe with a Jewish star around her neck; a woman in Jacksonville who made her Christian husband buy a home in a Jewish neighborhood because she doesn't feel comfortable around gentiles; the man in Florida, married to a Mennonite woman, who is raising his small son to speak Yiddish; the inmates of Graterford Prison, who raise money for orphans in Netanya; the yuppie mystics in the Hollywood midrash class; the young leaders of the UJA who can't understand their love for Israel; Marty Gaynor, the Jewish cop with a yarmulke under his crash helmet.

As Americans, these people have nothing in common; but as Jews, they share something they often cannot articulate, even to themselves. It is an emotional tie—to places they have never lived, a history they barely remember, other Jews they have never met. For some this feeling is an intense and constant flame; for others, an occasional and mystifying flicker. But when it occurs it is undeniable and powerful, a reminder that even in America, in the promised land of personal freedom and individualism, they are still, somehow, Members of the Tribe.

GLOSSARY

Aliyah Literally "ascending." The Hebrew term for immigration to Israel.

Ba'al tshuva A newly orthodox Jew.

Bikur Holim In Hebrew, literally "sick visit." Such visits are considered a religious obligation.

Bocher The Hebrew and Yiddish word for boy.

Bris The Yiddish term for the circumcision ceremony (in Hebrew, "Brit" or "Brith").

Chabad A Chasidic group, also known as Lubavitcher Chasidim.

Chai In Hebrew, "life."

Chanukah Jewish Feast of Lights, commemorating the victory of the Maccabees over the Greeks.

Chasid (plural Chasidim)   A member of a Chasidic group.

Chavura movement   A movement in the late 1960s and 1970s by young Jews trying to establish smaller, independent, more egalitarian and more participatory Jewish congregations, either independently or within synagogues.

Cheder   Literally "room," a cheder is a primary school for observant Jewish children.

Cholent   A traditional Sabbath dish usually made with meat and beans.

Eretz Israel   Hebrew for "the land of Israel."

Felafel   Fried chick-pea balls common in Israel and the Middle East.

Glatt   An especially strict form of kashrut.

Hadassah   American women's Zionist organization.

Halacha   The body of Jewish law and commandments.

Havdalah   The prayer service that marks the end of the Sabbath and the beginning of the week.

Humos   A chick-pea dip common in Israel and the Middle East.

Kaddish   The Hebrew prayer for the dead.

Kashrut   (also spelled **Kashruth**) The Jewish dietary laws.

Klezmer music   Eastern European Jewish music, often played at weddings or other festive occasions.

Kotel   The Western Wall of the Temple in Jerusalem, also known as "the Wailing Wall."

Kreplach   Jewish ravioli.

Lag B'Omer   The twenty-third day of the counting of the omer; the only day between Passover and Pentecost on which observant Jews may marry.

Latke   A potato pancake usually eaten at Chanukah.

Le'hitraot   In Hebrew, "see you again."

Makher   Yiddish for "big shot."

Marrano   An underground Jew. The term is usually associated with Jews forcibly converted to Christianity during the Spanish Inquisition.

Mazel   Luck.

Midrash   A body of literature containing rabbinic interpretations of biblical texts.

Mensch   A Yiddish term for an honorable and decent person.

Meshuggeh   Crazy.

Mikvah   Ritual bath.

Mincha   Afternoon prayers.

Minyan   Hebrew term for the ten-man worship quorum (Conservative and Reform Jews count women as well).

Mitzvah   In Hebrew, literally a commandment. A mitzvah is a religious obligation.

Ner tamid   Hebrew for "eternal light"; a light that hangs over the ark in synagogues.

Nosh   In Yiddish, a snack.

Payes   The Yiddish pronunciation of "payot" or sidelocks worn by Chasidic Jews.

Purim   Holiday commemorating the salvation of the Jews of ancient Persia from a genocidal enemy.

Reb   A term of respect that may be applied to any Jewish male.

Rebbe   The leader of a Chasidic group.

Schnapps   An alcoholic drink.

Seder   Ritual Passover service.

Shabbes   Yiddish pronunciation of "Shabbat," the Hebrew Sabbath.

Shema   A Hebrew prayer of divine affirmation.

Shikseh   Yiddish for gentile female.

Shmooz   Yiddish for "shoot the breeze."

Shonda   Yiddish for "a shame."

Shtetel   A Jewish village in Eastern Europe.

Shul   Yiddish term for synagogue.

Simchas Torah   (also spelled **Simchat Torah**)—The Rejoicing in the Law, a holiday celebrated shortly after the Jewish New Year.

Strimel   The fur hat worn by Chasidic Jews.

Succah   A boothlike structure decorated with agricultural produce in which Jews take their meals during the holiday of Succot.

Succot   (also spelled **Succoth**)—The Feast of Tabernacles.

Ta'am   Hebrew and Yiddish for "taste" or "flavor."

Tallis   Yiddish pronunciation of the Hebrew "tallith" or "tallit," prayer shawl.

Talmud   The commentaries on the Torah.

Tanya   A book of eclectics written by the first Lubavitcher Rebbe and studied by his disciples.

Tisha B'Av   The ninth day of the Hebrew month of Av, on which the destruction of the Temple is commemorated.

Tzaddik   (plural **Tzaddikim**) The Hebrew term for a righteous man.

Tzedaka   The Hebrew word for charity.

Tzitzes   Yiddish pronunciation of ''tzizit,'' the fringed garment worn by observant Jews.

Yeshiva   School where Orthodox Jews study Talmud; higher yeshivot offer rabbinical ordination.

Yidden   The Yiddish word for Jews.

Yiddishkeit   A Jewish heart or, more generally, subjects pertaining to Jewish life.

Yahrzeit   The Yiddish term for the anniversary of a death.